The Latin American Development Debate

Series in Political Economy and Economic Development in Latin America

Series Editor
Andrew Zimbalist
Smith College

† Available in hardcover and paperback.

The Latin American Development Debate

Neostructuralism, Neomonetarism, and Adjustment Processes

edited by
Patricio Meller

Routledge
Taylor & Francis Group

LONDON AND NEW YORK

First published 1991 by Westview Press, Inc.

Published 2019 by Routledge
52 Vanderbilt Avenue, New York, NY 10017
2 Park Square, Milton Park, Abingdon, Oxon OX14 4RN

Routledge is an imprint of the Taylor & Francis Group, an informa business

Library of Congress Cataloging in Publication Data
The Latin American development debate : neostructuralism,
neomonetarism, and adjustment processes / edited by Patricio Meller.
    p. cm. — (Series in political economy and economic
development in Latin America)
   Includes bibliographical references and index.
   ISBN 0-8133-7971-7
   1. Latin America—Economic conditions—1982– 2. Latin America—
Economic policy. I. Meller, Patricio. II. Series.
HC125.L3479 1991
338.98—dc20   90-45811
                                                                          CIP

ISBN 13: 978-0-367-29345-1 (hbk)
ISBN 13: 978-0-367-30891-9 (pbk)

Contents

Tables

Figures

Acknowledgments

The Corporación de Investigaciones Económicas para Latinoamérica (CIEPLAN) in Santiago, Chile, thanks those individuals whose support has made possible a major portion of the research contained in this book. CIEPLAN is particularly indebted to the International Development Research Center (IDRC) of Canada and the Ford Foundation.

About the Contributors

Sebastián Edwards holds a Ph.D. in Economics from the University of Chicago and is a full professor at the University of California, Los Angeles.

Ricardo Ffrench-Davis holds a Ph.D. in Economics from the University of Chicago and is a senior economist at CIEPLAN in Santiago.

Nora Lustig holds a Ph.D. in Economics from the University of California, Berkeley. She is a full professor at El Colegio de México and a visiting fellow at the Brookings Institution in the Foreign Policy Studies Program.

Patricio Meller holds a Ph.D. in Economics from the University of California, Berkeley, and is a senior economist at CIEPLAN in Santiago.

Oscar Muñoz holds a Ph.D. in Economics from Yale University and is a senior economist at CIEPLAN in Santiago.

Carlos Ominami holds a Doctor (of State) degree in Economics from Paris University and is involved as a research economist in the ECLAC program on Latin American International Relations (RIAL).

Mauricio Rojas holds a Doctor in Economics degree from Lund University in Sweden and is a professor there.

Andrés Velasco holds a Ph.D. in Economics from Columbia University and is an assistant professor at New York University.

Roberto Zahler is a Ph.D. candidate in Economics at the University of Chicago and a research consultant at ECLAC.

Introduction

Patricio Meller

Since the 1980s Latin America has undergone its second-worst economic crisis of the century. Today, its average per capita income is about 10 percent less than it was in 1980; this regional average means that in some Latin American countries per capita income is the same as it was ten years ago, while in others it is the same as fifteen years ago. That is why it has been said that "the 1980s is a lost decade for Latin America." The crisis has affected all Latin American countries, irrespective of their economic policies; in other words, "reasonable" economic policies have not saved any of the countries from the crisis, although they may have lowered the cost of adjustment and improved future development prospects.

The reasons for and lessons to be derived from the vulnerability of the Latin American economies need to be reviewed. The strategy of Latin American development should therefore be reexamined and the old structuralist-monetarist debate restudied, in the light of new theoretical knowledge and recent economic events. In addition, the adjustment processes applied in Latin America during the 1980s must be probed. The purpose is twofold: Such analysis will contribute to an academic understanding of why things happened the way they did, in order to improve the theoretical instruments for studying the operation of Latin American economies. But even more important is the quest for a "package" of economic measures that will help remedy the situation—measures that will not only prove viable politically and socioeconomically but also promote democratic regimes and greater social justice.

The essays in this book focus on various aspects of the above topics. In Chapter 1 ("Latin America Economic Development and the International Environment") Ricardo Ffrench-Davis and Oscar Muñoz delineate the general trends of economic evolution in Latin America. The next three essays deal with the controversy surrounding the structuralist paradigm: In Chapter 2 ("From Structuralism to Neo-Structuralism: The Search for a Heterodox Paradigm") Nora Lustig examines the historical and theoretical roots of structuralist thinking in the period 1950–1980; in Chapter 3 ("Monetarism and Structuralism: Some Macroeconomic Lessons") Andrés Velasco reviews the macroeconomic debate between structuralism and monetarism that took place in the 1950s and compares it with the present debate; and in Chapter 4 ("Review of the Debate Over the Origins of Industrialization in Latin America and Its Ideological Context") Mauricio Rojas discusses the dependent developmentalist approaches to Latin American industrialization (in the context of the East Asian experience) as well as the renewal of current theoretical debates. The next two essays deal with the recent experience of Latin America in two key sectors, industry and finance: In Chapter 5 ("Deindustrialization and Industrial Restructuring in Latin America") Carlos Ominami identifies some of the elements in the crisis of the Latin American industrial sector and looks for relevant guidelines for designing new industrial-sector policies; and in Chapter 6 ("Financial Strategies in Latin America: The Southern Cone Experience") Roberto Zahler examines the financial liberalization reforms implemented in the Southern Cone countries, studies the results observed, and suggests factors to be taken into account in order to avoid the serious disadvantages of recent policies. The final two essays deal with the lessons derived from the recent Latin American adjustment process: In Chapter 7 ("Structural Adjustment Reforms and the External Debt Crisis in Latin America") Sebastián Edwards analyzes the long-term effects of structural adjustment reforms, focusing on the relationships among external opening, export promotion, and foreign trade liberalization; and in Chapter 8 ("IMF and World Bank Roles in the Latin American Foreign Debt Problem") Patricio Meller examines the existing problems and interrelations between the conditionality of multilateral institutions (IMF and World Bank) and the strategy based on adjustment with growth.

Some of the topics discussed in each chapter are described more specifically below.

For the Economic Commission for Latin America and the Caribbean (ECLAC), the main characteristic of Latin America in the early 1960s was economic instability in the face of changes in world economy. The import-substituting industrialization (ISI) strategy was intended to reduce such external vulnerability. In the period 1950–1980, all the criticisms aimed at the ISI strategy notwithstanding, Latin America grew steadily at the rate of 5.5 percent per annum in real terms; despite such growth, however, Ffrench-Davis and Muñoz point out that major inequalities continue in the distribution of economic and social benefits. Economic and social structures are persistently heterogeneous, thus causing social tensions in the region and resulting in profound economic crises. Thanks to the ISI strategy, the industrial sector grew by 6.5 percent per annum during 1950–1980; in other words, Latin America has achieved industrialization. Latin American countries, however, are no less vulnerable to external shocks, and a new kind of external dependency has arisen according to Ffrench-Davis and Muñoz: 86 percent of imports are intermediate or capital goods. Any shortage of foreign currency, therefore, brings down the level of output and investment, thus producing a negative effect on the evolution of the economy.

Nora Lustig explains the basic assumptions of structuralism as follows: (1) Society is *not* the sum of atomized consuming and producing units; economic policy measures affect the behavior of social actors, who, far from operating as single individuals, join together to form pressure groups. (2) Major social actors are not price-takers but price-makers and can therefore introduce significant rigidities into certain markets. (3) The causal relationship is not from savings to investment but the reverse. (4) Money supply is passive and adjusts to inflation, not the other way round. (5) Public investment is complementary and encourages private investment; there is no crowding out. (6) The development process is neither balanced nor harmonious. Trickle-down is slow; the free market system does not allow equitable distribution of the benefits of greater economic growth. (7) Intermediate inputs and capital goods are essential for economic growth. As they are basically imported into the region, foreign currency is a vital resource for growth; and, as foreign currency is scarce, efficiency considerations suggest that it should be used primarily in those areas where growth would be maximized. These basic assumptions of structuralism tend to explain the skepticism with which structuralists view orthodox recommendations for resolving short- and long-term economic problems.

The debate on inflation is a long-standing one among monetarists and structuralists. What have we learned after the recent experience of neomonetarism (a monetary approach to the balance of payments), whereby the exchange rate nominally anchors the system and whereby under the Law of One Price domestic and international inflation become equal; and after the recent experience of neostructuralism with the heterodox shock, whereby the inertial component of inflation is suppressed by means of generalized price controls and inflation is thus reduced to a low reasonable range; and, finally, after observing the failure of both anti-inflationary approaches to stabilization? Andrés Velasco is optimistic in this respect and suggests four lessons drawn from stabilization policies with which economists of different stances would agree: (1) Attacking inflation by controlling a single variable only creates greater imbalances in the medium term; (2) control of aggregate demand may not be a sufficient condition for stabilization, but it is certainly a necessary one, or all complementary policies would be doomed to failure; (3) interest rates can neither be kept artificially low (or negative in real terms) nor be allowed to shoot up during stabilization; (4) policy credibility is crucial for their success. Inconsistencies among the various measures adopted and unforeseeable changes of direction are to be avoided at all costs. The targets set for stabilization programs should be feasible and therefore credible. Overly ambitious announcements, if not complied with, only create uneasiness and distrust.

According to Mauricio Rojas, several changes have taken place in the analysis of Latin American industrialization. (1) With respect to *break or continuity*, the idea of "industrial revolution" prevailed in the development theories of the 1940s and 1950s. This is the notion of a break resulting from an abrupt change in society (as in Rosenstein-Rodan's "big push" theory or Rostow's "takeoff" theory). Today the notion of continuity prevails as a significant element, and the idea of a break is minimized. (2) Regarding *insertion in the world economy*, earlier theories based the description of types of development on external factors; that is, the "world economy" would be endowed with a kind of autonomous dynamics that would self-define the roles of "industrial centers" or "commodity-exporting periphery." Adherents of the prevailing approaches today contend that internal changes determine the specific way in which a given country takes its place in the world economy; this implies the replacement of "imperialism-" (or "dependency-") related views as a *deus ex machina* argument to hide our ignorance of the explanation for a given phenomenon. (3) With respect to *paradigmatic models and comparative economic history*, comparative economic history analysis would replace the analyses based on "industrialization models" or "development models." The comparative historical method would be best used to examine the complex problem of industrialization whereby each new industrialized nation has followed its own pattern instead of copying another nation's model.

Why is industrial evolution different in Argentina, Brazil, and Chile? The traditional answer is that in Brazil the large domestic market has played a very positive role; but in Argentina and Chile the adoption of neoliberal free trade policies has had a negative effect. In addition, Carlos Ominami identifies various kinds of industrialization in these three countries: Argentine industry suffers from industrial sclerosis, compounded by government passivity and lack of private-sector dynamics. Brazilian industry has a high degree of internal productive articulation and has increased its international competitiveness; moreover, its capacity for transformation is clearly progressive. Such capacity is measured by the existing relation between production of capital goods and production of traditional goods. Chilean industry exhibits regressive international specialization, with highly active domestic private agents and a highly passive public sector. The latter is linked to a relative fall in the production of capital goods and intermediate goods, and to a relative expansion of industry-producing traditional goods. In his examination of these types of industrial evolution, Ominami argues that Latin America must reopen the debate on the role of industry, because to let the market freely take care of all decisions concerning new investments, international specialization, or technological options would simply mean giving up on the future.

In the traditional Latin American context of "financial repression" (controlled interest rates, quantitative allocation of credit, barriers to the entry of new financial institutions, etc.), a policy of deregulation and capital market liberalization was applied in the 1970s in the Southern Cone. Roberto Zahler points out some of the results observed. (1) For five years the real interest rate was relatively high, both in absolute terms and relative to international standards, thus suggesting that a free interest rate is not the mechanism for self-regulation of the capital market. (2) The rising interest rate did not help to increase savings, nor did it lead to efficient allocation of resources. (3) Financial deregulation did not help to ensure the creation of a medium- and long-term credit market. (4) An explosive expansion of financial deepening may lead to internal overindebtedness, which worsens the economy's vulnerability and instability, especially during changes in interest rates or output levels.

Zahler further suggests that, in light of the Southern Cone experience, any reform designed to introduce greater liberalization of the capital market calls for the following measures: (1) Initial macroeconomic balances must be under control. Shorter maturities of financial transactions, excessive increase of interest rates, overindebtedness, and greater financial system vulnerability may considerably aggravate existing macroeconomic imbalances. (2) Ownership of firms (particularly large ones) in the productive sector of the economy should be separate from ownership of financial institutions. The state must monitor financial-sector operations so as to discourage speculative and potentially destabilizing management of the financial sector. In this context, the most effective financial regulation is qualitative and preventive, for in the event of serious problems of liquidity or credit-worthiness in a financial institution, the government will step in to save it from failing. (3) Because credit is a scarce commodity, each Latin American country must advance gradually toward a more liberalized financial market; rapid deregulation entails more expansion of consumption than of savings. If financial agents are to be prevented from suffering losses in the process of liberalization, lending rates, gradually followed by deposit rates, must be raised. External financial opening must be connected with the time sequence of lending and deposit-rate deregulation. Fairly high lending rates may encourage excessive external debt and lead to appreciation of the exchange rate; fairly low passive rates may encourage capital flight.

Trade liberalization policies are crucial in the debate over the adjustment-with-growth strategy. In this context, Sebastián Edwards points out that the notion of trade liberalization has changed over time. In the 1960s trade liberalization implied *some* relaxation of trade and exchange controls. In the 1970s trade liberalization meant more extensive use of price mechanisms so as to reduce the anti-export bias of the trade regime. Later on there was even talk of liberalization during the application of real devaluation to the context of quantitative constraints. Today, however, the notion of liberalization has acquired a rather extreme connotation. Trade liberalization involves the drastic suppression of all quantitative constraints together with rapid tariff reduction to a uniform level on the order of 10 percent; it has also become synonymous with policies based on free markets without government interference. Edwards examines (1) trade liberalization and its fiscal effects, given that taxes on trade are very often a major source of government revenue; (2) the implications of trade liberalization on employment (in this context, because physical capital is a fixed nonmalleable asset, when there are rigidities in the wage structure, a slower, more gradual tariff reform is preferable in order to engender less unemployment in the short run); and (3) the relation between devaluation and trade liberalization, whereby gradual tariff reforms require smaller devaluations in order to reduce the costs associated with abrupt devaluation.

There is a minor difference in the views of Sebastián Edwards and Patricio Meller on the subject of the required policies for export promotion. Based on World Bank studies, Edwards holds that (1) *some* form of trade liberalization is required if exports are to be promoted; countries in which export promotion has been successful have generally operated under less extensive export permit systems, lower average tariffs, less tariff dispersion, and a smaller number of instances of overvalued exchange rate. (2) There is a clear relationship between movements toward more liberalized trade regimes and better economic performance. Based on a study by Sachs (1987) regarding recent cases of successful Asian export expansion, I contend that the economic policy package applied by Japan occurred during the period of greatest export expansion (1950–1973). Of course, export promotion is not equivalent to import liberalization, nor is import liberalization a requirement for export promotion. Something similar may be said about the "pure" role of the market and of government. In brief, the economic policy package that produced the successful Asian export-promotion strategy is different from "liberalization plus deregulation."

Because of its foreign debt problem, Latin America will have restricted access to the international capital market. Accordingly, the multilateral organizations—the International Monetary Fund (IMF) and World Bank—will be the main sources of credit. This implies the joint presence of both institutions in several countries. Moreover, I suggest that in the immediate future the Latin American nations are going to be faced with the double conditionality of the IMF and the World Bank. Latin American economists should therefore present their suggestions and views *a priori*, rather than criticizing *a posteriori* the nature and elements of this future double conditionality. Such possible double conditionality would contain the following elements: (1) liberalization of markets and of the foreign sector (a major component in the latter case is import liberalization); (2) incentives to encourage export expansion through devaluation, maintenance of a stable real exchange rate, and reduction of export taxes; (3) privatization of public enterprises; (4) stable and permanent economic rules, which imply the reduction of government intervention in the economy.

This future double conditionality may be questioned in various ways. (1) There is a substantive discrepancy in the approach to the future double conditionality. Its main objective is to achieve equilibrium in the balance of payments of a less developed country (LDC) consistent with flows of service payments on foreign debt and the amounts of new foreign credits received; in this scheme, the economic growth rate of the LDC is residual. But the LDC view of a new strategy based on adjustment with growth should be different; given a minimum appropriate level of growth needed for the development of an LDC, what is the volume of necessary foreign funds? In this case, the flow of external credits is residual. Then the crucial question becomes, Where will those funds come from? (2) Future IMF–World Bank double conditionality will hinder a Latin American country's negotiations with the multilateral organizations, for the country cannot complete one negotiation until it has completed the others. (3) The degree of a country's sensitivity will be affected when there is obvious meddling in crucial economic and political issues such as liberalization, deregulation, privatization, and foreign investment.

In short, this collection of essays covers a range of topics associated with the general theme of development, with special emphasis on the economic policies needed to remedy the current situation in Latin America. This debate, on both the analytical and the empirical levels, is likely to continue in the near future.

1

Latin American Economic Development and the International Environment

Ricardo Ffrench-Davis
Oscar Muñoz

The suspension of the external debt service by Mexico in 1982 was a resounding signal of what would be the second most serious financial crisis of the century in Latin America—a crisis that determined the characteristics of the region's economic evolution during the 1980s. Mexico's action marked the end to a long period of expansion that, with some ups and downs, started in the postwar period and lasted until the early 1980s. This expansion had continued even during the 1970s, when, after the first oil crisis, the advanced industrial countries entered into a stagflation process.

The relatively sustained economic growth permitted an increase of the Latin American per capita gross domestic product (GDP) at a yearly rate of 2.8 percent between 1950 and 1980; it also facilitated the modernization of the production and social structures, and contributed to an increase in the standard of living of a population approaching 400 million. These outcomes occurred in a region with the fastest growing population in the world.

Population growth started to accelerate in the 1950s. It reached its highest rate in the early 1960s and has declined slowly ever since. Between 1950 and 1980 Latin America had an annual average rate of population growth of 2.7 percent, higher than any other region of the world. As a consequence, total population more than doubled, increasing from 163 to 359 million and thus rising from 6.5 to 8 percent of world population.

This process of demographic transition—declining mortality rates, followed by falling birth rates—had a dramatic effect on the age composition of the population. In 1980 individuals 15 years or younger accounted for 40 percent of the total population, those over 64 for 4 percent, and the active population in between for 56 percent. In other words, the latter group had to support a passive population that represented nearly 80 percent of its own size—thus indicating not only the formidable social problems faced by Latin America but also the enormous task faced by an economy that has to generate employment opportunities for the large and rapidly growing population of younger people reaching working age. By 1980 an estimated 20 percent of the labor force was underutilized in Latin America, both because of unemployment and because of the underemployment associated with the informal sectors of the economy.

Another profound and rapid change has been the massive transfer of rural people to cities. In the 1950s about half the increased rural population of Latin America emigrated to urban areas. Between 1950 and 1980 urban centers of more than 20,000 inhabitants grew fourfold in size, from 40 million to more than 160 million, at a rate of 4.4 percent per annum. In 1950 there were six or seven cities in Latin America with a population of more than a million but none with a population larger than 10 million. In 1980, by contrast, there were twenty-five cities with more than a million inhabitants, four cities larger than 10 million people (Mexico City, Buenos Aires, Rio de Janeiro, and São Paulo), and several metropolitan areas of unprecedented size. The share of urban population in Latin America increased from 41 percent in 1950 to 63 percent in 1980.

The economy of the region has also changed and grown considerably. In 1980 average GDP reached about $2,000 per capita (at the 1980 dollar value).[1] This level placed Latin America in an intermediate position among the countries of the world, above most underdeveloped regions of Africa and Asia, and below the industrialized countries of Europe and North America as well as the socialist economies.

Between 1950 and 1980 the economic growth of Latin America reached an average rate of 5.5 percent per annum (see Table 1.1). This rate was above that in other developing regions (except for the oil-exporting economies and the group of Southeast Asian countries) and well above the average for the industrialized countries (4.2 percent), except Japan (7.9 percent) and the socialist countries. The GDP of Latin America in 1980 was five times that in 1950. Growth was associated with a sizable rise in the investment ratio. Gross fixed capital formation rose from 17 percent of GDP in 1950 to 22 percent in the second half of the 1970s (see Table 1.2). The dynamic economic growth and development of the region have resulted in both greater availability of consumer goods and improved social conditions in health, education, and housing. Private

TABLE 1.1 Latin America: Annual Real Growth Rates of GDP (in percentages)

	1950–1960	1960–1970	1970–1980	1950–1980	1980–1986
Argentina	2.8	4.3	2.6	3.2	-1.2
Brazil	6.8	6.1	8.7	7.2	2.8
Chile	4.0	4.2	2.5	3.6	0.7
Colombia	4.6	5.2	5.4	5.1	3.1
Mexico	6.1	7.0	6.5	6.5	0.9
Peru	5.5	5.0	3.9	4.8	1.3
LATIN AMERICA[a]	5.1	5.7	5.6	5.5	1.3
Oil exporters	6.3	6.4	4.8	5.8	0.7
Non-oil exporters	4.5	5.2	6.2	5.3	1.7

[a]In this category are nineteen Latin American countries: ten South American countries, six Central American countries, and Mexico, the Dominican Republic, and Haiti. Growth rates are weighted according to GDP country levels (at 1980 constant prices).

Source: CEPAL (1987b).

TABLE 1.2 Latin America: Gross Fixed Investment Coefficients (as percentages of GDP, in 1980 dollars)

	1950–1959	1960–1969	1970–1981	1982–1986
Argentina	15.1	18.4	20.9	13.1
Brazil	21.9	19.1	22.5	16.7
Chile	20.6	19.0	15.2	13.3
Colombia	19.6	16.3	16.1	16.9
Mexico	16.7	18.3	22.1	18.0
LATIN AMERICA	18.4	17.4	21.3	16.8

Source: CEPAL (1987b).

consumption per capita rose nearly 2 percent a year in the 1950s and more than 3.5 percent in the 1970s (CEPAL, 1984 and 1988).

Various social indicators have also exhibited sustained advances throughout this period. The average mortality rate, which was roughly 16 per 1,000 in 1950–1955, dropped to 8 per 1,000 in 1980–1985. Life expectancy at birth increased from 52 years in 1950–1955 to 64 years in 1980–1985. This progress in social conditions must be attributed largely to the more active role of the public sector in Latin America. Although the public sector has been oriented toward fostering capital accumulation and growth, public institutions designed to improve social conditions developed widely, thus reflecting the increasing concern of governments with social welfare.

These improvements, however, have not overcome the strong inequities that characterize the distribution of economic and social benefits in Latin America. The economic and social structures of the region are still heterogeneous, in terms of both differences among countries and differences among social groupings and regions within countries. It is a well-established fact that living conditions in urban sectors are much better than those in rural areas. By the early 1970s, 26 percent of the urban population was living below the poverty line, compared to 62 percent of rural households. Urbanization rates are a good approximation of the degree of modernization and improvement of social conditions achieved by various countries. For instance, by 1980 the countries of the Southern Cone (Argentina, Chile, and Uruguay) exhibited high urbanization rates (i.e., between 79 and 84 percent). At the other extreme, the small countries of Central America as well as Bolivia and Paraguay revealed urbanization rates below 50 percent. At an intermediate level of urbanization were most of the other countries of the region. These countries, which also exhibited the fastest rates of change in this respect, started from low levels in 1950.

Strong heterogeneities can also be seen within areas of a given country. Note, for instance, the contrast between rich São Paulo and poor northeastern Brazil, or that between the province of Buenos Aires and northern Argentina. Prevailing economic structures and institutions tend to concentrate the benefits of growth and modernization in small areas that enjoy high levels of technology, productivity, and income. These areas are thus able to achieve consumption styles and urban designs similar to those of the most affluent societies in the industrial countries. The people in these areas coexist with large masses of urban and rural poor, who must endure precarious living conditions, often below the level of minimum subsistence. The resulting social tensions have created deep political crises as well as instances of authoritarianism in several countries of the region.

Another fundamental characteristic of Latin American development has been the permanent interaction of external and domestic conditions. Latin America's economy has long been linked to the international economy. This dependent relationship was reinforced by the boom of international trade that occurred near the end of the nineteenth century. The result was consolidation of a production structure specializing in raw materials for export. Since the end of World War II, the region's development efforts have been devoted to reducing this commercial dependence, especially with respect to exports of primary products and

TABLE 1.3   Latin American Industrial-Sector Annual Growth Rates (in percentages)

	1950–1960	*1960–1970*	*1970–1980*	*1950–1980*	*1980–1986*
Argentina	4.1	5.6	1.6	3.8	–1.2
Brazil	9.1	6.9	9.0	8.3	1.1
Chile	4.7	5.3	1.1	3.7	0.0
Colombia	6.5	6.0	6.0	6.2	2.0
Mexico	6.2	9.1	6.9	7.4	0.0
Peru	8.0	5.8	3.3	5.7	1.0
LATIN AMERICA	6.4	6.9	6.2	6.5	0.5
Oil exporters	7.1	8.1	5.7	7.0	0.3
Non-oil exporters	6.1	6.4	6.4	6.3	0.6

Source: CEPAL (1987b).

imports of manufactures. Indeed, this asymmetry in foreign trade has been a central target of Latin America's industrialization and investment policies.

Although the region was able to grow and derive positive results from its industrialization process (see Table 1.3), import substitution and export diversification—new forms of dependency on the international economy—have increased the area's vulnerability.

In the 1950s and 1960s, for example, the intensification of industrial growth and the diversification of consumption patterns made the countries more dependent on imported technologies, thus creating production imbalances, especially in labor markets. Import substitution of consumer goods, by contrast, was highly dependent on imported inputs. By 1980 intermediate and capital goods accounted for almost 86 percent of the total value of imports. Hence foreign currency shortages tended to discourage economic activity and domestic investment.

During the 1960s a significant inflow of direct foreign investment concentrated on the production of manufactured import substitutes. Given a high import intensity of output, the net savings of foreign currency were sometimes negligible in the trade balance, and profit remittances were high due to effective protection.

From a more positive viewpoint, the international trade boom of the 1960s favored the diversification of Latin America's exports and allowed a dynamic growth of manufactured exports of those countries that had made more progress in their industrialization. This was especially the case in the region's largest countries, such as Brazil and Mexico, but it was also true of Argentina, Colombia, and Chile. They all diversified

TABLE 1.4 Intra- and Extraregional Exports from Latin America (annual rates of change, in constant dollars)

	Intraregional				Extraregional			
	1965–1970	1970–1975	1975–1979	1965–1979	1965–1970	1970–1975	1975–1979	1965–1979
Basic and primary commodities	2.8	4.8	7.0	4.7	3.6	3.4	5.0	3.9
Fuel	0.4	16.9	–0.6	5.7	0.7	13.8	8.8	7.4
Manufactures	15.9	13.5	9.9	13.3	11.9	4.7	7.9	8.2
Other	20.4	3.9	–7.8	5.8	9.0	30.9	0.8	13.8
TOTAL	6.4	11.6	6.2	8.2	4.1	6.4	6.7	5.7

Note: Current dollars were deflated by the unit price of exports index of non-oil Latin American countries, as estimated by CEPAL.

Source: BID (1984), Table II.5.

exports of manufactures within Latin American markets and abroad (see Table 1.4).

In the 1970s the international financial diversification allowed most Latin American countries (LACs) an easy access to external funds. Accordingly, the foreign exchange constraint was relaxed, even though it coupled Latin American economies to the fiscal and monetary policies of advanced countries. In fact, because of the large debt it had accumulated, the region became more dependent on changes in the availability of new loans and in international interest rates applied to the debt service. These pervasive circumstances eventually led to the crisis faced by the region during the 1980s.

In short, Latin American economic growth is deeply linked to the evolution and characteristics of the international economy. There are four phases of this growth, insofar as it has been affected by international economic trends. The first of these phases lasted from the 1950s until the early 1960s; the second, from the mid-1960s until 1973; and the third, from the 1970s until the financial crisis of the early 1980s. The fourth phase constituted the subsequent period of recessive adjustment.

Postwar Instability and Accelerated Inflation: The 1950s and Early 1960s

This period witnessed the implementation of industrialization programs in most of the region's countries. Under the theoretical and programmatic inspiration of the Economic Commission for Latin America (ECLA), Latin Americans felt that the traditional structures of primary exporting economies would leave the countries in a state of permanent instability and worsening terms of trade.

As a result of strong fluctuations in the prices of raw materials, the instability of those markets was transferred to the domestic economies. This was historically the case with all the nations of the region during the Great Depression of the 1930s, World War II, and the 1950s. This instability generated the acceleration of domestic inflation and unemployment.

Indeed, the period from 1950 to 1955 was characterized by the instability created by the Korean War. Latin America's terms of trade deteriorated and fiscal revenues, which were largely dependent on export proceeds, were subsequently depressed. To the extent that governments tried to avoid these recessive effects, they usually appealed to inflationary financing.

Argentina, Brazil, and Chile underwent strongly accelerated inflation during this decade. The pressures caused by this inflation prompted the first stabilization plans of the postwar period. For their implementation external financing had to be sought under the aegis of agreements with the International Monetary Fund. But such financing was conditional upon the enforcement of a set of macroeconomic policies inspired by a monetarist diagnosis that disregarded the structural sources of inflation. This approach was the subject of great controversy and was strongly questioned by the ECLA.

One of the main concerns of the structuralist school was that orthodox stabilization policies could endanger industrialization objectives as well as the growth of investment and employment. The emphasis of those policies on the restriction of aggregate demand tended to create a recessive climate that discouraged investment in countries that were engaged in an effort to increase their capital formation. Thus created was a contradiction between the objectives of stabilization and those of growth. According to the structuralist approach, inflationary de-acceleration should be sought through policies promoting production and expanding supply— especially in agriculture, which was viewed as one of the main bottlenecks in the economy. Toward this end, modernization of agriculture and of land tenure structures was considered to be imperative.

A series of international events had great influence on Latin American development. During the 1940s and 1950s industrialization was encouraged for the following reasons: First, restrictions on external supply reduced the availability of imported manufactures in LACs, thus fostering the domestic output of import substitutes. Second, the foreign supply subsequently normalized. However, the Latin American countries faced obstacles in expanding and diversifying their exports to world markets. Their access was more limited then than in the 1960s. Thus, the trade policies of the 1950s cannot be assessed in terms of the world markets of the 1960s. Again, it should be noted that the performance of the world markets encouraged import substitution.

During the 1950s unsophisticated and inefficient controls on imports were used. The period also witnessed a great variety of tariff and nontariff import restrictions, sharp real exchange-rate revaluations, and varied price and administrative deterrents to exports.

In the early 1960s the Cuban revolution had a wide political and ideological impact on the rest of the continent. Proposed reforms in the distribution of property and power acquired strength. In Brazil, for instance, popular and peasant movements sought revolutionary transformation. Paradoxically, the greatest degree of encouragement for these structural changes came from the United States through the Alliance for Progress promoted by President John F. Kennedy. Faced with the Cuban challenge and risking ideological radicalization, the U.S. government launched a program that sought to reconcile long-term financial assistance for development with the reform of traditional structures of property (especially in the agricultural sector), to be carried out by the countries themselves. In addition, the countries were expected to incorporate the concept of long-term planning in order to determine priorities and justify the use of resources. The object, in short, was to implement a concerted conditionality of loans.

The resulting controversy at the level of both short- and long-term policies had implications for the orientation of industrialization policies. The fact that various countries were experiencing decreasing growth rates in their industrial development was interpreted as a symptom of exhaustion of import-substitution industrialization (see Table 1.3). Likewise, unemployment and poverty problems persisted, thus creating wide frustration in social sectors. The conduct of industrial policies came under criticism that focused on the impossibility of continuing Latin American industrialization according to the "watertight compartments" concept.

Several facts formed the foundation of this concept. First, it was obvious that domestic markets were too small to take full advantage of scale economies in several manufacturing activities, particularly the area of intermediate goods. Second, the advanced industrial nations provided an example of trade integration by establishing the European Common Market and the successive rounds of tariff liberalization within the framework of the General Agreement on Tariffs and Trade (GATT).

The support for Latin American regional integration began to spread as a way to promote industrialization. By the end of the 1950s two groups of countries had organized the Latin American Free Trade Association (LAFTA) and the Central American integration scheme. These were followed by the Andean Pact in the late 1960s. The fact that these initiatives achieved some important results was reflected in the high growth of intrarregional exports of manufactures: 13.3 percent in 1965–1979 (see Table 1.4). From a broader perspective, however, the outcome of the Pact was quite different from that originally expected.

The Commercial Boom of the 1960s

The decade of the 1960s was a dynamic period for the world economy. Between 1960 and 1973 world production and trade grew at yearly rates of 5 and 8 percent, respectively. Per capita GDP growth was triple the rate achieved by developed nations in the previous two and a half centuries (Kuznets, 1966). Reciprocal trade liberalization among advanced industrial countries was the central feature of the international economy and the basis of an intensive technological and intra-industrial specialization change. Among the six countries of the Organization for Economic Cooperation and Development (OECD) with the largest GDPs—the United States, the U.K., France, Germany, Italy, and Canada—productivity increased by 5.3 percent annually between 1960 and 1973, as compared to 1.7 percent in 1870–1950 and 4.2 percent in 1950–1960 (Maddison, 1985). This growth was associated with the vigorous trade of manufactures made possible by the organization of more open economies. In the above-mentioned industrial countries, the proportion of exported merchandise increased from 12.6 percent of GDP in 1950 to 15.4 percent in 1960 and 17.5 percent in 1973 (Maddison, 1985). Moreover, the increasing role of transnational corporations was conducive to a more dynamic trade growth. Their effect, however, was double edged: Whereas in some sectors they increased competition, in others they captured marketing channels that limited the access of new competitors from LDCs.

In this context of commercial dynamism, two major regional circuits were strengthened. The first was that within Europe and between Europe and the United States; the other was formed by the East Asian countries under Japan's leadership (namely, South Korea, Taiwan, Hong Kong, and Singapore). The main characteristic of these circuits was the industrialization achieved through promotion of manufactured exports. The principal instruments of the advanced OECD countries were the reduction of tariffs and the transnationalization of capital, which allowed the transfer of technologies from the United States to Europe. In the East Asian countries the most important instruments were the active state-guided industrial policies set forth to define the priority sectors in which those countries intended to undertake technological learning. In place of across-the-board import liberalization, these countries tended to grant similarly effective protection to producers for domestic and foreign markets, but with a broad heterogeneity among products. Despite their low levels of income and productivity at the end of the war, it was by this means that they achieved spectacular growth in the area of industrial exports.

These trends exerted some influence on the orientation of Latin America's industrial policies, but they did not alter the region's development patterns, which were based on import substitution within the local markets. They complemented import substitution with export promotion, seeking to integrate both dimensions of trade policy. Consequently, they stimulated the implementation of export-promoting policies, a higher selectivity in the substitution of imports, and more efficient use of such economic policy tools as the exchange rate, interest rates, and investment policies. Regional integration also gained a fresh impetus in the early 1970s as a result of the Andean Pact.

Of particular note in this context were the exchange-rate reforms in Chile (1965), Colombia (1967), and Brazil (1968). These nations were following systematic crawling-peg policies, which represented policy innovation. Such innovation contributed to the stabilization of price relations between domestic and foreign products, and encouraged nontraditional exports that were more sensitive to the stability of real exchange rates. The new exchange-rate policy contributed to a reduction of redundant protection, which was previously preserved as a defense against recurrent artificial appreciation in inflation-prone countries.

The expansion of international trade and of the world economy favored the Latin American countries, as reflected in the significant improvement of the terms of trade. Between 1960 and 1970 the terms of trade improved by more than over 10 percent in the non-oil-producing countries of Latin America, even though the oil producers were temporarily affected by a fall in the terms of trade. The positive net effect reinforced the acceleration of the economic growth rate, which was already relatively high.

The improvement of the terms of trade, the easier access to international markets for manufactures, the stronger industrial base of several LACs, and the decrease in the relative export bias in the structure of incentives gave way to a significant rise in the rate of manufactured exports. Between 1965 and 1979 Latin America increased the real value of manufactured exports to other regions by 8.2 percent per year (11.9 percent in 1965–1970), thereby exceeding the growth rate of total exports for the region (5.7 percent) (see Table 1.4).

The positive contribution of economic integration is reflected in the 13.3 percent annual growth recorded for intraregional exports of manufactures. In response to world trends and to import-substitution industrialization, exports of manufactures rose much faster than those of commodities from 1965 to 1979. This difference, not surprisingly, was sharper in intra–Latin American trade. In the midst of this positive trend, however, was a series of imbalances in the world economy. These imbalances had a negative effect in the following decade.

Macroeconomic Imbalances and Financial Crisis

The reorganization of the international economy, particularly that of the financial system agreed upon in Bretton Woods following World War II, led to an option for an approach involving an important factor of imbalance—namely, the leadership and responsibility attributed to the U.S. economy in the expansion of international payments. Thus world liquidity, which had to finance the growth of international trade, depended on capital outflows from the United States to the rest of the world. These capital outflows could be achieved only by means of a deficit in the balance of payments of that country. As long as its competitive position was sound, the United States could obtain a commercial surplus that would permit it to finance capital outflows allocated either to foreign aid or to direct private investment abroad. During the 1940s and 1950s its competitive position was virtually unrivaled. The United States accounted for 60 percent of the industrial production of the world, and its gross productivity per working hour was almost twice that of the European countries and nearly six times the level reached by Japan (Maddison, 1985).

The growth of the industrial economies and the changes in competitive positions drastically altered that situation, however. The United States gradually lost its productivity advantage vis-à-vis its commercial rivals. As the trade surplus continued to decline, new financial liabilities in the United States derived from its international policy and military commitments in the rest of the world (U.S. Government, 1983).

The domestic economy of the United States was also subject to other progressive imbalances that translated into an increase in inflation. During the first half of the 1960s consumer prices exhibited a yearly increase ranging from 1 to 2 percent, whereas in 1969 the increase exceeded 6 percent.

The maladjustments affecting the major economic world power resulted in progressive uncertainty regarding the stability of the dollar. The financial adjustments culminated in 1971 with the dollar's nonconvertibility and subsequent devaluation. These actions completed the disarticulation of the fixed parity system agreed upon in Bretton Woods, and a new phase of exchange-rate instability began in response to the attempt by the industrial countries to avoid the deterioration of their competitive positions.

Among the other shocks that followed the dollar devaluation in the early 1970s was the sharp increase in oil prices. The prices of raw materials rose until the peak year of 1973. The terms of trade of non-oil-producing countries in Latin America improved by 7 percent between 1970 and 1973, whereas those for oil-producing countries improved by 134 percent in 1970–1974. Two-digit inflation had become a general feature in the industrial countries by 1974, and, as a result, implementation of stabilization policies with a marked recessive orientation was reestablished. Because the inflationary pressures were mainly of a cost-push nature, the traditional approaches toward stabilization based on demand control intensified the recession and failed to check inflation significantly. Stagflation became widespread, unemployment increased, and investment declined.

At the same time, the recycling of the surplus of the oil-producing countries expanded and diversified the sources of supply in international capital markets. The increase of supply, coupled with a low demand for funds in the industrial world, generated a strong flow of financial funds into the developing countries—especially those in Latin America, which was considered to be an increasingly credit-worthy region.

The two oil shocks in 1973–1974 and 1979–1980 had affected the region significantly. In terms of balance of payments, Latin America, as a net oil exporter, was benefited by the price increases. The net oil exports rose from US$3.2 billion in 1973 to US$22.8 billion in 1981 (see Table 1.5).

The sharp rise in oil prices increased the diversity among LACs. It was only in Venezuela that oil represented more than half of all exports previous to the sharp price increases that had occurred since 1973. The increases in price and output of oil also affected Ecuador as well as Mexico, which had lost its status as an oil importer. Peru became an oil exporter as well, but its expectations of becoming a significant producer were frustrated inasmuch as the actual reserves were smaller than expected. Most other LACs were net importers. Brazil in particular accounted for 44 percent of oil imports in 1981.

The main Latin American producer of oil, Venezuela, experienced a sizable increase in domestic disposable income and supply of foreign currency. Its exports increased from US$3.1 billion in 1972 to US$11.1 billion in 1974, with a terms of trade effect roughly equivalent to one-fourth of GDP (CEPAL, 1987b). As Venezuela was an "old oil exporter"

TABLE 1.5   Trade in Oil and Derivatives (1973–1985) (in millions of dollars)

	1973	1981	1985[a]
Net oil-importing countries	1,704.6	15,030.8	6,845.1
Net oil-exporting countries	4,936.7	37,861.3	31,882.0
Argentina	—	—	652.2
Bolivia	48.9	3.3	—
Colombia	61.4	—	—
Ecuador	207.1	1,710.0	1,728.4
Mexico	—	13,902.5	14,793.1
Peru	—	672.2	481.1
Trinidad and Tobago	161.0	2,221.8	1,164.2
Venezuela	4,458.3	19,351.5	13,063.0
Latin America	3,232.1	22,830.5	25,036.9

[a]Preliminary figures.

Source: BID (1986).

and a member of OPEC, it reduced output in order to help sustain world prices. (Other OPEC members did likewise.) As a consequence, even though Venezuela experienced much larger export returns and an increased national welfare, GDP at *constant prices* stagnated after the oil shock. The non-oil sector grew, but it was compensated by the decline in oil output.

Two other oil exporters—Ecuador and Mexico—reaped significant benefits from the increased export price. Both countries were able to maintain an output pattern different from that of Venezuela. Ecuador's output was more or less constant throughout the remainder of the 1970s. Mexico, with the help of large, newly discovered reserves, made a substantial and persistent gain: Whereas it had produced 9 percent of the regional output in 1973, its share climbed to 44 percent in 1982 (BID, 1986).

Oil producers increased their borrowing abroad instead of decreasing it. Their decision to do so was fostered by their improved credit-worthiness, which encouraged lenders to exert stronger pressures over these countries so that they could accept larger loans and liberalize the movement of capital. The prevalence of both free access to the foreign-exchange market and appreciating exchange rates prompted a significant flight of capital. Nonetheless, domestic investment vigorously increased in Ecuador, Mexico, and Venezuela.

Oil importers faced the shock in different ways from 1973 to 1974. Those countries with better access to bank loans and a declared preference for growth borrowed heavily. This was true of Brazil, which continued to grow and to increase its capital formation in what was called a case of "debt-led growth." At the other end of the spectrum, Chile, which faced a sharp fall in the price of copper, reduced its economic activity and curtailed investment sharply.

During the shock of 1979–1980 these approaches were reversed. Brazil experienced some difficulty in gaining access to bank loans and, with an already large debt stock, chose to reduce economic activity in 1981; Chile, by contrast, maintained a large aggregate demand and continued to borrow heavily until the commercial banks reduced their lending in 1982.

After the financial shock of 1982, the changes in the price of oil more directly influenced the macroeconomic performance of the LACs. In fact, given the abrupt reduction of voluntary loans by bank creditors, changes in oil prices have affected the foreign-exchange shortages of all the countries in the region.

Also affected were the current accounts of the industrial countries. Their surplus, which in 1973 had reached $10 billion, was replaced by a deficit of $15 billion in the following year. The current-account deficit of non-oil-producing developing countries rose from $9 billion in 1973 to $21 billion in 1974 (World Bank, 1985). These countries, however, contracted a massive debt with the international private banks, which intermediated the surplus of the oil-producing countries. These capital flows allowed non-oil-exporting LDCs to maintain their rates of growth and to expand imports of manufactured goods from the industrial countries, which in turn quickly reestablished the equilibrium of their trade balances (World Bank, 1985).

This trend structurally involved the developing countries, particularly those of Latin America, in the economic policies adopted by the industrial countries. Traditionally, this relationship had operated on the basis of commercial flows. The economic activity of the industrial countries affected the growth of the periphery through the demand for exports. Under the new conditions, a financial link was established as a result of the external debt contracted with the international private banks at floating interest rates and with short- and medium-term maturities. The short-term policies of the leading industrial countries can thus be held accountable for the worsening of both the debt terms and the balance-of-payments current account of the LDCs.

In short, the inability of the stabilization policies to curb the inflationary pressures and to reactivate growth in the industrial countries in the second half of the 1970s, in combination with the second oil shock of

1979–1980, further contributed to the dynamic imbalances under way in the Latin American economic structures.

In 1979–1980 inflation was reactivated in the industrial countries. The balance of their current account showed a deficit of $6 billion in 1979 and close to $39 billion in 1980 (World Bank, 1985). In addition, their fiscal deficits increased, for both cyclical and long-term reasons.

Under these circumstances, the economic authorities in most of the industrial countries intensified their restrictive monetary policies. Fiscal deficits were not successfully controlled, however. although a similar outcome was not attained as regards the control of fiscal deficits. Especially serious were the conditions of the economic policy of the United States, whose fiscal deficit increased from 1.3 percent of GDP in 1980 to 3.8 percent in 1982 (Maddison, 1985), even though monetary policy was tight. These conditions culminated in an unprecedented increase in real interest rates. The cost of the instability and excessive expenditures incurred by the industrial countries was thus transferred to the periphery via the high interest rates on a floating debt.

Latin American debt grew rapidly from $96 billion in 1976 to $288 billion in 1981. During the same period most LACs accommodated a large transfer of funds from abroad, thus inducing a deficit in the trade balance of the region.

In several nations the large supply of foreign funds fostered a re-valuation of real exchange rates. In addition, import liberalization strengthened the adjustment of the domestic economies to the growing availability of foreign currency. The process was most intense in countries that, like Argentina and Chile, implemented monetarist experiments, and in new oil-exporting countries, like Mexico, whose foreign currency increased as a result of loans and enlarged oil export proceeds.

Notwithstanding real exchange-rate revaluations, the adjustment of LACs during the 1970s was performed by means of a growing exports volume that kept rising until 1981. The continued development of markets for the manufactured exports of the LDCs more than compensated for the dwindling of overall international trade in the 1970s. Indeed, international trade declined from a yearly growth of 8.0 percent in the 1960s to 5.5 percent in 1970–1981 (UN DIESA, 1984). Oil-exporting LACs achieved a rate of 6.6 percent in the latter period, combined with strong domestic demand. As a consequence, the LACs were able to maintain a significant economic growth until the early 1980s. Fast-rising indebt-edness was utilized by the LACs partly to finance a vigorous investment drive. In fact, the rate of capital formation increased from 17 percent in the 1960s to 22 percent in the second half of the 1970s.

More than 80 percent of the debt was contracted with private bank creditors. As a result of the increase in interest rates in 1980–1981, these payments, as a proportion of exports of goods and services, rose from 17 percent in 1979 to 38 percent in 1982 (CEPAL, 1986)—an effect that was aggravated by the sudden curtailment of foreign credits by mid-1982. Latin America was thus forced to start a drastic adjustment process in order to release the real resources that had to be transferred abroad to pay the higher financial cost of its debt. This adjustment meant the end of the steady economic growth that the region had succeeded in maintaining until the early 1980s.

Recessive Adjustment in the 1980s

In the 1980s Latin America faced a deep crisis arising from both the large debt it had accumulated during the 1970s and the worsening of the international markets of goods and finance. The abrupt reduction of the sources of external financing, concentrated in bank loans, was one cause of the low level of economic activity since the beginning of the 1980s. Together with the deterioration of the terms of trade, this reduction brought about such a shortage of foreign exchange that an intense recession in the region's national economies was provoked and the utilization rate of the available productive resources declined steeply. At the same time, the scarcity of foreign exchange, the recessive framework, and the adjustment policies that had been adopted discouraged investment. As a result, the rate of capital formation likewise diminished throughout the region after the early 1980s.

Since 1982 capital inflows to Latin America have experienced a sharp drop. The outflow of profits and interest has consequently become larger than capital inflows. The subsequent net negative transfer amounted to an annual average of US$27 billion in 1983–1988. Moreover, the negative net transfer of funds represented 24 percent of exports of goods and services in 1988. (Exports had declined owing to the deterioration on terms of trade.) By contrast, in 1978 (the year in which the largest net inflow of funds occurred) positive transfers were equivalent to 26 percent of exports. The difference is equivalent to 50 percent of the exports in 1988.

During the process of adjustment, several countries increased their export quantum, but Latin America as a whole did not succeed in raising the value of sales in foreign markets. Indeed, exports were lower in 1987 than in 1981.[2] During a six-year period of adjustment, and after a notable increase in real exchange rates (real depreciations), Latin America was unable to surmount the barriers presented by the world economy—namely, restricted access and markedly lower prices.

Following the significant downswings of per capita GDP in 1982 and 1983, some recovery did take place. Nonetheless, in 1987 per capita GDP was 4 percent below that achieved in 1981; only Brazil, Colombia, Panama, and the Dominican Republic exceeded the 1981 levels. The productive setback of the region resulted in the underutilization of its installed capacity. Labor, land, and factories were utilized on a reduced scale relative to 1981. Similarly, capital formation suffered from the recessive situation as well as from external financial stringency.

Rates of investment rose significantly during the increasing indebtedness of the 1970s, thus suggesting that foreign resources contributed to the development of the region as a whole. There were differences between countries, however, in terms of volume and quality. For example, those nations (such as Chile) that liberalized capital inflows, domestic financial markets, and imports tended to show both lower investment and reduced domestic savings. Yet a better performance was attained by those countries (such as Brazil and Colombia) that reformed their trade and financial policies in a moderate and selective manner.

Regardless of the effectiveness of the use of external borrowing, investment was limited by the shortage of funds following the shock of the reversal in net financial flows. Both the private and the public sectors have had to channel a sizable proportion of their savings into interest payments on the foreign debt. In fact, the net transfers abroad in 1983–1986 were roughly equivalent to one-half of the net capital formation recorded in those years.

In this adjustment process, investment and imports of capital goods fell substantially below pre-crisis levels. The recessive domestic setting, the notable uncertainty as to the duration of the recession, and the restrictions hampering public investment all contributed to a decline in the rate of capital formation. Investment ratios in 1983–1986 were about six points below the average achieved in 1975–1981. Social factors also worsened. There was a widespread drop in real wages; employment in formal sectors declined; the number of informal jobs increased; and public social expenditures were curtailed in several countries.

Three factors account for the costly adjustment that took place between 1982 and 1988: (1) the unfavorable world trade setting, (2) the abrupt cessation of funds from private lenders, and (3) the difficulties faced by debtor countries in designing a development strategy consistent with domestic structural adjustment and the actual shortcomings of the world economy. In short, Latin America finds itself in the middle of a debt crisis and far from reinvigorated development, notwithstanding its seven years of costly adjustment.

Notes

The authors are grateful for the helpful comments made by O. Sunkel, O. Altimir, O. Rosales, and V. Tokman, and for the efficient assistance provided by M. Cabezas and M. Paz Avalos.

1. With 1986 exchange rates, the figure drops to $1,800 per capita in 1980 and to $1,700 in 1986.

2. The quantity of exports of goods increased 42 percent between 1980 and 1987, whereas unit prices fell 29 percent. In the case of non-oil countries the quantity increased by 44 percent and the decrease in unit prices was 22 percent. See CEPAL (1987b, table 8).

References

BID (1984, 1986), *Progreso económico y social en América Latina*. Washington, D.C.

CEPAL (1984), *Estudio económico de América Latina 1982*. Santiago: CEPAL.

———(1986), *Relaciones económicas internacionales y cooperación regional de América Latina y el Caribe*, División de Comercio Internacional, LC/G. 1422. Santiago: CEPAL.

———(1987a), "Balance preliminar de la economía latinoamericana, 1987" (December). Santiago: CEPAL.

———(1987b), *Anuario Estadístico de América Latina y el Caribe 1987*. Santiago: CEPAL.

Kuznets, S. (1966), *Modern economic growth: Rate, structure and spread*. New Haven: Yale University Press.

Maddison, A. (1985), "Naturaleza y causas del estancamiento económico: Un examen de seis países," *Comercio Exterior*, Vol. 35, No. 1, Mexico.

UN DIESA (1984), "Major economic indicators showing historical development trends" (April), United Nations, New York.

U.S. Government (1983), *Economic Report of the President*. Washington, D.C.: Government Printing Office.

World Bank (1985), *World Development Report*. Washington, D.C.: World Bank.

2

From Structuralism to Neostructuralism: The Search for a Heterodox Paradigm

Nora Lustig

Among the numerous intellectual efforts undertaken by Latin American authors to understand the economic phenomena of the region, the current of thought known as *structuralism* stands out for its originality and persistence. Although structuralist ideas have sometimes been incomplete or unrigorous, over the years they have enriched our comprehension of certain economic processes in the region and suggested fruitful alternative approaches for policy design.

In what follows I shall outline the theoretical roots and summarize the historical evolution of structuralist thought from its inception at the end of the 1940s to the more recent emergence of what is called *neostructuralism*. Although this chapter reveals some of the shortcomings and qualities of structuralist ideas, it does not assess the analytical and empirical validity of structuralism either by itself or vis-à-vis alternative theories.

The Theoretical Roots of Structuralism

At the risk of sounding redundant, one can start by saying that structuralist thought views *structural* characteristics as the basic determinants of a society's evolution. These structural factors include, for example, the distribution of wealth and income, the land tenure regimes, the type and degree of foreign trade specialization, the density of productive linkages, the degree of market concentration, the control of the means of production by different types of actors (i.e., the private sector, the state, and transnational capital), the functioning of financial mechanisms, and the penetration of technological innovation, as well as the socio-political factors associated with the degree of labor organization, the organization of other classes or influential sectors, and the geographic and sectorial distribution of the population and its skill level. In structuralism, these characteristics determine the specific functioning of the causal mechanisms and the predictable success of any development strategy.

Structuralist thought—either in its most radical form associated with the Marxist tradition, or in its reformist version linked to the Keynesian and institutionalist schools of thought—falls within the realm of political economy. In the structuralist framework, the conception of society as the sum of family units and atomized firms that face given economic parameters has no meaning. On the contrary, economic policy measures are thought to affect the behavior of social actors who, far from functioning as isolated individuals, tend to join together and generate pressure groups (on either an organized or a spontaneous basis).

The classical roots of structuralist thought can be traced back to the Schumpeterian/Marxist view of free-enterprise capitalism as an inherently conflictive rather than harmonious system, and to its development as an irregular series of jumps that generate countless other imbalances. Although no version of the theory of exploitation appears explicitly in any of the structuralist literature, the notions of surplus generation and appropriation do emerge—along with identification of the losers in this process: the periphery versus the center, workers versus capitalists, campesinos versus the urban sector, and, finally, the very poor versus the rest of society. Nonetheless, the main difference between structuralist and Marxist thought is that structuralist authors do not necessarily conclude either that capitalism will tend to destroy itself or that encouragement of its destruction is necessarily convenient or desirable.[1]

The theoretical precursors of structuralism are various. As I mentioned earlier, the most evident ties are with the Marxist/Schumpeterian tradition, with respect to the vision of the functioning of the whole system. At the level of the specific mechanisms determining prices and product, the link is clearly with the Keynesian and post-Keynesian theories, with Kalecki, and, more recently, with the analytical developments of neoRicardian thought. Thus, one can identify some of the assumptions that structuralist analyses have in common. The most important of these are as follows:

1. The most relevant social actors are not price takers; these social actors thus create important rigidities in the markets.
2. The causal relation does not go from savings to investment but, rather, in the opposite direction.
3. In general, the money supply is passive and is adjusted to inflation, not the other way around.

4. Public investment is complementary and encourages private investment.
5. The development process is neither balanced nor harmonious, and it arises from the incorporation and dissemination of technical progress. New investment is the principal instrument in this process.
6. From a technological point of view, imported goods may be fundamental; hence the foreign exchange to purchase them becomes an indispensable requirement for sustained growth.

As a group these assumptions produce what can be called "critical skepticism" toward the recommendations that arise from economic orthodoxy for solving short- and long-term economic problems. In particular, structuralist thought greatly mistrusts the unanimous orthodox recommendation of correctly aligning relative prices as a sufficient (or sometimes even necessary) means of remedying all evils.

This distrust derives from some of the assumptions already mentioned. Due to the intrinsic rigidity of some markets, the adjustments induced by the orthodox recommendations more often change output levels, or income distribution, than prices.[2] Moreover, even if the assumption of price flexibility is accepted, the reallocation of resources that results from the change in prices may not be the best one. For example, partial liberalization in noncompetitive economies does not necessarily lead to a position of greater welfare than that resulting from price intervention. This result has been expanded on and accepted by orthodox welfare theory: The second-best option is not obtained by a partial approach toward the freeing of markets.

Furthermore, even in the case of a competitive world, the alignment of domestic prices with international ones is theoretically not the best policy for long-term growth. It is true that under competitive conditions the correct alignment of prices results in welfare improvement, as measured by static profits. However, it has been demonstrated that, in a dynamic model, a productive specialization different from the one dictated by international prices may result in increased growth over time. Two such circumstances are the presence of increasing economies of scale (Scitovsky, 1954) and uneven technical progress between productive sectors (Ros, 1987). Such productive specialization can also occur when the price and income elasticities of exports and imports as well as the capacity utilization rate reach certain magnitudes (Taylor, 1987).

Regardless of whether these ideas were developed with the same rigor during the first years of structuralist thought, they were clearly behind Raúl Prebisch's notion of industrial development as the best way to achieve sustained growth. Even if this policy meant a loss of welfare, due to the inefficiencies it introduced over the short term, industrial development was considered to be the most effective way of attracting and instituting dynamic comparative advantages.

The First Stage of Structuralist Thought:
The 1950s

It can be said that Latin American structuralist thought officially began at the end of 1949 and the beginning of 1950 with the publication by the Economic Commission for Latin America (ECLA) of two documents: "The Economic Development of Latin America and Some of Its Main Problems" and "The Economic Study of Latin America 1949." In spite of the fact that they are official documents of an organism dependent on the United Nations, the ideas set forth in them can be attributed primarily to one author, Raúl Prebisch.

These papers developed, for the first time, the original concept of the center-peripheral system. According to the analysis presented in them, the capitalist world can be conceptualized as consisting of two types of countries: the center, conformed by those economies in which capitalist production techniques first predominated; and the periphery, which is "constituted by economies whose production continues to lag behind in an organizational and technical point of view,"[3] and in which "technical progress only occurs in a few sectors of its enormous population. Generally, it only penetrates those sectors where food and raw materials must be produced at a low cost for large industrial centers."[4]

One of the consequences of this process is that the structure of the periphery acquires two fundamental characteristics. On the one hand, the peripheral economy is specialized, inasmuch as development occurs almost exclusively in the primary-goods export sector whereas other goods and services are usually imported. On the other hand, the peripheral structures are heterogeneous. Those sectors that use advanced techniques imported from the centers, and in which there is a comparable level of labor productivity, coexist with others in which obsolete, old-fashioned techniques are used, thus leading to productivity levels very much inferior to those in analogous activities in the centers.

However, the most important aspect of the central-periphery concept is the idea that these characteristics of the peripheral productive structure, far from disappearing as capitalism advances in the centers, tend to perpetuate and reinforce themselves. One of the determinants of this increasing gap between the two poles is that technological change is much more pronounced in the industrial sector than in the primary sector. Under conditions of constant terms of trade, the former leads to an increase in the productivity and to an income gap between the center and the periphery. This polarization tends to increase given that the centers are able to keep the fruits of technical progress due to the degree of organization of the working class and the oligopolist power of the private business sector. In the periphery, by contrast, productivity increases are not translated into lower prices owing to the structural labor surplus. Furthermore, the income elasticity of raw materials is smaller than that of industrial goods. In other words, there are inherent forces that cause a secular deterioration of the terms of trade, to the continual disadvantage of the periphery.

In view of this interpretation, the development of the periphery has fundamentally depended not on continuing with the historical pattern of specialization based on exploiting static comparative advantages but, instead, on promoting industrial development. Such development can be achieved through import substitution. It can also be achieved if the *infant industries* are furnished with the necessary protection.

The theory of the *deterioration of terms of trade* gave rise to a long theoretical and empirical debate, which experienced various changes later on.[5] Apart from the empirical validity of this theory, the relevance of structuralist thought in its initial stages had to do with the emphasis it placed on the limitations associated with a development pattern based on static comparative advantages. According to the ideas of the period, the productive specialization arising from that pattern would condemn the periphery to remain underdeveloped.

The predominant idea, then, was that development implied industrialization, inasmuch as this was the only course that allowed the peripheral economies to break with the negative characteristics of their productive structure and to make full use of the advantages derived from technical progress.

As Fishlow (1985) has noted, structuralism found fertile ground for its ideas in the postwar Latin American economies. In these economies, during the 1930s and 1940s, the combination of controls on international trade, restrictions on foreign exchange, and expansive demand policies resulted in a rapid recuperation led by the industrial sector after the Great Depression. The economic policy recommended by structuralism was also congruent with modernization in its broadest sense: It implied encouraging the growth of an urban labor sector and strengthening the position of the industrial businessmen vis-à-vis the oligarchical agro-export sector. It was assumed that industrialization through import substitution would lead the peripheral economies to a more independent, democratic, and egalitarian growth path than growth based on primary goods exports. Industrialization created expectations of higher development, but this outcome did not occur.

There is, it seems, a certain paradox in what was initially stated in structuralist thought as a justification for an import-substitution industrialization policy and the results of that process. In theory, such a policy was the only way to achieve independent development, as the specialization in the production and export of primary products would lead to an inevitable deterioration of the terms of trade. The periphery, therefore, would have to resign itself to growing at lower rates (owing to the transference of the surplus to the center) or else sustain its growth with external savings (which, in fact, constituted the same surplus transformed and returned to the periphery as another's property).

However, the implementation of the import-substitution strategy (which took place in the 1950s) placed the countries in a more vulnerable situation vis-à-vis the external market than they had been in before. On the one hand, the overvaluation of the exchange rate that accompanied the substitution process discouraged exports and, on the other, the evolution of the substitution process increased the dependency of complementary imports (intermediate and capital goods), which became more and more essential.[6]

This growing vulnerability paved the way for what is known as the structuralist interpretation of the external deficit.[7] In modern language, the structuralist hypothesis is that external imbalance is intrinsic to the process of late industrialization, owing to two characteristics of the first stages of industrialization via import substitution. First, the income elasticity of demand for imports is high (greater than one), as the majority of imports are essential intermediate and capital goods that are relatively expensive and sophisticated. Second, the price elasticity of imports is low, due to the fact that most imports are complementary.

On the other hand, exports are unable to grow at the necessary rate. With industrialization, the domestic demand for exportable goods grows (as these are the raw materials used by local industry), and, on the international level, the demand for primary goods tends to decrease, given Engels' Law and the fact that natural raw materials are substituted by synthetic materials. Furthermore, fledgling manufacturing industries in the periphery are not able to export because they cannot compete on the international market (Villarreal, 1976).[8]

It is thus clear that whereas some of the structuralist authors viewed the "failure" of import substitution to generate a less foreign exchange–dependent growth as an unpleasant surprise, for others it was clear from the start that industrialization via import substitution would *inevitably* lead to greater external imbalance.

The following question then arises: If it was clear that industrialization via import substitution would imply a deterioration in the trade balance over a long period of time (meaning that someone had to be willing to finance this imbalance), what was the advantage of industrializing in this manner? One could think that structuralist thought has suffered, and that it suffers from some sort of industrialist fetishism.

However, in the original structuralist framework (which continues to be in effect, though with certain modifications), the *equation* between development and industrialization was accepted because historical experience indicated that industrialization had been the most efficient means of introducing the technological and organizational changes that guaranteed the development of the advanced countries. Moreover, structuralists were firmly convinced that continuation of the model of primary goods specialization would tend to produce external imbalance as well (depending on the degree to which the income and price elasticities of their international demand decreased), with the additional problem that this tendency would never revert itself.

In contrast, industrialization via import substitution, once completed, would eventually lead to the disappearance of the structural external imbalance. This perception of industrialization was the basis for the rejection of the orthodox position that the Latin American countries would be better off specializing in the production of primary goods and using the foreign exchange generated from their exports to import the necessary manufactured goods. In the 1950s, the reader should note, it was unclear that import substitution could lead to the diversification and development of exports. Although various Asiatic countries were following this policy, they could not go *directly* to diversification and development of exports.

For most structuralist authors, exchange devaluation was not an adequate mechanism for adjusting the trade balance. Given the relative magnitudes of the income and price elasticities of imports (and exports), a very pronounced devaluation would also be needed in order to restore equilibrium. Because devaluation makes noncompetitive imports more expensive, it would result in inflationary pressures and a contraction of output. For the structuralist school of thought, then, it was more sensible to resort to import controls (quotas or tariffs) and to complete the industrialization process. Once this process was completed, the income elasticity of the imports would substantially decrease and the economies would be in a position to grow without being limited by the current-account restriction.

Before moving on to the next decade, I should note another significant component of structuralist thought that emerged during the 1950s—namely, the interpretation of the causes of the inflationary process and the ways to combat it. It was during this period that the structuralist theory of inflation began to take shape, leading to debates and controversies that continue today. The initial premises of this theory were developed by Noyola (1956) and Sunkel (1960).

According to Noyola, inflation resulted from two types of components: "basic" inflationary pressures caused by the existence of sectoral imbalances that placed pressure on a key price (e.g., agricultural prices and the exchange rate) and "transmission mechanisms" that transferred the initial price increase to the rest of the economy. Among the latter, he cited the adjustment of monetary and fiscal policies and the existence of some type of salary indexing process. These mechanisms facilitated the transmission of the price increase of a certain commodity, or productive factor, to the rest of the economy.

This interpretation of inflation led its proponents to reject the policy of combatting inflation through demand cuts, as the origin of the inflationary pressures was believed to be *structural* in nature. Hence inflation could be eradicated only through elimination of the bottlenecks found in the basic components of the inflationary process. Although the orthodox measures might decrease the rate of inflation, they would imply a sacrifice in the level of activity and a deterioration in income distribution. This point of view is partly responsible for both the complacency of the structuralists regarding inflation and their disdain for short-run stabilization policies. As inflation was a consequence of structural imbalances, one had to learn to live with it and confront it as part of a long-term policy toward the elimination of bottlenecks.

Structural Pessimism: The 1960s

The relative failure of industrialization via import substitution became evident in three areas: First, the problem of external imbalance became more acute for the reasons referred to already. Second, serious sectoral imbalances appeared. For example, the agricultural sector became less dynamic, resulting in bottlenecks in the production of foodstuffs (and, hence, in inflationary pressures); the use of capital-intensive techniques in industry led to the surfacing of urban impoverishment because industry was unable to absorb quickly enough the labor force that was arriving in the cities in search of a better standard of living; and because more priority was placed on physical goals than on those of efficiency, plants were constructed that would always operate at excess capacity. Finally, as the import-substitution process advanced, the real resources initially transferred to industry by the agro-industrial sector decreased (as a consequence of the stagnation of agricultural production), and the process depended more and more on state intervention and subsidies.

At the same time, public expenditures that were complementary to the industrialization process increased (owing to infrastructure projects, for example, or because the government became the last-resort employer), and the potential growth of government income became restricted. An imbalance in the public finances was thus unleashed, resulting in demand pressures that contributed to the inflationary process.[9]

Disappointment with the results of the import-substitution process gave way to new currents of thought within structuralism. One group placed its hopes on regional integration.[10] During this period several efforts were made to bring about subregional integration; this position continues to be held today among the advocates of south-south commerce as the best option for indebted countries.

Another group believed it was necessary to resort to official capital from abroad to palliate the scarcity of foreign exchange and alleviate the fiscal imbalances—a vision embedded in the Alliance for Progress.[11] And a third group, one that probably had more impact in academic and political circles, continued to base its strategy on the development of the internal market. Within this group, however, many different positions have been taken concerning the specific means of implementing an inward-looking development strategy. Adherents of the most radical position considered the possibility of development within the capitalist system to be nonexistent. Inasmuch as the development of capitalism at an international level resulted in underdevelopment in peripheral economies, the only way of overcoming the limits to growth was by changing the system.[12]

Another group of authors considered the possibility of growth within the capitalist system to be possible indeed, but only if a redistributive mechanism mediated the process.[13] Finally, yet another group deemed growth within capitalism to be feasible but claimed that such growth implied inequality and impoverishment.[14]

A common thread among these three visions is the importance given to the relationships among the distribution of income, consumption, and growth. What follows is a synthesis of some of the central ideas concerning these relationships. According to some of the structuralist authors who wrote during the mid-1960s and the beginning of the 1970s, the evolution and characteristics of the accumulation of capital during the "difficult" stage of import substitution led to the emergence of stagnation tendencies. This point was stated principally by Furtado (1966), who considered Latin American countries to be victims of a "vicious spiral" triggered by the interaction between growth and income distribution. The prevalent growth model generated a high concentration of income, which in turn oriented the demand structure toward durable consumer goods. This orientation then induced the productive structure to lean toward sectors with greater capital density (i.e., a greater capital-output relation) and higher import requirements, thus impeding the possibility of sustaining a certain growth rate.[15]

Furtado's (1966) pessimism with respect to the possibilities of continued growth was not shared by other structuralists (such as Sunkel and Paz, 1970; Pinto, 1970, 1974; and Vuskovic, 1974). Although they recognized that the productive structure had become more and more inclined toward sectors with higher capital and import coefficients, they contended that this fact did not preclude growth altogether. However, these authors argued that the resulting resource allocation implied a worsening of the external imbalance and of inequality.[16]

In short, these authors considered the restrictions on sustaining a certain growth rate to be fundamentally supply-side in nature. The supply constraints emerged during the "difficult" stage of import substitution, when the productive structure moved increasingly toward the "modern" sectors.[17] These sectors used relatively more capital-intensive techniques and had higher import requirements. Their resource allocation was the result of an unequal distribution of income that generated a demand profile biased toward those sectors.

This basic characteristic of the growth pattern heightened the problems of inequality, impoverishment, and foreign dependency, because these sectors have not only a lower labor requirement and higher import coefficients but also a higher participation rate on the part of multinational companies. Within this framework, then, a more equal distribution of income would be accompanied by increased output and employment growth rates as well as a higher degree of national control over the productive apparatus.

The third set of authors, those belonging to the group who believed that the growth path had to be based on the expansion of the domestic market, fundamentally disagreed with adherents of the previous position. Tavares (1973) and Serra and Tavares (1974), for example, claimed that the accumulation of capital during the industrialization process was stimulated by the expansion of the "modern" sector, owing to the magnitude of its dynamic linkages and the external economies it produced. For these authors (in contrast to the previous ones), this "modern" sector was perceived to be the leading sector of the economy in the Shumpeterian sense of the word, and accumulation could continue only if the "realization" problems found in the "modern" or durable consumer goods sector were resolved.

In other words, the decreased growth rate during the "difficult" stage of import substitution was the result of a realization crisis in the leading sector, brought about by an "underconsumption" of the goods produced there. This underconsumption was a direct result of the distributive profile, which induced a saturation of the demand for these goods. If the crisis was to be overcome, then, income needed to be concentrated in the middle groups.[18]

Given that the durable consumer goods sector was the leader of the economy, these authors contended that income concentration was necessary to guarantee an adequate market. The "redistributionists," on the other hand, took the position that the durable consumer goods sector was exactly the one that should not expand, as it had the greatest import requirements and capital-labor ratio. In both conceptions, however, growth based on the expansion of the "modern," or durable consumer goods, sector meant that the underdeveloped character of the growth path would continue to manifest itself both in the impoverishment of vast sectors of the population and in foreign dependency.

The ideas outlined above triggered a series of studies and empirical analyses. Interestingly enough, the empirical studies that have analyzed income distribution and growth have found evidence of a positive, yet *small*, relationship between the two variables (Cline, 1972; Wells, 1977; Berry, 1981; Lustig, 1981; Bonelli and Viera da Cunha, 1983).

In addition, the socialization experiences in Chile and Nicaragua, as well as the populist attempts to improve the relative income position of salaried workers in Argentina, Brazil, and Mexico (to name just three countries), indicate that, in practice, a redistributive process can generate strong sectoral imbalances and have serious consequences for the balance of payments. Income redistribution turned out to be much more difficult than anticipated, even from a strictly economic point of view.

These difficulties may arise because the demand for certain products (food, for example) can have an outcome very different from that expected, given the observed elasticities. Moreover, reformist or revolutionary redistributive processes entail conflicts that cause financial and physical decapitalization, both of which negatively affect output.

In combination with international economic and political pressures, redistributive policies—far from resulting in self-sustained growth—may exacerbate imbalances that heighten instability. My point is not that the struggle for a more equal society should be abruptly suspended but, rather, that it cannot be waged on fragile bases and with naive hypotheses. If the redistributive strategies fail to take into account the reactions that can surface during these processes, the result can be the exact opposite of what is sought.[19]

The Emergence of Neostructuralism:
The 1970s and 1980s

In the time since the positions on growth and income distribution were elaborated, structuralist thought seems to have concentrated more and more on short-term problems and policies. Perhaps this is a natural reaction to the "orthodox" stabilization packages applied in the Southern Cone during the 1960s under the aegis of military regimes. It may also be a response to the difficulties involved in implementing structural change along the lines recommended by the redistributionists, as exemplified by the Chilean case.

An alternative current of economic thought could not dismiss the problem of galloping inflation with the argument that its only feasible solution was profound structural change, the results of which would become clear only over the long term. Such an attitude could only lead to intellectual inaction and practical irrelevance.

Maybe one of the most important characteristics that distinguish neostructuralism from its forerunner is the awareness that recommendations for long-term structural change cannot be made in the absence of knowledge about what their possible effects may be during the transition period or about how to deal with them.

Moreover, neostructuralists are aware that a successful long-term policy cannot be made in a world plagued with uncertainty—a world in which the largest outlay of intellectual energy made by society is directed toward finding ways of evading the inflationary tax.[20]

Within the structuralist theory of inflation mentioned previously, we distinguished two types of components: the basic inflationary pressures that emerge from relative price adjustments caused by sectorial imbalances, and the transmission or reproduction mechanisms by which inflationary pressures are translated into an increase in the general level of prices in the entire economy. The emphasis of structuralist thought in its original form was on the first component, resulting in a complacent attitude toward inflation as an inevitable evil of late industrial development. The neostructuralist analyses, on the other hand, has focused primarily on the transmission mechanisms and on designing economic policy packages that might generate stability while minimizing social costs and damage to the productive apparatus. These analyses have been the foundations for the so-called heterodox stabilization programs, which direct the bulk of the measures toward eliminating "inertial" inflation and distributive conflicts by freezing prices and salaries.[21]

In clear contrast with structuralism, in fact, it might be said that neostructuralist thought has the opposite bias: a lot of emphasis on short-term analysis and relatively little emphasis on the long run. The reason for this might be that the short-term problems are so pressing that intellectual energy has been directed toward them rather than toward long-term problems. It may also be that adequate long-term strategies are less clear. The negative consequences of recommendations in the more "naive" version of structuralism (i.e., regarding the efficiency of the public and private productive apparatus) have resulted in more skepticism concerning direct or indirect state intervention in the allocation of resources. Democracy has reappeared in many countries, and the desire to maintain this form of government has made economic policy more cautious. Years of dictatorship and repression are evidence of political fragility and of the sensitivity of many societies to conflictive measures. In neostructuralist thought there is the clear perception that solutions must be reached through consensus.

Finally, the opinion that a viable long-run strategy is impossible under the current conditions of foreign debt servicing seems to make long-term analyses irrelevant until the conditions change. However, the existence of this restriction demonstrates the urgency of finding new formulas that make more equitable growth strategies a viable option. In other words, formulas must be found that permit the original proposals of structuralist thinking to observe real-world examples.

Notes

1. De Janvry (1985) presents some interesting ideas regarding the ideological/political position of structuralism.

2. A rigorous presentation of these adjustment mechanisms as well as other theoretical aspects of structuralism and their implications for economic policy can be seen in Taylor (1983).

3. Rodríguez (1980), p. 26.

4. CEPAL (1949), from Rodríguez (1980), p. 26.

5. According to Rodríguez (1980), there are three versions of this theory: the accounting, the cyclical, and the "industrialization" versions.

6. See the ground-breaking discussion of the "failure" of the substitution process presented by Hirschman (1968) and the more recent analysis by Fajnzylber (1983).

7. In fact, this idea appeared during the 1940s in the work of the Mexican economist Juan Noyola entitled "Fundamental Imbalance and Economic Development" (Noyola, 1949).

8. In other words, late industrialization will always imply an external imbalance because, "due to the delayed character of its industrialization the domestic production of the country was unable to compete in the internal and external markets for manufactured goods to the same degree at which the internal demand for these types of goods increased" (Bazdresch, 1984, p. 571).

9. Fishlow (1985), p. 144.

10. Within the group promoting regional integration, it was expected that "the freest possible commerce between Latin American countries could motivate business to divert towards competitive imports and increase the amount of foreign exchange available for complementary imports from the industrial countries . . . [and] free up the restrictions on foreign exchange, as well as reap benefits from a higher degree of specialization" (Fishlow, 1985, p. 145).

11. However, it was soon discovered that the goals of the Alliance were incompatible with structuralist objectives (Fishlow, 1985, p. 146).

12. Frank (1969).

13. Pinto (1970); Vuskovic (1974).

14. Serra and Tavares (1974).

15. Furtado (1969).

16. According to Vuskovic (1974), for example, the growth obstacles that resulted from the orientation of the productive structure toward durable or "modern" consumer goods were surmountable, despite the fact that these areas had lower labor coefficients and higher rates of transnational participation than the traditional sectors.

17. Above all, the productive structure moved toward the durable consumer goods sector.

18. Serra and Tavares (1974).

19. Chile under the Allende government was a painful case in point.

20. This has intermittently been the case in several Latin American countries.

21. For further details on heterodox stabilization programs, the reader is directed to the works of Fanelli and Frenkel (1987); Heymann (1986); Arida and Lara-Resende (1985); Bacha (1987); Lopes (1986); Modiano (1987); Ros (1987); Alberro and Ibarra (1987); and Ocampo (1987).

References

Alberro, J., and D. Ibarra (1987), "Programas heterodoxos de estabilización, Presentación," *Estudios Económicos*, El Colegio de México (October).

Arida, P., and A. Lara-Resende (1985), "Inertial inflation and monetary reform in Brazil." In J. Williamson, (ed.), *Inflation and indexation: Argentina, Brazil and Israel*. Cambridge, Mass.: Institute of Technology Press.

Bacha, E. (1987), "La inercia y el conflicto: El Plan Cruzado y sus desafíos," *Estudios Económicos*, El Colegio de México (October).

Bazdresch, C. (1984), *El pensamiento de Juan E. Noyola*. México: Fondo de Cultura Económica.

Berry, R. (1981), "Redistribution, demand structure and factor requirements: The case of India," *World Development*, Vol. 9.

Bonelli, R., and P. Vieira da Cunha (1983), "Distribuçao da renda e padroes de crescimento: Um modelo dinamico de economia brasileira," *Pesquisa e Planejamiento Económico*, Vol. 13, No. 1.

CEPAL (1949), *El desarrollo económico de América Latina y algunos de sus principales problemas*. Santiago: United Nations.

⸻ (1950), *Estudio económico de América Latina, 1949*. Santiago: United Nations.

Cline, W. (1972), *Potential effects of income redistributions on economic growth: Latin American cases*. New York: Praeger.

De Janvry, A. (1985), "La desarticulación social en la historia de América Latina," *Investigación Económica*, Vol. 44, No. 172, México (April).

Fajnzylber, F. (1983), *La industrialización trunca de América Latina*. México: Nueva Imagen.

Fanelli, J. M., and R. Frenkel (1987), "El Plan Austral: Un año y medio después," *El Trimestre Económico*, Vol. 54 (September).

Fishlow, A. (1985), "El estado de la ciencia económica en América Latina." In *Progreso económico y social en América Latina. Deuda externa: crisis y ajuste*, Banco Interamericano de Desarrollo, Informe de 1985.

Frank, A. G. (1969), *Capitalism and underdevelopment in Latin America*. New York: Modern Reader.

Furtado, C. (1966), *Subdesarrollo y estancamiento en América Latina*. Buenos Aires, Argentina: Editorial Universitaria.

_____ (1969), *Um projeto para o Brasil*. Río de Janeiro, Brasil: Editorial Saga.

Heymann, D. (1986), "Inflación y políticas de estabilización," *Revista de la CEPAL//xit,//* No. 28, Santiago.

Hirschman, A. (1968), "The political economy of import substituting industrialization in Latin America," *Quarterly Journal of Economics* (February).

Lopes, F. (1986), "Inflaçao inercial, hiperinflaçao e desinflaçao: Notas e conjectura," *Revista de ANPEC*, No. 9. Río de Janeiro: Asociación Nacional de Perquises Economicos (ANPEC).

Lustig, N. (1981), *Distribución del ingreso y crecimiento en México: Un análisis de las ideas estructuralistas*. México: El Colegio de México.

Modiano, E. (1987), "El Plan Cruzado: Bases teóricas y limitaciones prácticas," *El Trimestre Económico*, Vol. 54, México (September).

Noyola, J. (1949), "Desequilibrio fundamental y fomento económico," thesis, Universidad Nacional Autónoma de México, México

_____ (1956), "El desarrollo económico y la inflación en México y otros países latinoamericanos." In L. Solís (ed.), *La economía mexicana*, Vol. 2, Lecturas de *El Trimestre Económico*, No. 4, Fondo de Cultura Económica, México (1973).

Ocampo, J. A. (1987), "Una evaluación comparativa de cuatro planes antiinflacionarios recientes," *El Trimestre Económico*, Vol. 55, México (September).

Pinto, A. (1970), "Naturaleza e implicaciones de la heterogeneidad estructural," *El Trimestre Económico*, No. 145, México (January).

_____ (1974), "El modelo de desarrollo reciente en América Latina.," In Serra, J. (ed.), *Desarrollo latinoamericano: Ensayos críticos*, Lecturas de *El Trimestre Económico*, No. 6, Fondo de Cultura Económica, México.

Rodríguez, O. (1980), *La teoría del subdesarrollo de la CEPAL*, Siglo 21, México.

Ros, J. (1987), "On models of inertial inflation," World Institute for Development Economics Research of the United Nations (WIDER) (July), mimeo.

Scitovsky, T. (1954), "Two concepts of external economies," *Journal of Political Economy*, No. 62.

Serra, J., and M. C. Tavares (1974), "Más allá del estancamiento: Una discusión sobre el estilo del desarrollo reciente en Brasil." In J. Serra (ed.), *Desarrollo latinoamericano: Ensayos críticos*, Lecturas de *El Trimestre Económico*, No. 6, Fondo de Cultura Económica, México.

Sunkel, O. (1960), "Inflation in Chile: An unorthodox approach," *International Economic Papers*, No. 10.

Sunkel, O., and P. Paz (1970), *El subdesarrollo latinoamericano y la teoría del desarrollo*, Siglo 21, México.

Tavares, M. C. (1973), "Distribuçao de renda, acumulaçao e padroes de industrializaçao." In *A controversia sobre distribuçao de renda e desenvolvimento*. Río de Janeiro: Zahar Editores.

Taylor, L. (1983), *Structuralist macroeconomics*. New York: Basic Books.

———(1986), "Economic openness: Problems to the Century's End," WIDER, *Macroeconomic Policies Project* (May), mimeo.

———(1987), "El Plan Austral (y otros choques heterodoxos): Fase II," *El Trimestre Económico*, Vol. 55 (September).

Villarreal, L. (1976), *El desequilibrio externo en la industrialización de México (1929–1975)*, Fondo de Cultura Económica, México.

Vuskovic, P. (1974), "Distribución del ingreso y opciones de desarrollo." In J. Serra (ed.), *Desarrollo latinoamericano: Ensayos críticos*, Lectura No. 6, Fondo de Cultura Económica, México.

Wells, J. (1977), "The diffusion of durables in Brazil and its implications for recent controversies concerning Brazilian development," *Cambridge Journal of Economics*, No. 1.

3

Monetarism and Structuralism: Some Macroeconomic Lessons

Andrés Velasco

This chapter surveys the macroeconomic theories and policies that have emerged in Latin America during recent years. Its main purpose is not to recapitulate country experiences (many of which have been described at length elsewhere) but, instead, to focus on the contrasting approaches of monetarism and structuralism, the policy experiments they have spawned, and the lessons that can be extracted from them.

Two restrictions are imposed to make this broad task manageable. First, only short-run variables and policies are considered. In the past, there has been considerable confusion over the distinction between the short run and the long run among both orthodox and heterodox Latin Americanists. At one time, structuralists of the old school believed that the key to restraining inflation was agrarian reform, given that rising agricultural prices are responsible for rising aggregate prices. More recently, advocates of liberalization have insisted that Latin American countries cannot achieve price stability without privatizing most state enterprises and drastically shrinking the public sector. In both cases the short run has been replaced by the long run, thus introducing into the policy debate factors whose effect on macroeconomic outcomes is far from clear. This is not to say that structural or long-run tendencies lack importance or do not have macroeconomic implications. Nor does it mean that the state of certain Latin American countries is not in need of an overhaul.

Second, this chapter emphasizes the closed-economy aspects of the macroeconomic debate. Although references are made to exchange-rate and commercial policy, the focus is on two other areas: the behavior of prices (on the supply side) and monetary and fiscal policies (on the demand side).[1]

Old Problems, Old Ideas: The 1950s and 1960s

The controversies between structuralists and monetarists reached their peak during the 1950s and 1960s. The debate is summarized in a volume edited by Baer and Kerstenetsky (1964).[2] Structuralist theories were based on the work of Sunkel (1960) and Seers (1962), who stressed the crucial role of real supply and institutional factors in the initiation of inflation. On the other side, the monetarist arguments of the 1950s and 1960s, referred to as old orthodoxy, have their most lucid exposition in the well-known paper by Harberger (1963) on inflation in Chile. The principal origin of inflation, Harberger argues, lies in excessive rates of monetary expansion, generally attributed to the fiscal deficit. In this connection,, monetarists reaffirmed the argument of Milton Friedman that inflation "is always, and above all, a monetary phenomenon." Fiscal reform, monetary prudence, and a devaluation of the fixed exchange rate are necessary and sufficient conditions to end inflation. This prescription was put into practice in various stabilization programs, including those in Chile (1956–1958), Argentina (1959–1962), and Peru (1959).

Friedman's notion is correct in a very basic sense. To sustain high, persistent inflation, the Central Bank must follow an accommodating monetary policy. Otherwise, rising prices would erode the real value of money balances, thereby reducing aggregate demand and eventually inflation. This conclusion is confirmed by observations of the correlation between increases in prices and increases in money supply in an inflationary economy: Over medium to long periods, the correlation is always significant and close to unity. After estimating this relationship for a group of Latin American countries, Cardoso (1987) showed that during the years from 1960 to 1985, the most inflationary Latin American countries were invariably those in which the Central Bank had acted in an excessively "generous" manner.

The measured correlation is suggestive, but it does not answer two fundamental questions. First, if monetary expansion causes inflation (at least in the long run), why do the governments of these countries insist on following such policies? This behavior cannot be attributed to ignorance or simple irresponsibility. The fiscal deficit might be part of the reason, but it does not necessarily have to be financed through the printing of money. And if the deficit were at the root of the problem, there should be a one-to-one correlation between the size of the deficit and the rate of monetary expansion, but such a correlation is not always the case.[3] (See Figure 3.1.)

To tackle this question, we will find it helpful to inquire about the possible costs of a more contractionary monetary policy. In a neoclassical

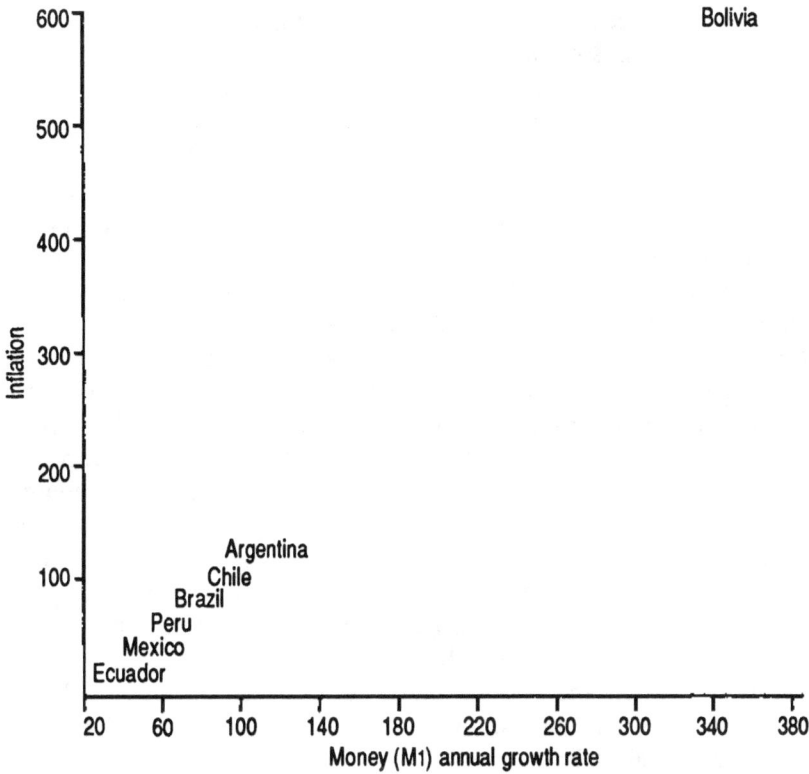

FIGURE 3.1 Inflation and Money Supply (1960–1985) (in percentages). *Source:* Cardoso (1987).

model of perfectly flexible prices and full government credibility, this cost is zero. But, as structuralists have argued, price increases in Latin American economies tend to reflect frequent and uncontrollable shocks on the supply side: Devaluations, wage increases, and rising food prices have been the factors frequently mentioned by critics of orthodoxy. Moreover, as wages and controlled prices are indexed to past inflation, supply shocks tend to be quite persistent over time. In this context inflation can become inertial, and trying to stop it by means of monetary policy alone can be costly in terms of employment or output.[4] Therefore, it is likely that monetary authorities are not causing an expansion *motu proprio*; rather, they are simply accommodating monetary pressures originating outside the money market. Indeed, a principal hypothesis of the structuralists was that money is effectively "passive" (Olivera, 1970).

Structuralists have also argued that the persistence of shocks on the cost side can be attributed to a distributive struggle[5] among different sectors of society. Everyone makes his or her own plans acting on the assumption that there will be inflation. And inflation is in fact perpetuated through wage adjustments, exchange-rate devaluations, and increases in public-sector prices. Economic agents attempt to maintain the real value of their income at the cost of perpetuating the inflationary spiral. Paradoxically, if all groups in society were to behave in this way, the real income of each one would be the same as that without inflation. Inflation therefore acts as a costly and inefficient mechanism to avoid or ease internal conflicts over the distribution of real income. Neo-structuralists rediscovered this idea in the 1980s.

Only closed-economy versions of the "old orthodoxy" and their corresponding critiques have been mentioned so far. In more general versions the economy is open to international trade and finance such that exchange-rate policy acquires a central role. A simple and elegant version of the resulting model is found in the work of Dornbusch (1982).[6] In this model only one combination of the real exchange rate and the fiscal deficit (defined strictly as the ratio of the deficit to output) allows the economy to achieve internal and external equilibrium. At the same time, the fiscal deficit has to be monetized, and the resulting inflation rate depends on the elasticity of the demand for money with respect to inflation. If the country has a trade deficit at the beginning of the stabilization plan, the deficit can be corrected through the combination of a real devaluation and a reduction in the fiscal deficit. These policies will also result in an automatic reduction of inflation, given that only a smaller deficit must be financed through the inflation tax.

As Dornbusch (1982) points out, this model is essentially long run and has little to say about the dynamics that immediately follow the implementation of the stabilization plan. A program of this sort must meet two requirements in order to be successful: (1) The nominal devaluation should reduce real wages and thereby enhance competitiveness; and, (2) when relative prices change, resources should quickly move to the tradeable goods sector. Only in this way will the adjustment take place with minimal output and employment costs. Even if there is no indexation and condition (1) is met, condition (2) is often delayed by costs of adjustment and uncertainty over the definitive structure of relative prices. During the transition period, wage earners may find themselves in the worst of both worlds, experiencing both unemployment and a drop in the purchasing power of wages.

This dynamic can explain why adjustment programs designed by the International Monetary Fund (IMF) and based on this framework have been strenuously resisted by countries of various political leanings. In many countries there is generally a marked improvement of external accounts, but at the cost of sizable domestic output and employment losses. This is explained by the fact that short-run external adjustment is obtained primarily through import contraction and very low expansion of exports. The examples of Chile in 1975–1976 and Brazil in 1982–1983 stand out, but similar problems were encountered by the orthodox stabilization programs of the 1950s and 1960s.

Old Problems, New Ideas: The 1970s

The problems faced in stopping inflation, as well as the growth slowdown in a number of countries of the region,[7] led certain orthodox economists to convert to a type of structuralism—that is, if simple structuralism is understood to blame macroeconomic problems on the structure and institutions of the economy. As Alejandro Foxley (1982) observed with respect to the liberalizing Southern Cone experiments of the 1970s, "the orthodox policies put a heavy emphasis on changing the more fundamental ways in which the economy works. In a curious parallel to structuralist thinking, inflation is increasingly viewed as the result of an economic system that does not work."

In spite of this new conviction—or perhaps assuming that structural reforms and liberalizations had eliminated all imperfections in the relevant markets—the monetarist policymakers of the Southern Cone of the late 1970s adopted a daring approach to stabilization that relied on the existence of a great degree of flexibility in the economy. The results of applying the "monetary approach to the balance of payments" to several countries of the region have been widely analyzed. Different perspectives are found in Díaz-Alejandro (1982), Foxley (1982), Edwards (1985), Calvo (1986), and Ramos (1987).

The old and the new orthodoxies differed in their assumptions concerning the degree of openness of the economy. If complete openness in the goods market is assumed, the "law of one price" should hold:

$$P = E\,P^*,$$

where P = price of the one good in local currency, P^* = world price, and E = the nominal exchange rate. If it is also assumed that international inflation is exogenous and negligible, then:

$$\dot{P} = \dot{E},$$

where the "." above the variables indicates percentage change over time. That is, domestic inflation is essentially attributed to a persistent devaluation of the nominal exchange rate. Therefore, the rate of change in domestic prices should rapidly converge to the international rate when repeated devaluations are ended. It is on this principle that the stabilization approach applied in the Southern Cone was based. Note that in this case money supply is endogenous because, in circumstances of capital mobility, the government must buy and sell its own currency at the fixed exchange rate.

These experiments, which to varying degrees were accompanied by trade and financial liberalization, ended in failure. Carlos Díaz-Alejandro (1979) succinctly describes the perverse dynamic that took place:

> The liberalization of domestic financial markets tends to increase real returns on financial assets. Domestic and foreign wealth owners will increase their net holdings of those assets. While that portfolio adjustment is taking place, the real exchange rate will appreciate relative to what it would have been without financial liberalization. During this period financial liberalization will work at cross-purposes with export promotion. . . . Authorities in those countries have announced the crawling peg with respect to the U.S. dollar for several months ahead of time, hoping that such information will cluster inflationary expectations around a lower path. Domestic interest rates . . . substantially exceed foreign dollar interest rates after adjusting for expected devaluation of the peso relative to the dollar. Massive financial inflows occur, expanding Central Bank and the money supply, yet domestic interest rates react only sluggishly. . . . Exporters and previously protected producers of importables will find these short-run dynamics singularly perverse, and will clamor for faster devaluation or subsidies. Authorities will point to bulging reserves as evidence that faster devaluation is unnecessary.

It is now known that real exchange-rate appreciation led to unsustainable trade and current-account deficits, which could no longer be financed when external capital flows dried out around 1982. Díaz-Alejandro's main point was that financial liberalization (whether domestic or international) can be a cause of real appreciation. Today, the idea that the capital account should be kept closed during a period of stabilization/liberalization has become quite common,[8] in sharp contrast to the advice given by orthodox economists a decade earlier.

Aside from financial liberalization, two crucial factors complicated the use of active exchange-rate management to combat inflation. The first was the apparent inertia of domestic prices, particularly in the non–tradeable goods sector, associated with the backward wage indexation that was applied in Chile during the period under consideration. In Chile, and in many other countries of the region, the government employed a wage readjustment rule of the form:

$$\dot{W}_t = a\dot{P}_{t-1},$$

where "a" is a positive parameter. That is, the wage readjustments of the current period correspond to a portion of the inflation accumulated

in the previous period. Under a markup equation, prices rise according
to

$$\dot{P}_t = b\dot{W}_t + d\dot{E}_t \qquad\qquad b, d > 0$$

Substituting the wage indexation rule into this equation, and keeping
in mind that the nominal exchange rate is fixed,[9] we arrive at

$$\dot{P}_t = ab\dot{P}_{t-1}$$

Under these institutional arrangements, prices develop a dynamic of
their own, independent (in the short run) of the course of aggregate
demand variables. If $ab > 1$, the system can even be unstable, leading
to a permanently rising inflation rate. In these circumstances, it is not
surprising that domestic inflation took a long time to converge to the
world rate, in spite of the fixed nominal exchange rate. In the meantime,
the real exchange rate tended to appreciate, and the trade balance
deteriorated.[10]

A second crucial factor in determining success or failure was the
perceived consistency and credibility of the policies that were applied.
Presumably, pre-announcement of the exchange rate serves to anchor
inflationary expectations. If this policy is to be effective, agents must
expect that the announced policy will be in force during a long period
of time. But how are such expectations about the survivability of policy
formed? There are several possibilities. One is that the announced policy
is credible in that it does not induce disequilibria that are unsustainable
over the long run. In Argentina, for example, the *tablita* (a table listing
the future values of the exchange rate) was applied in the absence of
a previous reduction of the fiscal deficit. Moreover, the loss of inflation
tax revenue may have effectively increased the nonmonetary financing
required by the deficit. Therefore, agents may have foreseen that the
government would eventually have to devalue again, resorting to the
inflation tax to equilibrate its accounts.[11] As Calvo (1986) argues, such
lack of credibility produces a distortion in intertemporal prices and
possibly induces an increase in current consumption, current-account
deficits, and debt accumulation.

The credibility question is complex for two reasons. First, the problem
of dynamic inconsistency suggests that all optimal policies are "non-
credible" almost by definition,[12] as long as there are some underlying
distortions in the economy. For instance, the inflation tax is more effective
when it is not anticipated by the public; otherwise, real balances—and
the tax base—are reduced. A benevolent Central Bank that is worried
about financing the fiscal deficit in the least distortionary fashion has
an incentive to "surprise" the public as soon as the demand for money
has been determined. But this inevitably means that the announcements

of the Central Bank concerning future levels of the money supply lack credibility.

The other problem with credibility is that it is intimately linked to self-fulfilling prophecies. If everyone expects inflation to rise, price-setting firms will tend to raise the prices of their own products; the result, of course, will be more inflation. If everyone expects a devaluation, agents will run to the Central Bank to buy foreign exchange, thereby precipitating a balance-of-payments crisis. In this sense, the logic of failed stabilization is similar to that of bank runs. In both cases, an inefficient outcome with high inflation or a bankrupt bank can occur even if the underlying fundamentals (the credit-worthiness of the government and the bank) are sound. Because it is so difficult for the government to attain credibility, it is extremely risky to base overall macroeconomic policies on the assumption that exchange announcements will be fully believed. For the monetarist economists, particularly in Argentina, the bet proved to be an excessively risky one.

New Problems, New Ideas: The 1980s

The debt crisis that erupted in 1982 dramatically increased the net transfers abroad carried out by Latin American countries. At the same time, inflation increased in many countries in the region. Both monetarists and structuralists of the old school had reason to regard this debt-inflation correlation as proof for their old theories.

From the monetarist point of view, the rise in world interest rates was equivalent, *ceteris paribus*, to an expansion of the fiscal deficit, given that a large portion of the debt was public. As the government tried to monetize the additional deficit, inflation increased. This occurred to a certain extent in several countries, but Bolivia provides the quintessential example. Finding itself in a weak political position, the government of Siles Suazo sought to accommodate internal pressures (interest group demands) and external pressures (increased interest rates and falling export prices) by printing money. The ensuing hyperinflation was the highest ever in the continent: an annual rate of almost 15,000 percent during a few months in 1985.[13]

From the structuralist point of view, the fall in real disposable income exacerbated the distributive struggle that is often associated with persistent inflation. Indexation was extended not only to the labor market but also to foreign exchange, goods, and financial markets. On a theoretical level, the old concept of "inertial inflation" took on renewed strength (Arida and Lara-Resende, 1986). Its practical importance was reinforced by the observation that, in Brazil and other countries, the growth of the money supply was substantially lower than that of prices between 1980 and 1984 (Cardoso, 1987).

In the mid-1980s a serious attack against inflation had to address both fiscal and "inertial" problems, regardless of the theoretical perspective of the policymaker. The heterodox shocks applied in Argentina and Brazil were directed at these two objectives.

Many analysts recognize that inflationary inertia is plausible, at both the theoretical and the empirical levels. Disagreements arise among them when they try to determine the most appropriate method to eliminate it. According to the "rational expectations" school, inflationary expectations and the indexation mechanisms that contribute to its perpetuation are only a reflection of fiscal and monetary policies that signal to agents that they should expect inflation in the future. From this point of view (Sargent, 1986), a credible fiscal reform is sufficient for stopping inflation. It must have two components: a halt in the exponential growth of the public debt and a reduction in the deficit to a level that can be financed with a small inflation tax. If these outcomes are possible, and if the program enjoys full credibility among the public, the inertial mechanisms simply become obsolete and disappear as inflationary expectations decrease. This was the lesson extracted by Sargent (1986) from his study of four European hyperinflations between the two world wars.

By contrast, the authors of the heterodox plans have argued that the credibility of fiscal and monetary policies is a necessary, but not sufficient, condition to stabilize prices. Another crucial source of uncertainty arises from the expected reaction of all the other economic agents to the stabilization program. For example, cautious workers or union members will think twice before reducing the growth rate of their nominal wages; if others fail to moderate wage demands as well, they will be left in a relatively disadvantaged position. The same thing is true of firms that set prices in monopolistic markets.

Simonsen (1987, pp. 5–6) addresses this very problem:

In the late sixties and early seventies, inflationary inertia was explained by combining the natural unemployment rate hypothesis with Cagan's adaptative expectations formula. Although empirically convincing, the explanation was soon eclipsed by the rational expectations revolution that dismissed backward-looking inflationary expectations as an "ad-hoc" assumption. Painless inflation cure appeared as a strong possibility, provided a credible monetary rule was announced, and provided some gradualism was accepted to bridge the temporary inertia caused by staggered wage and price-setting. Empirical evidence never supported this optimism, but it appeared as the outcome of sound economy theory. Once wage and price-setting decisions are viewed as a play of a B_2 game (where either the number of participants is too large to make them all trust the others as Nash strategists, or where information on payoffs is incomplete), the rational expectations optimism goes to pieces. Even if the Government commits itself to a credible program of nominal output stabilization, price-setters have no serious reason to stop price increases until they are assured that other price-setters will behave as Nash strategists. "Expectations" now appear as an imprecise concept that attempts to summarize how rational economic agents face strategic interdependence problems. In fact, what is involved is how to play a B_2 game. From this point of view, the old-fashioned adaptative expectations hypothesis deserves some rehabilitation, since it describes a trial and error approach to a Nash equilibrium.

Simonsen (1987) maintains that, under these circumstances, prudent players will follow "maximin" strategies: They will choose the path that minimizes losses in the worst possible case—the case in which other players do not cooperate. If this outcome occurs, the period of convergence to an equilibrium with low inflation and full employment will be long and painful. In the short run, increases in nominal wages will exceed the pace of monetary expansion, and the economy will suffer a recession. The risk is that the costs associated with this initial adjustment will be so large that the government will decide to abandon its anti-inflationary effort, leaving the economy with high inflation and in a recession.

Income policies can serve to mitigate this problem, as the policymakers behind the "heterodox shocks" in Argentina, Brazil, and Israel had hoped (Arida and Lara-Resende, 1986; Dornbusch and Simonsen, 1987). If the government supports the new fiscal and monetary policies with price and wage controls, it can effectively play the role of the absent Walrasian auctioneer. By establishing a target around which prices and wages can converge, the government helps to coordinate the behavior of price and wage setters. As Dornbusch and Simonsen (1987) note, price and wage controls do not coerce the economy away from equilibrium but, instead, guide it to the best of several feasible equilibria. This logic escapes the classical criticism that price controls are based on the false assumption that the government knows more and acts in a more rational manner than do actors in the private sector. In this case the government "does not discover the optimum strategies of the private sector, but only coordinates the strategies that are simultaneously chosen" (Simonsen, 1987).

Actors often do not fix prices or wages at the same time; but they do so at varying intervals that do not coincide with each other. Taylor (1979), for instance, analyzed a staggered wage-setting scenario. As is well known, this type of institutional arrangement ensures that even credible monetary policies have real effects. In addition, contracts of this sort make it more difficult to apply income policies. At a given moment in time, and assuming a constant inflation rate, some of the workers receive more than the average real wage and others receive less. The same is true of the prices of various goods. If the structure of relative prices were to be frozen at this instant, income would be redistributed, leading to shortages, bankruptcies, political pressures, and so on. The implication is that, in order to be successful, designers of income policies should pay strict attention to micro and sectorial factors and should probably readjust certain selected prices when imposing the freeze (Meller, 1987). Brazil and Argentina tried to achieve this readjustment of prices, but numerous problems arose—inevitably, perhaps, given the magnitude of the task.

In the Bolivian case, price controls were not imposed but inflation fell as rapidly as it had in Argentina and Brazil. Does this mean that such controls are unnecessary or redundant? Quite the contrary. An interesting hypothesis is that when hyperinflation is as high as it was in Bolivia, medium- and long-term contracts tend to disappear, and domestic prices become instantly indexed to the dollar. In a situation like this, fixing the exchange rate in a credible manner—as was done in Bolivia—is equivalent to controlling prices, inasmuch as all prices are already linked to the exchange rate.

It is important to note that all arguments in favor of such income policies (i.e., price control or exchange-rate policies) are predicated on the assumption that authorities have adopted—in addition to the freeze—fiscal and monetary policies that are compatible with price stability in the medium run. In Brazil, this crucial requirement was not met.

The stabilization programs were initially quite successful. In Argentina the monthly rate of inflation fell from more than 30 percent to 2 percent, and in Brazil it dropped from 20 percent to less than 2 percent. Furthermore, these gains were achieved during a period of vigorous economic expansion—in contrast to what had happened in other countries under more orthodox programs. Real output in Brazil grew more than 8 percent in the year following the application of the program. In Argentina the economy also expanded at a respectable rate, although unemployment rose slightly. This success elicited considerable social support, which, in turn, increased the effectiveness of the stabilization policies. But in Brazil it soon became evident that aggregate demand policy was not consistent with official inflation targets. Shortages began to crop up, and many firms accumulated stocks of durable goods in anticipation of renewed inflation. By the beginning of 1987 inflation had risen to levels comparable to those in the pre-Cruzado period. A failure of the political will necessary to keep the deficit under control was chiefly responsible for the Brazilian collapse.

The same can be said of Argentina. In that country, high rates of return on domestic assets were used to support the Austral from mid-1986 onward. The strategy worked in the short run, but at the cost of a snowball effect on the fiscal deficit and a subsequent loss of credibility in the program.[14] In both cases, the effects of the fiscal deficit were very different from the effects of "excess aggregate demand and overheating" found in the old orthodox theories. In the Argentine case, the deficit affects the expectations of future monetization, not the level of current demand.[15] An overly large deficit can coexist with a recessionary economy, as occurred in Argentina and Brazil throughout much of 1987.

Toward a Consensus?

In view of the enormous difficulties with these programs, is generalized skepticism the only rational response? Not at all. The advantage of experiments as "pure" as those carried out by several Latin American countries in the past few years is that they permit each school to empirically test its favorite theories. With luck, certain lessons will be learned.

Indeed, an optimistic view of this process suggests that at least four lessons concerning stabilization policies can be taught by the economic analysts discussed throughout this chapter:

1. Attacking inflation by controlling only one variable creates even greater disequilibria in the medium run. This lesson is valid for strategies that are uniquely focused on control of the quantity of money, nominal exchange rates, or prices and wages.
2. Control of aggregate demand is not a sufficient condition for stabilization, but it is certainly a necessary condition. If aggregate demand is not controlled, all complementary policies are destined to fail.
3. Interest rates can neither be maintained at artificially low levels (or at negative levels in real terms) nor be allowed to shoot up during the stabilization period. Excessively high interest rates can result in an accumulation of debts that governments and firms cannot service, jeopardizing not only the stabilization effort but also the financial system as a whole.
4. The credibility of policies is essential for their success. Inconsistencies among the various measures adopted should be avoided at all costs. The stated goals of the stabilization program should be achievable and credible. Excessively ambitious announcements only create disappointment and lack of confidence when they are not realized.

Even if these four criteria are met, neither the success of an anti-inflationary program nor the transition to a period of sustained growth is guaranteed. To achieve a successful anti-inflationary program and the transition to sustained growth, a country must adopt the proper trade, savings and investment, and external debt policies--all of which are even more controversial issues than the ones considered in this chapter.

Notes

1. See, for example, Ffrench-Davis and Feinberg (1986) and Díaz-Alejandro (1984).

2. For a more detailed review of this debate, see Wachter (1976).

3. On this point, see the recent paper by Kiguel and Liviatan (1988).

4. This "inertial" view of inflation was rediscovered by northern neo-Keynesian economists in the 1970s and by neostructuralists in Latin America in the 1980s.

5. This concept seems to imply that the total sum of sectorial claims exceeds the available output, such that people are fighting over a pie that is "too small." This proposition is not a necessary component of the argument that follows, however. Inflationary inertia can be created simply by the failure of price setters to coordinate their pricing strategies, as several authors—among them Simonsen (1987)—have argued.

6. The International Monetary Fund has traditionally used an analogous analytical framework in its stabilization programs.

7. Growth slowdowns were particularly evident in Argentina, Uruguay, and Chile.

8. See, for example, the important work by Edwards (1985).

9. In other words, $E_t = 0$.

10. That is, old structuralist arguments about inertial inflation also proved to be relevant to the case of disinflation carried out through exchange-rate rather than monetary policy.

11. This argument is more applicable to the Argentinian case than to the Chilean case, given that the fiscal deficit of Chile was almost zero—unless we include *ex ante* the private-sector liabilities that the government had to assume *ex post*. See Velasco (1987b).

12. See Kydland and Prescott (1977) and Calvo (1988).

13. See J. Sachs (1987). Recently, Nicaragua surpassed this level.

14. See Calvo (1988) and Velasco (1988) regarding the possible theoretical links among interest rates, inflationary expectations, and deficits.

15. I am referring here to the process analyzed by Sargent and Wallace, in Sargent (1986).

References

Arida, P., and A. Lara-Resende (1986), "Inflación inercial y reforma monetaria: Brasil." In P. Arida (ed.), *Inflación Cero*. Bogotá: Oveja Negra.

Baer, W., and I. Kerstenetsky (1964), *Inflation and growth in Latin America*. New Haven: Yale University Press.

Calvo, G. (1986), "Fractured liberalism: Argentina under Martínez de Hoz," *Economic Development and Cultural Change* (April).

—— (1986), "Temporary stabilization: The case of predetermined exchange rates," *Journal of Political Economy* (December).

—— (1988), "Servicing the public debt: The role of expectations," *American Economic Review* (September).

Canavese, A., and G. Di Tella (1987), "Inflation stabilization or hyperinflation avoidance? The case of the Austral Plan in Argentina, 1985–87," *Documento de Trabajo*. Buenos Aires: Instituto Di Tella.

Cardoso, E. (1987), "Inflation and stabilization in Latin America." Paper presented at Seminario sobre Políticas de Estabilización, Quito (October).

Díaz-Alejandro, C. (1979), "Exchange rate management in developing countries: An introduction," *Journal of Development Economics* (December).

—— (1982), "Southern Cone stabilization plans." In Cline and Weintraub (eds.), *Stabilization policies in developing countries*. Washington, D.C.: Brookings Institution.

—— (1984), "Latin American debt: We are not in Kansas anymore," *Brookings Papers on Economic Activity*, No. 3.

Dornbusch, R. (1982), "Stabilization policies in developing countries," *World Development* (September).

Dornbusch, R., and M. H. Simonsen (1987), "Inflation stabilization with incomes policies support," Rio de Janeiro, mimeo.

Edwards, S. (1985), "Stabilization and liberalization: Ten years of Chile's economic experiment," *Economic Development and Cultural Change* (January).

—— (1985), "The order of liberalization of the external sector," *Princeton Essays in International Finance*, No. 156.

Ffrench-Davis, R., and R. Feinberg (1986) (eds.), *Más allá de la crisis de la deuda: Bases para un nuevo etlnfoque*. Santiago: Ediciones CIEPLAN.

Ffrench-Davis, R., and O. Muñoz (1988), "El desarrollo económico de América Latina y el marco internacional: 1950–86," *Colección Estudios CIEPLAN*, Vol. 23, Santiago (March).

Foxley, A. (1982), "Experimentos neoliberales en América Latina," *Colección Estudios CIEPLAN*, Vol. 7, Santiago (March).

Harberger, A. (1963), "The dynamics of inflation in Chile." In C. Christ (ed.), *Measurement in economics*. Stanford: Stanford University Press.

Kiguel, M., and N. Liviatan (1988), "Inflationary rigidities and orthodox stabilization policies." Paper presented to the Eighth Latin American Meeting of the Econometric Society, San José, Costa Rica (August).

Kydland, F., and E. Prescott (1977), "Rules versus discretion: On the inconsistency of optimal plans," *Journal of Political Economy* (June).

Meller, P. (1987), "Apreciaciones globales y específicas en torno al Plan Cruzado," *Apuntes CIEPLAN*, No. 62, Santiago (March).

Olivera, J. (1970), "On passive money," *Journal of Political Economy* (July).

Ramos, J. (1987), *Neoconservative economics in the Southern Cone of Latin America*. Baltimore: Johns Hopkins University Press.

Sachs, J. (1987), "The Bolivian hyperinflation and stabilization," NBER Working Paper, Cambridge.

Sargent, T. (1986), *Rational expectations and inflation*. New York: Harper and Row.

Seers, D. (1962), "A theory of inflation and growth in underdeveloped economies based on the experience of Latin America," *Oxford Economic Papers* (June).

Simonsen, M. H. (1987), "Rational expectations, game theory and inflationary inertia." Paper presented to the Seventh Latin American Meeting of the Econometric Society, São Paulo (August).

Sunkel, O. (1960), "Inflation in Chile: An unorthodox approach," *International Economic Papers*, Vol. 10.

Taylor, J. (1979), "Staggered wage-setting in a macro model," *American Economic Review* (May).

Taylor, L. (1983), *Structuralist macroeconomics*. New York: Basic Books.

Velasco, A. (1987a), "Políticas de estabilización y teoría de juegos," *Colección Estudios CIEPLAN*, Vol. 21, Santiago (June).

———— (1987b), "Financial crises and balance of payments crises: A simple model of the Southern Cone experience," *Journal of Development Economics* (October).

———— (1988), "Government debt and real interest rates during stabilization." Paper presented to the Eighth Latin American Meeting of the Econometric Society, San José, Costa Rica (August).

Wachter, S. (1976), *Latin American Inflation*. New York: Lexington Books.

4

Review of the Debate over the Origins of Latin American Industrialization and Its Ideological Context

Mauricio Rojas

Ideological Change and the Origins of Latin American Industrialization

The origins of industrial development in Latin America have increasingly drawn the attention of numerous historians, sociologists, and economic historians. In my view, this new focus is both a symptom and a result of the weakening of the ideological and theoretical trends that in one way or another have characterized the Latin American political and intellectual environment.

Earlier answers, in the context of ideas prevailing at the time, are no longer assisted by a self-evident certainty. The preceding ideological environment was dominated by the "developmental" school of thought outside the Marxist sphere and by the "dependence school" within it. Beyond their differences, both trends emphasized a number of common topics and provided answers in the field of economic history that were to some extent coincidental. They were in fact two opposing poles in a common paradigm—that is, in a common set of problems within which debate and research had their place.

Developmentalism and Dependence

The developmental school of thought, basically but not exclusively associated with the Economic Commission for Latin America and the Caribbean (ECLAC), originated in doubts aroused by the inclusion of Latin America in the world market through the export of primary commodities and import of manufactured goods. The deterioration of the terms of trade had been going on for centuries in the countries of the region. According to the theories put forth by Raúl Prebisch (1949) and Hans Singer (1950), this deterioration pushed these countries to a dead end from which the sole means of escape was "forced" industrialization, even at the cost of violating the "laws" of free international competition, and bringing about a loss in the overall product obtained. The criticism that Prebisch and Singer aimed at the traditional theory of international trade questioned not the earning of absolute profits as a result of international specialization but the distribution of such profits via international prices.[1] The application of supplementary resources in an effort to offset the drop in prices with a higher volume of exports would only aggravate the deterioration in the terms of trade and thus raise the relative price of manufactured goods imported by Latin America. For that reason the region should persevere, whatever the costs, in the policy of government-driven, tariff-protected industrialization that had arisen spontaneously since the crisis of the 1930s.

On the Marxist side, the late 1950s saw the beginning of what was later to be called the Dependence School. In its simplest but also most influential version, this "school" posited the existence of a close relationship between the Latin American economies and world capitalist economy, on the one hand, and the industrial backwardness of the former, on the other. The closer the link with the world capitalist economy, the greater the underdevelopment. This, indeed, was the main thesis of Paul Baran (1959)[2] and A. G. Frank (1967).[3] The link between Latin America and an asymmetric international economic and power structure would have led to an increasing loss of "economic surplus" as well as to structural deformation of dependent societies. The thesis implied that periods of relative unlinkage (whether forced or voluntary) from the world capitalist economy should generally coincide with periods of more dynamic, harmonious, and industrializing development in peripheral nations.

Both schools of thought necessarily led to a view of the economic history of Latin America whereby the period before the 1930s crisis, characterized by free trade and high integration into the world economy, was deemed a time of "frustration" by some (e.g., Pinto, 1962), and one of open retrogression and "development of underdevelopment" by others (Frank, 1967). In turn, the crisis of the 1930s was construed as a positive event, the forced breaking point between a basically exporting model and the subsequent attitude that, in spite of evident flaws rather acrimoniously criticized according to the ideological position taken, was nonetheless superior to that of the preceding period.

Background of the Recent Ideological Movement

The first event of note is the industrial export boom offensive regarding manufactured goods that was conducted by a number of European,

Asian, and Latin American countries (including Spain, Finland, South Korea, Taiwan, Brazil, and Mexico). These countries have revealed the flexibility and capabilities of the world economy in sharp contrast to the closed scheme of metropolis-satellite or center-periphery relations peculiar to dependence or developmentalist theories. They are countries with a high degree of integration into the network of international capitalist relations and with a significant penetration by transnational capital. This fact would affect the credibility of theories that based their argumentative force on questioning the prospects of periphery industrialization founded on a more active integration with the international capitalist economy. This "pessimistic" view is quite problematical, to say the least; indeed, it may even be said that the opposite trend prevails today, and that the old pessimism is being replaced by excessive optimism and overestimation of the possibilities of generalizing new "development models." Be that as it may (and this is what should be stressed in the present context), a debate of top importance that will influence our view of history has been opened.

Second, I should mention the now widely recognized difficulties that surrounded the highly protected Latin American "model," which was almost exclusively oriented toward captive internal markets. This industrializing project should not be characterized by import substitution (as it so often is), for the simple reason that since industrialization was consolidated in England, no attempt at industrial development has failed to undergo a major stage of substituting previously imported goods. Import substitution is therefore neither a distinction of Latin American industrialization nor the source of its problems. Emphasis should instead be directed to the following elements: (1) relative abundance of non-industrial exportable items in the first stage of Latin American industrialization; (2) strong protectionism and dependence of industry upon the political system; and (3) orientation of industry almost exclusively toward the domestic market.

One of the most significant traits of Latin American industry has been its lack of exporting ability and its resulting seclusion in the framework of domestic markets. This was the most generalized and enduring feature of the industry until recently, and it originated, of course, well before 1930. Industry in the region was thus established on a basis from which it would sooner or later come face to face with very difficult problems. It is worth noting that, although the organization and development of this industry resulted in a growing need for imported capital goods and industrial inputs, the industry itself has seldom, if ever, generated the foreign exchange required for such imports. Paradoxical though it may seem, Latin American industrial development has been totally dependent on the exporting ability of the primary sector—an ability severely questioned by the ECLA and dependence theorists.

Expansion of industrial development inevitably led to a critical situation, particularly in the 1960s, characterized by pressure on the trade balance and ever more difficult access to increasingly necessary foreign exchange. Inflation, devaluation, speculation, and protectionism pushed beyond all reasonable limits; and industrial growth, which became daily less effective and eventually raised the price of industrial items to intolerable levels, resulted from the fundamental weakness in an industry incapable of generating an autonomous flow of international means of exchange.

Exclusive orientation toward the domestic market caused yet another set of equally serious problems. One was the degree of dependence and patronage that emerged with respect to the political system, for both the predominance of domestic industry in the domestic markets and the associated profit margins have been almost exclusively governed by political measures (customs regulations, differential exchange rates, preferential government purchases, subsidies, etc.). The rationale of the resulting industry has increasingly diverged from international criteria. The limitations of Latin American domestic markets, dependent on population size and the distribution of income, also resulted in an easily monopolized, scarcely dynamic industry that failed to generate sufficient jobs and in a significant percentage of idle installed capacity. The restricted size of such markets became particularly obvious as the industrialization process progressed toward the production of more complex goods and optimum production scales, usually larger than the absorption capacity of most Latin American economies (as well as that of many small and medium-sized European countries).

These features very soon engendered an extremely problematic "industrializing profile." The successive expansion of captive areas of domestic markets determined a broadly diversified industrialization process, particularly in consumer goods. Such breadth was offset by lack of depth and by growing dependence upon imports of technically complex manufactured items. These factors are two of the major differences from more successful industrialization projects, in which the ability to export industrial goods is based on specialization and increased processing of industrial production—and, hence, on increased capacity for technological innovation, together with more concentrated and effective utilization of restricted domestic resources.

The progress (as described above) of Asian and European peripheral economies, in which the income distribution profile is more egalitarian than that in Latin America (see Fajnzylber, 1987), reflects the effectiveness of an alternative to Latin American import substitution. These countries are characterized by their ability to go from production of relatively simple to more complex manufactures, to export new kinds of products, and therefore to reshape continuously their position in the world economy.

Relatively similar economic policy instruments (e.g., industrial protection and government intervention) have been used in a radically different way, encouraging rather than inhibiting innovative ability, deeper industrialization, and export of manufactured goods. These policy instruments must be insisted on, in view of the trend—simplistic in theory and disastrous in practice—of reducing everything to a quasi-doctrinaire conflict between protectionism and free trade.

The significance of the foregoing for the topic under discussion here lies above all in questions about Latin America's development, history, and prospective links with the world economy. Here the resort to comparative economic history—that is, to the wide variety of historic experiences that contemporary research makes available, the better to understand our own history—becomes especially important.

The third and last element in this context is particularly relevant to understanding the evolution of the Marxist school of thought. The dependence school was closely linked to the fate of socialist experiences, from the Russian revolution to the Cuban revolution. The ascent of Fidel Castro to power, especially his openly socialist policy from 1961 on, was for Latin America a political cataclysm of a magnitude that cannot be overestimated. This event, which shook the awareness of an entire generation of young Latin American intellectuals, was, in historical terms, equivalent to the political movement that Lenin and Trotsky led in Russia in 1917. The latter, together with Chinese, Yugoslav, and other experiences, cast doubts upon critical elements of classical Marxist orthodoxy, which emphasized the evolutionary aspects of transition to socialism—above all, the previous development of industrial capitalism in the country or area in question, which in turn laid down the material and social bases that the industrial proletariat would subsequently take over.

Encouraged by this spectrum of revolutionary experiences in industrially backward countries, several theories sprang up, each more esoteric than the last with respect to classic Marxism, which sought to explain and validate those revolutions. An ideological and practical field thus took shape; for the sake of simplification I shall call it Leninism. A fundamental fact for the present discussion is that in such theories the classical Marxist posture regarding the historically progressive role of colonialism and imperialism was gradually reversed.[4] In time, a view of the expansion and influence of industrialized metropolises as merely predatory and destructive began to prevail and was consecrated in the theses of Paul Baran, André Gunder Frank, and Samir Amin. Only a drastic breakdown, a radical revolution among the peripheries, could start the process of industrial and economic development that was blocked by "imperialist domination," which simultaneously paved the way for the transition to socialism. The slogan "underdevelopment or revolution"[5] summarized these ideas; there was no middle of the road, only radically opposed alternatives.

This universe of ideas was profoundly shaken, not only by the speedy capitalist development of several peripheral nations but also by the fact that the Leninist experiences or "models" had led to a set of problems at least as serious as those they had attempted to resolve. "Fraternal" invasions, "socialist" wars, Pol Pot–style terror regimes, and a most worrisome lack of social and economic freedoms and dynamism have provoked increasing and understandable skepticism about the Leninst idea as a whole as well as a gradual return to more classical Marxist attitudes. Such events and difficulties have driven many Marxist theoreticians and historians to question both the analytical methods and the very view of history that stemmed from Leninist theories in general and from dependence theories in particular.

New Ideological Trends

To round out the foregoing, I shall comment on the ideological trends that have come to fill the predominant place of the previous ones. Of particular relevance to our present discussion are the concerns, questions, and topics that these trends have brought to light, thus influencing academic activity.

Three major trends stand out very clearly, however: neoliberalism, neoclassical Marxism, and ecologism, or neoromanticism.

Neoliberalism may be understood as a response to the sustained advance of government and corporate apparatus and intervention. To this, neoliberalism opposes a view whereby the individual, civilian society, business, and the market fill the leading roles. In my opinion, neoliberalism has posed a number of real and very significant problems not to be lightly dismissed with a mere reference to the more extreme political expressions inspired thereby.

The vitality and influence of such ideas may be observed in many fields. To take just one example of purely academic interest, there is a revival of interest in the theories of Joseph Schumpeter and a concurrent decline in the influence of Keynes. Schumpeter's emphasis on the crucial role of entrepreneurs, innovations, and markets as well as his concern for the microeconomic breakdown mechanisms of steady states are clearly very different from the Keynesian (or developmentalist) approach, with its insistence on the leading role of the state and macroeconomic regulations. It does not seem too hazardous to equate this replacement of Keynes by Schumpeter with an overall change in the ideological setting, where a greater awareness of the limitations of planning attempts and government regulation coincide with a reassessment of the role of entrepreneurs[6] and markets.

In the field of Marxism now, though with obvious implications outside Marxism, a broad range of ideological upheavals can be observed. For the most part they are epiphenomena of the limitations and frustrations of Leninist experiences. As these problems go beyond the scope of this chapter,[7] a few comments will be made regarding trends critical of dependence ideas.

In the 1970s there emerged a number of paradigms that aimed to interpret the problems of the Third World. They were mostly marked by an attempt to return to Marx and nineteenth-century European Marxism, which is why the term *neoclassical Marxism* seems appropriate for the new trends. Neoclassical Marxism stands out clearly, for instance, in the Althusser-inspired School of Modes of Production,[8] or, in Latin America, in the Marxist critique that had its starting point in the writings of Ernest Lachau (1971) and Agustín Cueva (1974). No one, however, has expressed the pure and simple (even exaggerated) return to the spirit of pre-Lenin Marxism more forcefully and authoritatively than the deceased British Marxist, Bill Warren.

Warren's famous article of 1973 in the *New Left Review* and his posthumous book *Imperialism, Pioneer of Capitalism* (Warren, 1980) unleashed a frontal attack on all tradition from Lenin to the modern Dependence School. These works restate with singular vigor the progressive role of capitalism and its fundamental forms of world expansion—that is, "colonialism" followed by "imperialism." In a tone that brings to mind the unconcerned language of the *Communist Manifesto*, which dealt with the "civilizing" effects of European expansion on "barbarian" and "semibarbarian" peoples, or of Engels when he described the annexation of Algiers by France as a "significant and fortunate event for the progress of civilization,"[9] Bill Warren proposes a historical view whereby capitalism is only just dawning and must still fulfill the most important parts of its "historic and civilizing mission" before a true transition to socialism can take place among the nations on the periphery of the world capitalist system. The fulfillment of this undertaking would have been substantially aided in the period following World War II, thanks to the activity of the new Third World nation-states and the large transnational corporations. These manifestations would be contemporary with an "imperialism" that would be acting everywhere as the "pioneer of capitalism" and thus breaking the ground for a future move to socialist society. In short, according to Warren, first Leninism and then dependence theories would have ignored what Engels termed the ABC of Socialism[10]—that is, the inability of most of the world to undertake the transition to socialism (which has taken a thousand shapes in the dramas and frustrations of "real socialism").

The interest of the foregoing lies above all in a restatement of a set of fundamental postulates of Marxist thinking that has led many Marxist theoreticians to take a fresh "recourse to history"—that is, to reexamine history in light of new questions, concerns, and premises. The fact that so many Marxists show increasing interest in the origins of Latin American industrial development is, in my view, obviously related to the general debates outlined above.

Ecologism is the third ideological trend that has clearly emerged in the recent past. It involves a broad challenge to the industrialist ideology and technological optimism shared by almost all modern trends of thought, from liberalism to Marxism. Ecologist thinking has brought up topics of vital importance and cast doubts on much that had long been considered evident. From the very idea of progress to that of the overall feasibility of industrialization, all such thinking has been submitted to a critical scrutiny that will doubtless become more stringent as industrialism continues to reveal that it produces useful items for human life but also causes such serious damage to the earth's biosphere that the very survival of our species is jeopardized. Such scrutiny has not failed nor will it fail to influence significantly the direction taken by social and historical research.

Coincidental Topics in European and Latin American Economic History

The coincidences observed among recent trends of research into economic history in Europe and Latin America are grouped below under three major themes. First there is the problem of continuities and breaks in the history of industrialization; second, the reasons that might account for the perceived variety of forms of linkage with the world economy; and, third, the setting aside of "industrialization models" and the growing interest in comparative economic history.

Breaks and Continuities

The evolution of economic history as a discipline has always been associated with the way in which the starting point of all modern industrial development (i.e., industrialization in England) is viewed. It might even be said, without too much exaggeration, that economic history is but one of the many by-products of the industrialization process, on which it continues to be dependent to this day. Traditionally, however, that process has been seen as a more or less abrupt disruption, a clearly defined discontinuity, a dramatic, overwhelming invasion of new technologies and production ratios, so well synthesized that even today, in spite of everything, the phrase *industrial revolution* is used to designate it.

There is no question that this phrase, will always retain some degree of validity, just as *neolithic revolution* and similar terms that refer to fundamental changes in the economic history of mankind are still valid. Nevertheless, the notion of industrial revolution has always meant more than that. As noted, it embodies the idea of a sudden occurrence over a few decades that drastically changed the face of society. In this context, the concept of industrial revolution crucially influenced the development theories of the 1940s and subsequent decades. Starting from Paul Rosenstein-Rodan's famous paper of 1943, in which he posed the idea of the "big push," followed by Walt Whitman Rostow's (1962) "take-off" and Alexander Gerschenkron's (1962) "great spurt," an orthodoxy was put forth whereby an industrializing effort comparable to the so-called British industrial revolution was proposed for the countries then known as underdeveloped, at least in the sense that transition to "self-sustained growth," which was based on industrialization, was seen as an abrupt break that would alter in a few decades the course of the society concerned.

Ideas of this sort did not, of course, clash with the majestic projects of planners and policymakers of the time, from the Marshall Plan in Europe, to Mao's "great leap forward" in China, to the impressive plans of Prasant Chandra Mahalanobis in India. Today, not only has there been a loss of faith in the effectiveness of great leaps, breaks, or revolutions, but the historic justification that many saw for such leaps— that is, the notion of the British process as a true industrial revolution is being questioned more and more.

In an article published in *The Economic History Review*, Rondo Cameron (1985) has summarized what is today a vast body of literature that questions the traditional idea of the industrial revolution, both in Britain and in Europe generally. Cameron points to the discovery of numerous coincidences that belie that picture of abrupt, clearly defined disruption that used to describe both the British process and its alleged duplication in the European continent. What is becoming increasingly clear is the initial prolonged period of gestation, followed by a transition to the new forms of production. Economic growth was remarkably modest throughout the period, and no dramatic acceleration, nothing remotely like a big push, a take-off, or a great spurt has been observed.

As a less common example of this changeover from break to continuity, consider Swedish economic history. Swedish industrial development was traditionally thought to have been triggered by outside influence and of short duration, with a possible beginning in the 1850s and a crucial period lasting from 1870 to 1914, at the latest. Such a view, which conforms to the notion of industrial revolution, is being undermined today by recent studies that paint a picture of much greater evolution, thus underscoring the extensive transformation of Swedish agriculture in the first half of last century, the considerable deepening of the domestic market, the expansion of cottage industries, and the gradual rise in income levels until the middle of the century. All of these factors would have led to sustained long-term economic growth, wherein the creation of modern industry took its place as of the mid-nineteenth century.[11]

The pioneering attempts to estimate the dynamics and share of nonmarketed production during the period preceding the so-called take-off at the end of last century have been very significant for this reassessment of Swedish development. In this context it has been shown that the notion of dramatically accelerated development had been based to a considerable extent on a substantial underestimation of the previous size of the Swedish economy, owing to the use of an accounting system that systematically undervalued nonmarketed production.[12] As this issue is of crucial importance, future research into the origins and evolution of Latin American industrial development would stand to gain a great deal if cottage industries and artisanal operations were given their proper place. It would then be possible to prove that the replacement of artisanal and cottage industries for home consumption by industrial production was at least as important for industrial development as was the highly praised import substitution.

Recent research into Latin American economic history reveals a remarkable similarity to the evolution described above in terms of the trend toward placing the inception of industrial development further and further back in time, and toward "dedramatizing" the breakdown of the 1930s. Continuity is accordingly deemed a significant element in the search for links between the pre- and post-1930s. Latin American industrialization emerges as a much more gradual, evolutionary, and extended process than was previously recognized. Indeed, the answers to the 1930s crisis and to the problems posed by World War II are much better understood if they are seen as the development of previous trends rather than as a true break. The industrial structure applied before the crisis, with all its singularities and flaws, is what will condition and crucially orient the subsequent evolution.

Ortega (1987), following others such as A. W. Frank, places the beginning of Chilean industrialization as early as 1879–1883 (before the War of the Pacific). For that period he describes a significant and varied industrial sector whose major core is composed of metal-working industries. In fact, many of the presentations made during the Consejo Latinoamericano de Ciencias Sociales (CLACSO) symposium of 1987 followed similar lines, inasmuch as they offered concrete evidence that the idea of a supposed incompatibility in principle between a commodity-exporting economy and industrial development is being replaced by empirical studies of the various possible links among such activities and of the features of industrial development during the period of "outward growth."

Quite apart from the above symposium, ample material illustrates the new trends affecting many countries of the region. In the interests of brevity I shall offer only the example of research dealing with the Chilean industrial development process.

Starting with the pioneering studies of Oscar Muñoz (1968) and Marcello Carmagnani (1971),[13], much has been published on the subject of industrial development before the 1930s crisis.[14] Muñoz (1968) described a substantial degree of industrial development, at least since the outbreak of World War I, whereas Carmagnani (1971) showed that such development had its roots in the final decades of the nineteenth century. A little later, Henry Kirsch (1977) stated that the War of the Pacific marked the "great divide" in Chilean economic history and that, since then, the preconditions have been set for considerable industrial development in Chile. The latest works along these lines are those by Luis Ortega (1979, 1981), who fixes the beginning of Chilean industrialization as early as the 1850s.

This change in viewpoint has clearly been accompanied by a much more extensive theoretical and ideological change. Carmagnani's work, for example, is still framed by the dependence paradigm. To use Thomas Kuhn's terminology, he attempts to "standardize" the fact of industrial development during the "primary commodity-exporting phase"; that is, he tries to make this "anomaly" consistent with the dependence theory. To this end Carmagnani makes a distinction between development and industrial growth, and concludes that Chilean industrialization was only part of the general development process of underdevelopment arising from the dependence to which Chile was subject. Remarkably, however, later authors not only make a more or less clean break with dependence or developmental assumptions, but they also see their work as part of an explicit criticism of the central issues of the previously prevailing paradigm. In this context, Gabriel Palma (1978) is the most outstanding international exponent.

Three of Palma's (1978) conclusions summarize much of what we have said here: (1) that it is false to say that industrial development in Chile began with the 1930s crisis (in fact, by the 1920s the industrial sector had taken up "the role of 'driving force' of local economic development"); (2) that the transition from "free trade" development to "protectionist" development began before the 1930s and proceeded gradually—a conclusion that was recently reaffirmed by Sergio Villalobos and Rafael Sagredo (1987), who cast definitive doubts on the existence of a true "free trade period" in Chilean economic history; and (3), notwithstanding the findings of such authors as Frank (1967), it is not true that "the Great Depression was unmistakably 'positive' for peripheral economies, such as Chile" (Palma, 1978, p. 86).

The Problem of Insertion in the World Economy

I would like to approach this second set of problems through a personal experience. In the late 1970s, when I began to study the economic history of Scandinavia, I discovered an amazing fact that became a growing source of concern—namely, that the same kind of explanation that the dependent-developmental paradigm provided for backwardness in Latin America was upheld by more traditional theoreticians to explain exactly the opposite situation for the Nordic countries (i.e., successful industrial development in Sweden, Denmark, Norway, or Iceland).

In the mid-nineteenth century these countries were in an archetypical peripheral position, exporting raw materials and foodstuffs to Britain and importing manufactured goods therefrom. By the outbreak of World War I, however, they were already small but burgeoning industrial economies. In the case of Sweden, the traditional interpretation[15] was that industrialization had been the result of more active incorporation into the world economy, given the effect of exports of raw materials and foodstuffs. The dynamic side of this "model," known today as *export-led industrialization*, was composed of factors external to the Swedish economy. Social scientists observed that Sweden (as well as Norway and Denmark) had succeeded in adapting to increased international demand and altered terms of trade, progressing from exports of raw materials in the mid-1800s to exports of items with more and more processing before shipment (from raw to sawn lumber, pulp, and paper; from run-of-mine iron ore to special steels and fabricated items; and from oats, via grain imports and development of agriculture and animal husbandry, to butter). In the process, domestic demand for both consumer and capital goods have risen, thus internally disseminating the effects of higher international demand. By the 1890s industry, though aimed at the domestic market, was playing a predominant role—but without excluding a growing flow of industrial exports.

What became a source of concern for many young Swedish historians, who had also undergone a "dependent phase" of thinking, was that the same world economy that had been so abundant in "virtuous circles," and had supposedly resulted in spectacular development for Scandinavia, was held responsible for the "vicious circles" of the underdeveloped world. The problem was compounded by the fact that the difference could be accounted for either by geographical proximity to the British market (think of Australia, New Zealand, South Africa, or Japan) or by the fact that Sweden belonged to the "European center" of the world economy. Other European countries (e.g., Ireland, Portugal, Spain, Greece, Romania, and, among the Nordic countries themselves, Finland) had not been able to follow in the footsteps of Scandinavia.

The result of this remarkable paradox could be none other than a general questioning of the argument that focused the explanation on outside causes and endowed the "world economy" with a kind of autonomous dynamics that defined the roles of "industrial centers" or "commodity exporting" peripheries. Researchers of economic history have wondered about the various factors responsible for deciding the kind of insertion in the world economy, the latter being seen as a flexible set of conflicts, relations, and possibilities rather than as a metastructure with a logic of its own. The demythification of this figment called "world economy" has led to a resurgence of history with all its diversity, its constant surprises, and its incurable "indiscipline."

In the international field, many of these difficulties were highlighted by Brenner's (1977) criticism of Wallerstein's (1979) "world system" theory. In Sweden, as in many other countries in Europe, a research trend arose in keeping with the endeavor to understand the successful insertion of Sweden into the world economy of the time, in light of national, regional, and even local transformations. This research trend resulted in extensive questioning of the previous approach, the over-simplification of which has been increasingly revealed. The trend today is to recognize, in the first place, that structural changes in the Swedish economy were not caused but only reinforced and reoriented by external elements; and, second, that such internal changes were precisely what determined the specific form of Swedish insertion into the international economy.

In my view, the economic history of Latin America reflects a similar, though less pronounced, trend. The CLACSO symposium referred to above was itself an example of a major change in this respect. The papers presented only occasionally resorted to the kind of pseudo-explanations that were so common some time ago, when "imperialism" and "dependence" served to obscure economists' true ignorance about concrete circumstances or actual forces that accounted for a specific event. It is a matter not of denying the existence of asymmetric international relations but of examining the actual components and forms of such ever-changing asymmetry, and determining the actual degree of its influence on the course followed by our nations. Broadly speaking, it seems that most Latin American nations have the resources to decide their own fate. The governing elites and the wealthy classes must assume some responsibility if the region has lost the option to develop in a different way. Investigation of such sectors and the structures on which their power has rested will surely provide crucial answers for understanding our history.

The papers on Brazil by Lobo and Levy (1987) and von der Weid (1987) may be taken as examples of this pursuit of the complexity of historical processes. They outline a movement in the field of Brazilian economic history that shows much promise, emphasizing issues that not only step beyond the previous paradigm but also show critical maturity in the rediscovery of the export/industrialization dynamics. These papers insist on the diverse situations that existed simultaneously within the Brazilian economy before the 1930s; their various logics cannot be reduced to a single type, such as the Paulista coffee economy, which, though the most extensive, nonetheless failed to account for many other highly autonomous forces that gave the Brazilian process its particular shape. To the extent that studies of this kind multiply and knowledge increases on the various regional and local processes, a degree of information will certainly be achieved that will doubtless make it difficult, if not impossible, to come up with the "heroic generalizations" that were so common in the recent past. The knowledge obtained will probably be more "undisciplined" and more refractory to the schematization, but no less solid and reliable for that.

Models and Comparative Economic History

In a third area of problems, a degree of convergence may be observed between certain trends in economic history in Europe and Latin America. I am referring here to the movement from the idea of industrialization or development "models" toward the relative predominance of comparative economic history. This issue is clearly related to the previous one—that is, to our increased knowledge of an ever-growing diversity of industrialization experiences.

The general evolution of economic history might be described as a discipline, as a gradual expansion of a horizon of problems and references that started from the "British model" and became more and more complex as other major countries came on the scene with their own substantial differences relative to the "original model." Such countries as France, Germany, the United States, Japan and the Soviet Union, with their industrial development, set up as many "development models." Expansion of knowledge has made matters even worse by bringing into the debate a vast number of regional and local experiences. The whole European periphery was suddenly brought into comparative studies, which now include the Belgian, Swiss, Swedish, and Norwegian models.

Obviously, the conclusion to be derived from above could not be other than a gradual giving up of the very idea of the development model as a "natural" result of its own uselessness. Now, to avoid any misunderstanding, we should note that abandoning the use of models, or simply returning them to the normative, axiomatic, or experimental disciplines capable of making proper use of them, does not imply abandoning the theory (as some seem to think); quite the contrary, truly historic theoretical and methodological approaches are recovered. The choice, then, is not between "models or empiricism" but between the use of historic methods or dubious loans from nonhistoric disciplines.

Economic historians have a broad field of work in which to establish generalizations, periodizations, and regularities in the "chaos" of history, and to prove various explanatory hypotheses and theories dealing with the relations among various aspects of social life. In the matter of industrialization they should establish the kind of requirements of the process during various periods and given institutional substitutions as well as possible combinations of diverse factors. Alexander Gerschenkron (1962), for instance, attempts to systematize this diversity in light of the degree of backwardness of the countries in question and establishes a true "substitution logic" based on the unique nature of the British case. This is not to say that Gerschenkron's hypothesis or scheme should be accepted, for it seems too deterministic and restricted; but it does contain an approach that is very stimulating.

Another example along similar lines is the typology presented recently by Dieter Senghaas (1985).[16] In this case, emphasis is directed to the transformations of agrarian structures in order to account for the wealth and diversity of all European experience, not only those of the more significant nations. The interesting point of Senghaas's attempt lies not only in its contribution to this veritable "discovery of Europe," which evidently focuses on European economic history, but also in its elucidation of the experience of non-European countries. In short, Senghaas discusses the problems of development theories in terms of a broader treatment of European industrialization.

What the study by Senghaas (1985) shows is the usefulness of these comparisons, particularly when applied to less well-known European experiences. The traditional comparative analysis has focused on countries whose central and dominating position in international relations makes them much less appropriate as reference points for comparing, for instance, the problems and prospects of Latin American nations. The experience of such countries as Sweden, Spain, Finland, Poland, Switzerland, Belgium, the Netherlands, Romania, Greece, and Portugal is obviously more appropriate for this purpose than that of Great Britain, France, or Germany. Indeed, this "discovery of Europe" and the comparative use of its vast historic variety open up a most promising historic diversity that calls for further research.

The article and book by Fernando Fajnzylber (1983, 1987), in the context of Latin America, are indicators of a growing interest in comparative studies, particularly in the use of international experience to enrich our understanding of the problems and history of Latin America. In the same context, mention should be made of the recent work of Donald Denoon (1983), who compares Australia, New Zealand, South Africa, Argentina, Uruguay, and Chile; of Tim Duncan and John Fogarty (1984), who compare Australia and Argentina; and of Nicos Monzelis (1986), who compares the Balkan countries, Chile, and Argentina. In my opinion, this path is a most fruitful one for Latin American economic history.

Notes

The author thanks Professor Oscar Muñoz as well as colleagues Christer Gunnarsson and Lennart Schon for their helpful comments. Thanks also go to the Humanistic and Social Research Council of Sweden (HSFR) for its financial support of the research project.

1. For a criticism of the empirical base of the Prebisch-Singer thesis, see the comment by Bela Balassa in Singer (1984).

2. See Baran (1959).

3. See the synthesis of ideas outlined by Nehru (1967) and other Indian theoreticians. In particular, see R. Dutt's work, *The Economic History of India* (1901, 1903).

4. See, for example, the articles written by Marx in 1853 on British domination in India and on European Marxism in the nineteenth century; Haupt and Reberioux (1967); and Carrere d'Encausse and Schram (1969). The transition from the classic to the Leninist view was discussed by Warren (1980).

5. See Frank (1967).

6. For an example of this reassessment, see Fajnzylber (1987). According to this distinguished ECLAC economist, the "scant social valuation and precarious leadership of domestic entrepreneurs" are sources of difficulty in the Latin American industrial development pattern.

7. These problems are discussed in my doctoral thesis, "Renovatio Mundi, Essaer om Marx, marxismen och marxismen kris," Studentlitteratur, Lund (1986). For Spanish articles, see Rojas (1981, 1985).

8. The most influential works of this school are Rey (1971) and Taylor (1979).

9. Engels (1964, p. 47) spoke even more forcefully, if that is possible, about the relations between the United States and Mexico, to the effect that the latter country "in the interests of its own development . . . should be placed under the custody *(Vormundschaft)* of the United States."

10. See the work written by Engels in 1875, reproduced in Spanish in 1965.

11. Among the exponents of the traditional view is the classic text of Montgomery (1939). For information on recent critical trends, see, for example, the paper by Schon presented to the 9th World Congress on Economic History (1986). For the Swedish version, see the same author (1982).

12. The ground-breaking work in this area was Schon's doctoral thesis (1979), which, together with the work by Olle Krantz (1987) on the historic evolution of the Swedish national product, gave rise to the project involving total reconstruction of Sweden's national accounts (1800–1980). The project is now in its final stage. A classic example of underestimation of the predindustrial Swedish economy is found in Sandberg (1979).

13. This topic was outlined, as Oscar Muñoz pointed out, in Lagos (1966) and Hurtado (1966).

14. Other works on this topic are Muñoz (1977, 1986), and Palma (1979, 1984).

15. This interpretation was formulated by the great Swedish economic historian Heckscher (1956) and was subsequently developed by Jorberg (1973) as an explanatory model.

16. See Senghaas (1985, published in German in 1982). A comparable approach was presented by Gunnarsson (1985).

References

Baran, P. (1959), *La economía política del crecimiento*. Mexico: Fondo de Cultura Económica.

Brenner, R. (1977), "The origins of capitalist development: A critique of neo-Smithian Marxism," *New Left Review*, Vol. 104.

Cameron, R. (1985), "A new view of European industrialization," *Economic History Review* (February).

Carmagnani, M. (1971), "Sviluppo industriale e postsviluppo economico: Il caso cileno 1860–1920," Luigi Einaudi, Torino.

Carrere d'Encausse, H., and S. Schram (1969), *Marxism and Asia*. London: Allen Lane.

Cueva, A. (1974), "Problemas y perspectivas de la teoría de la dependencia," *Historia y Sociedad*, Vol. 3.

Denoon, D. (1983), *Settler capitalism: The dynamics of dependent development in the Southern Hemisphere*. Oxford: Clarendon Press.

Duncan, T., and J. Fogarty (1984), *Australia and Argentina*. Melbourne: Melbourne University Press.

Dutt, R. (1901, 1903), *The economic history of India*, 2 vols. London: Routledge and Kegan Paul.

Engels, F. (1964), "Die Bewegungen vor 1847." In *Marx-Engels Werke*, Vol. 4. Berlin: Dietz Verlag.

_____ (1965), "Acerca de las relaciones sociales en Rusia," *Obras escogidas en dos tomos*, tomo 2. Moscú: Editorial Progreso.

Fajnzylber, F. (1983), *La industrialización trunca de América Latina*. México: Centro Editor de América Latina.

——— (1987), "Las economías neoindustriales en el sistema centroperiferia de los ochenta," *Pensamiento Iberoramericano*, second semester.

Frank, A. G. (1967), *Capitalism and underdevelopment in Latin America*. New York: Monthly Review Press.

Gerschenkron, A. (1962), *Economic backwardness in historical perspective*. Cambridge: Harvard University Press.

Gunnarsson, C. (1985), "Development theory and third world industrialization," *Journal of Contemporary Asia*, Vol. 2.

Haupt, G., and M. Reberioux (1967), *La Deuxième Internationale et l'Orient*. Paris: Cujas.

Hecksher, E. (1956), *An economic history of Sweden*. Cambridge: Harvard University Press.

Hurtado, C. (1966), "Concentración de población y desarrollo económico: el caso chileno," Instituto de Economía, Universidad de Chile, Santiago.

Jorberg, L. (1973), "The Nordic countries 1850-1914." In *The Fontana Economic History of Europe*, Vol. 4, No. 2. London: Fontana.

Kirsch, H. (1977), "Industrial development in a traditional society: The conflict of entrepreneurship and modernization in Chile," University Press of Florida, Gainesville.

Krantz, O. (1987), "Historiska nationalräkenskaper för Sverige 1800-1980," Stockholm.

Lachau, E. (1971), "Feudalism and capitalism in Latin America," *New Left Review*, Vol. 67.

Lagos, R. (1966), "La industria en Chile: Antecedentes estructurales," Instituto de Economía, Universidad de Chile, Santiago.

Lobo, E. M. Lamayer, and M. B. Levy (1987), "Providencia social da classe operaria e urbanizaçao: O papel das seguradoras," CLACSO, Buenos Aires, mimeo.

Montgomery, G. A. (1939), *The rise of modern industry in Sweden*. London: P. S. King & Son Ltd.

Monzelis, N. (1986), *Politics in the semiperiphery: Early parliamentarism and late industrialization in the Balkans and Latin America*. London: Macmillan.

Muñoz, O. (1968), "Crecimiento industrial de Chile, 1914-1965." Santiago: Instituto de Economía, Universidad de Chile.

——— (1977), *Estado e industrialización en el ciclo de expansión del salitre*. Santiago: Ediciones CIEPLAN.

——— (1986), *Chile y su industrialización*. Santiago: Ediciones CIEPLAN.

Nehru, J. (1967), *Glimpses of World History*. Bombay: Asia Publishers House.

Ortega, L. (1979), "Change and crisis in Chile's economy and society 1865-1879," Ph.D. thesis, University of London.

——— (1981), "Acerca de los orígenes de la industrialización chilena, 1860-1879," *Nueva Historia*, Vol. 1, No. 2.

——— (1987), "La coyuntura 1850-1879 y los orígenes de la industrialización chilena," CLACSO, Buenos Aires, mimeo.

Palma, G. (1978), "Dependency: A formal theory of underdevelopment or a methodology for the analysis of concrete situations of underdevelopment," *World Development* (July).

_____ (1979), "Growth and structure of Chilean manufacturing industry from 1830 to 1935," Ph.D. thesis, University of Oxford.

_____ (1984), "Chile 1914–1935: De economía exportadora a sustitutiva de importaciones," *Colección Estudios CIEPLAN*, Vol. 12, Santiago (March).

Pinto, A. (1962), *Chile, un caso de desarrollo frustrado*. Santiago: Editorial Universitaria.

Prebisch, R. (1949), "The economic development of Latin America and its principal problems." New York: United Nations.

Rey, P. P. (1971), "Colonialisme, néo-colonialisme et transition au capitalisme," Paris.

_____ (1976), "Les alliances de classes," Paris.

Rojas, M. (1981), "Socialismo real, desarrollo capitalista y crisis del marxismo," *Teoría*, Spain (July).

_____ (1985), "Marxismo y metafísica," *Revista Zona Abierta*. (January). Also published in *Estudios Sociales*, first semester.

Rosenstein-Rodan, P. (1943), "Problems of industrialization of Eastern and South Eastern Europe," *Economic Journal* (July).

Rostow, W. W. (1962), *The stages of economic growth*. Cambridge: Cambridge University Press.

Sandberg, L. (1979), "The case of impoverished sophisticate: Human capital and Swedish economic growth before World War I," *Journal of Economic History*, Vol. 1.

Schon, L. (1979), "Fran hantverk till fabriksindustri. Svensk textilltillverkning 1820–1870" (De la artesanía a la industria fabril. La producción textil en Suecia 1820–1970), Lund.

_____ (1982), "Industrialismens förutsättningar," Lund.

_____ (1986), "Market development and structural change in the mid-nineteenth century—with special reference to Sweden." In *Beiträge zur Wirtschafts—und Sozialgeschichte*, Vol. 33, No. 2. Wiesbaden: Verlag der Fachvereine.

Senghaas, D. (1985), *The European experience: A historical critique of development theory*. New Hampshire: Berg Publishers.

Singer, H. (1950), "Distribution of gains between investing and borrowing countries," *American Economic Review* (May).

_____ (1984), "The terms of trade controversy and the evolution of soft financing." In G. M. Mayer and D. Seers (eds.), *Pioneers in development*. New York: Oxford University Press.

Taylor, J. C. (1979), "From modernization to modes of production," London.

Villalobos, S., and R. Sagredo (1987), "El proteccionismo económico en Chile. Siglo XIX," Instituto Blas Cañas, Santiago.

von der Weid, E. (1987), "Estrategia empresarial e processo de industrializaçao," CLACSO, Buenos Aires, mimeo.

Wallerstein, I. (1979), *El moderno sistema mundial*, Spain, Siglo 21.

Warren, B. (1973), "Imperialism and capitalism industrialization," *New Left Review*, Vol. 81.

_____ (1980), *Imperialism, pioneer of capitalism*. London: Verso.

5

Deindustrialization and Industrial Restructuring in Latin America: The Examples of Argentina, Brazil, and Chile

Carlos Ominami

The Latin American debt crisis has given rise to a voluminous body of literature. A number of studies have thoroughly analyzed not only its various aspects but also the main factors that account for it. But it is sufficient to recall here that the crisis appeared at first to be external, determined by rising interest rates as well as dropping demand for, and prices of, main export items in the region. This pattern led to destabilization of the dynamics of indebtedness as a result of the spiraling increase in financial charges, together with a reduction of sales abroad and a reduction of loans from the private banking community. As a direct result of this process, import capacity was severely curtailed. In this context, it was inevitable that economic activity would have to adjust to the new conditions and external resources.

Reduction of import capacity brought about a severe fall in capital formation and in the rate of utilization of productive capacity, owing to a lack of intermediate goods. Adjustment policies thus emphasized the recessive trends because, according to the classic orthodox scheme, they required a reduction in real wages. The effect of this reduction, at the level of actual demand, induced an additional fall both in employment and in the degree of installed capacity utilization.

The industrial sector was particularly affected. Its income elasticity was higher than unity, thus causing a decrease in industrial production even greater than that in overall product. Bogged down in a process of cumulative recessions with enduring negative growth rates (1981, 1982, 1983), industry lost its ability to drive overall growth and became openly procyclical.

TABLE 5.1 Industrial Product Annual Growth Rates (in percentages)

	1950–1960	1960–1970	1970–1975	1975–1980	1980	1981	1982	1983	1984	1985	1986	Cumulative Variation 1981–1986
Argentina	4.1	5.6	3.4	–0.2	–3.8	–16.0	–4.7	10.8	4.3	–10.4	12.0	–7.4
Brazil	9.1	6.9	11.0	7.4	7.6	–6.5	0.2	–6.3	6.0	8.3	12.0	12.9
Chile	4.7	5.3	–4.9	7.6	6.2	2.6	–21.0	3.1	9.8	1.2	7.0	–0.7

Sources: CEPAL (1986, 1987).

This trend broke with historical precedent, whereby the industrial sector was the most dynamic core of the system. In this connection, the phenomenon of industrial regression affected practically all the economies of the region, irrespective of the extent of their industrial development. Even those countries that had achieved very different degrees of industrialization (e.g., Argentina versus Brazil, or El Salvador versus Bolivia) exhibited highly negative rates of industrial growth. The lack of correlation between growth rate and degree of industrialization reflected the fact that external restrictions were operating indiscriminately in most countries during this period. In other words, in spite of increased sophistication in the industrial apparatus of the larger economies, the fundamental features of the Latin American industrial development model apparently persisted—especially those associated with difficulties in reducing external vulnerability.

The industrial retrogression of Latin America had no precedent in the postwar period. By 1983 the degree of industrial development in the region had regressed to the level of 1966. In some countries the process was even more serious. In Argentina and Peru the degree of industrialization in 1983 was down to the level of 1960, whereas in Chile and Uruguay the equivalent of the 1983 level had to be sought in 1950.

Individual national responses to deindustrializing trends varied significantly. In some countries, the response has been passive; in others, restructuring attempts have been successful. The national experiences discussed in this chapter fall somewhere between these two extremes. As a starting point, consider the following differences in industrial behavior of Brazil, Chile, and Argentina:

1. Long-term growth (1950–1975) in Brazil (8.5 percent per annum) is more than twice the figures for Argentina (4.1 percent) and Chile (see Table 5.1).

TABLE 5.2 Manufacturing-Sector Product, by Country (in millions US$ of 1986)

	1960	1970	1980	1983	1984	1985	1986[a]
Argentina[b]	8,867	14,374	16,880	14,972	15,576	13,939	15,724
Brazil[b]	18,366	35,747	84,328	70,630	74,960	81,181	90,355
Chile	3,133	5,260	5,893	4,925	5,406	5,469	5,907

[a]Preliminary estimates.
[b]At factor cost.

Source: BID (1987).

2. The effect of the crisis (i.e., the drop in production) of the early 1980s was less serious in Brazil than in Argentina in 1981 (−16 percent) or Chile in 1982 (−21 percent).

3. Recovery was also highly uneven: The average growth rate for the period 1984–1986 was 8.8 percent for Brazil and 6 percent for Chile, but only 2 percent in Argentina. Accordingly, the cumulative variation for the period 1981–1986 was positive in Brazil (12.9 percent), but negative in Chile (−0.7 percent) and even more negative in Argentina (−7.4 percent).

4. Given these figures we find that, in absolute terms, manufacturing value added in Brazil (which in 1960 was 1.8 times higher than in Argentina and 6 times higher than in Chile) is now 5 and 15 times higher, respectively (see Table 5.2).

How can we account for these trends, which initially seemed to polarize Brazil on one side and Argentina and Chile on the other? Two reasons emerge: the size of the Brazilian economy and the application in Chile and Argentina of neoliberal policies with a strong anti-industrialist bias. These factors are undoubtedly very significant; they fail, however, to account for the divergences observed. A number of arguments may be cited in support of this position. To begin with, relative size per se cannot account for given industrial system's dynamism or ability to recover. A long-term comparison of industrial results in Brazil with those of other large developing countries (e.g., India and Pakistan) reveals substantial differences. Similarly, the capacity for industrial recovery exhibited by a country of significant size such as Mexico is considerably lower than that of Brazil. In fact, the cumulative variation of the Mexican industrial product in the period 1981–1986 is not more than 0.6 percent. Conversely, much smaller developing countries (e.g., South Korea, Taiwan, and Singapore) have shown exceptional dynamism and have even circumvented more successfully than Brazil the effects of the international crisis of the early 1980s.

The lower industrial dynamism of Argentina and Chile is a fact of long standing, prior to the adoption of open-economy and liberalization policies. Moreover, although the overall deindustrializing effect of neoliberal policies is beyond question, the comparison between Chile and Argentina points up specific industrial behaviors. Whereas industrial regression in Argentina has endured over time, Chile (even under the neoliberal policies preceding the 1980s crisis) has exhibited a period of some industrial dynamism (1975–1980) and its subsequent ability to recover has been greater than Argentina's.

The foregoing suggests a need to delve into the various factors that positively or negatively influence industrial behavior in individual nations. Hence the objectives of the following analysis are to determine the characteristics of industrial response to the crisis of the early 1980s in the three countries under discussion, and to identify the major elements that account for it. The central point here is that there have been three specific kinds of response. In Argentina, the response has been a type of "industrial sclerosis" encouraged by official passivity and undynamic private agents. Brazil's response has been vigorous reactivation supported by stronger internal productive linkages and improved international competitiveness, with substantial government involvement and greater productive commitment on the part of domestic and foreign private agents. And in Chile, industrial restructuring, based on regressive international specialization, has been promoted mainly by domestic private agents who have counted on governmental passivity.[1]

As illustrated by the data in Table 5.1, the early 1980s brought industrial breakdown to the three countries under consideration. In both Argentina and Brazil this breakdown was worst in 1981, when real industrial output dropped by 16 percent and 6.5 percent respectively, whereas in Chile industrial activity slowed down in 1981 and experienced an unprecedented fall (−21 percent) in the following year.

Recent Industrial Evolution

In the longer run, the industrial breakdown of Argentina appears to have been the worsening of a decline that began in the early 1970s and became acute in the second half of that decade, when already perceptible negative growth was evident. Then, on a purely quantitative basis, there is an argument in favor of the idea of industrial sclerosis; this is confirmed by the difficulty of ensuring subsequent sustained recovery in Argentina's industry. In fact, the new drop in industrial production in 1985 completely canceled the steps toward the recovery of 1983–1984, whereas the expansion of 1986 was not sufficient to recover the levels of 1980.

Brazil is at the opposite extreme from Argentina. The long-term trend of industrial growth in Brazil is characterized by a strong dynamism that has raised the country to the tenth place in industrial world power. In view of the country's subsequent recovery, the recession of 1981–1983 (in spite of its intensity) appears to have been a momentary check.

Compared with these two opposing cases, Chile's experience has been unique. By contrast to the situation in Argentina, Chile's crisis of the early 1980s was preceded by a short period of high growth. The same was true of Brazil, but there are some major differences as well. First, a deep industrial recession hit Chile in 1975 (industrial output dropped −25.5 percent) as a result of the failure of a large number of industrial firms (Mizala, 1985). Second, the early 1980s crisis was more intensive. These unique features of the Chilean case suggest that the economy, because it was incapable of moderating cyclical fluctuations, forced industry to make extreme adjustments. The intensity of recessionary pressures and the system's inability to distribute the appropriate adjustments over time hindered the development of scheduled reconversion processes and, instead, led to the destruction of uncompetitive production capacities. However, once more favorable conditions were restored (the recovery of real wages in 1976–1980, and more recently in 1983–1986, increased actual protection), partial reactivation processes set in with some vigor.

Yet both Chile and Argentina faced acute deindustrialization during the 1970s. As the main features of industrial regression in both Chile[2] and Argentina[3] have been described elsewhere, they will not be repeated here. A few comments are germane, however.

For Argentina, the provisional estimates of the 1985 *Censo Nacional Económico* (National Economic Census) confirm the diagnosis of deindustrialization. Comparison with the 1974 census data reveals a 14 percent decrease in the number of manufacturing establishments and a 13 percent decrease in the number of jobs; in absolute terms, this amounted to the closing down of 18,000 firms and the loss of nearly 250,000 jobs. Specific estimates concerning small- and medium-scale firms indicate that both the number of firms and the level of employment fell by 20 percent between 1974 and 1983.[4] This last figure is particularly significant because it largely accounts for the decline of a group of companies that had developed new technological advantages in the years preceding the open-economy policy, thus portending a change in the traditional international insertion pattern of Argentine industry (Katz, 1985). At the same time, this phenomenon contrasts with the greater capacity for resistance of such traditional industries as the automobile, steel, petrochemical, and shipbuilding industries—owing more to the oligopolistic power and political clout of these industries rather than to their ability to modernize.

Concomitant with deindustrialization was the stagnation of exports of manufactured items, whose share in total exports declined perceptibly.[5] Moreover, the structure of exports of manufactured goods became more dependent on the generation of exportable surpluses by the steel industry and on sales abroad of petrochemical products with little value added. Conversely, items with more technological content than those being exported by Argentina, such as certain kinds of machine tools and food industry equipment, lost their relative significance.

All diagnoses of Argentina's industrial development during the open-economy period are remarkably gloomy. The few perceptible positive elements were largely the result of modernization based on the possibility of purchasing imported capital goods at fairly low prices. The textile and petrochemical industries thus acquired more sophisticated equipment, even such state-of-the-art technology as digital control machine tools, CAD/CAMs, and robots (Chudnovsky, 1984). In any event, the significance of such positive effects was marginal by comparison with the extent of chaos in the industry as a whole.

The situation in Chile, though similar, exhibited certain peculiarities worth noting. Most of the indicators designed to measure the degree of industrialization showed an even steeper drop than had occurred in Argentina. For example, both the industrial product/gross domestic product (GDP) ratio and the industrial employment/total employment ratio fell severely.

The weakening of industrial employment was relatively more pronounced in Chile than in Argentina. Whereas the rate of industrial employment in Argentina declined from 24 percent in 1970 to 21.3 percent in 1980, the rate in Chile declined from 21.8 percent to 16.7 percent during the same period. The difference, as will be shown shortly, resulted from the greater intensity both of overall structural change in Chilean industry and of rationalization processes within firms that managed to survive the open-economy policy and the contraction of the domestic market.

In Chile, unlike Argentina, a change occurred in the late 1970s in the export breakdown—in favor of industrial items. Although exports are still considerably dependent on a small number of primary commodities sold in bulk or with little processing, access to international markets has allowed some branches of industry to grow at higher than the average rate for the sector. Such is the case with fishmeal, pulp, and nonferrous metals.

The Brazilian process is completely different. Here the decade of the 1970s was one of high and sustained overall industrial development. Brazil abstained from adopting an open-economy policy. In fact, in contrast to other countries in the region, the degree to which the economy was opened to the outside world following the first oil shock, as measured by the import coefficient, fell systematically from 8.6 percent in 1975 to 7.1 percent in 1980 and to 4.4 percent in 1984.[6]

Whereas the average rate of real industrial growth was less than 2 percent per annum in Chile and Argentina in the 1980s, Brazil exhibited a yearly growth rate of nearly 10 percent in the same period. "Growth at any cost" was the dominant strategy at the time; indeed, the will to make Brazil a first-rate industrial power, by investing in new technologies in order to acquire new comparative advantages, was the keystone of the Second National Development Plan (II PND), the application of which began shortly after the first oil shock (Tavares and Coutinho, 1984). In this context, sectoral priorities on the industrial plane were modified. The preference for durable consumer goods was replaced by priority granted to a group of intermediate inputs from metallurgy and petrochemicals, as well as to capital goods (Barros de Castro and Pires de Souza, 1983).

Access to abundant and low-cost external financing was undoubtedly a major condition governing the feasibility of the Brazilian option. Another significant difference is that the increase in external debt in Argentina and Chile involved a lower investment productive use of foreign resources than did the increase in Brazil.

The Architecture of the Industrial Apparatus

By the early 1970s the three countries under discussion had reached a comparable degree of industrial development (see Table 5.3), as a result of the systematic increase of the contribution of industry to GDP during the preceding decades. Subsequently, the individual trends of these countries began to diverge. A comparison with countries outside the region (see Table 5.3) points up certain important features of industrial evolution. To begin with, past a certain level the degree of industrialization tends to level off. Indeed, very few economies have broken the 30 percent GDP barrier; among those that have done so, a declining trend is particularly evident in the United Kingdom. Japan and South Korea are two notable exceptions, inasmuch as this trend affects not only the largest economies (the United States, the Federal Republic of Germany, France, Italy, and the United Kingdom) but also such rapidly indus-trializing countries as Singapore and to some extent Hong-Kong.

TABLE 5.3 International Comparison of the Evolution of the Degree of Industrialization
(Industrial Share of GDP in percentages)

	1973	1980	1984
France	28.4	27.8	27.0
Federal Republic of Germany	36.3	34.3	32.9
Italy	26.6	27.8	25.4
Japan	25.8	29.1	33.6
Spain	25.0	25.0	24.4
Sweden	26.0	23.7	24.1
United Kingdom	31.0	25.7	24.2
United States	23.9	22.3	22.5
South Korea	19.5	28.9	30.7
Hong-Kong	24.0	24.8	24.4
Singapore	27.3	27.4	22.7
Argentina	28.7	27.2	25.7
Brazil	27.0	29.1	27.0
Chile	26.3	22.2	21.4

Sources: ONUDI (1987) and CEPAL (1986, 1987).

From this standpoint, the characteristic evolutions of the three Latin American countries are undoubtedly part of a more general trend. However, at least two factors account for a radical difference between these countries and the developed countries. On the one hand, the characteristics of nonindustrial operations vary greatly. Agriculture in the industrial developed nations has reached remarkably high levels of productivity and technological uniformity, and, even more important, tertiary activities are experiencing rapid modernization. But this is not the case in Latin America. Here the agricultural sector is highly heterogeneous, and its integration with the rest of the productive system is for the most part defective. In turn, the tertiary sector continues to be extensively dominated by archaic low-productivity processes. On the other hand, the slowdown of the process happens when industrial systems are still far from attaining the degree of maturity pertaining to developed countries.

In this context, Table 5.4 provides useful information. A comparison of the structure of manufacturing value added in Argentina, Brazil, and Chile with that of the United States and Japan, in the period 1973–1975, reveals a well-known fact: In the first three countries traditional methods account for a significantly higher percentage of production, and the contribution of the technologically more sophisticated production of

TABLE 5.4 Changes in the Industrial Structure (percentages of manufacturing product)

| | 1973–1975 | | | | | 1982–1984[d] | | | | |
| | Machinery and | | | | | Machinery and | | | | |
	Tradi-tional[a] (1)	Inter-mediate[b] (2)	Transpor-tation[c] (3)	(4) (2)/(1)	(5) (3)/(1)	Tradi-tional[a] (1)	Inter-mediate[b] (2)	Transpor-tation[c] (3)	(4) (2)/(1)	(5) (3)/(1)
Argentina	38.3	13.8	21.9	0.36	0.57	37.5	13.1	23.4	0.35	0.62
Brazil	38.2	15.5	25.8	0.41	0.68	36.3	17.3	27.2	0.48	0.75
Chile	38.3	18.9	14.9	0.49	0.39	44.7	15.5	6.5	0.35	0.15
United States	30.1	15.7	36.4	0.52	1.21	28.1	14.7	35.1	0.52	1.25
Japan	28.1	17.3	34.0	0.61	1.21	25.8	15.7	39.3	0.61	1.52
South Korea	44.0	20.2	18.2	0.46	0.41	37.8	19.7	23.6	0.52	0.62

[a]Food (311/2), Textiles (321), Clothing (322), Footwear (324), Lumber (331), Furniture (322), Paper (341), Printing Press products (342).
[b]Chemicals (351, 352), Steel (371).
[c]Nonelectric machinery (382), Electric machinery (383), Transportation material (384), and Professional equipment (385).
[d]1982–83 for Argentina.

Source: UNIDO, *Industrial Statistics Yearbook*, various issues.

machinery and means of transportation is, symmetrically, much lower. In the United States and Japan the ratio of value added in these activities was thus twice as high as in Argentina and Brazil, and almost three times as high as in Chile (see column 5 of Table 5.4). If these results are compared with the figures for 1982–1984, it appears that, in Japan, production of both traditional items and intermediate goods loses significance in favor of production machinery and means of transportation[7]; as a result, the value-added ratio between the two kinds of production rises from 1.21 to 1.52.

In this context, the individual evolutions of the three countries under study differ widely. In Brazil, industrial structure transformations follow the same trend as in those in Japan, though at a less intensive pace. Thus the ratio between value added by industrial production and value added by traditional production in Brazil is still 50 percent less than that in Japan. Nonetheless, Brazilian industry is endowed with a clearly progressive transformation capability, whereas Chilean industry is a case of regressive transformation. Both the shares of intermediate goods (especially machinery) and the means of transportation have declined steeply in Chile, and Chilean industry has become much more traditional.

In Argentina, by contrast, industry has exhibited scant transformation capability. The relative roles of the three industrial branches remain almost unaltered—a fact that, in light of the substantial fall in manufacturing value added, points up the phenomenon of industrial sclerosis discussed earlier.

Finally, the evolution of the industrial process in South Korea, a country well known for its successful economic performance, confirms the idea that industrial dynamism is closely linked to the transformation capability of industrial structures, in terms of the pursuit of greater technological complexity. In this connection, production of machinery and means of transportation tend to increase very rapidly, and more traditional activities simultaneously decline.

The above analysis is further refined by reference to the information contained in Figure 5.1. Four elements are considered here: the degree of industrial development (manufacturing production/GDP), the extent of specialization of the industrial structure, the relative importance of exports of manufactured goods (with respect to total exports), and the degree of technological complexity. Regarding measurement of this last element, the ratio of production of the metalworking industry to total manufacturing production is traditionally deemed a reasonable approximation.[8]

The regressive nature of Argentine's industrial evolution is unquestionable. Between 1975 and 1984 the degree of industrial development, the quantity of industrial exports, and the extent of technological complexity exhibited systematic decline. Only the degree of specialization showed moderate progress.

In Brazil, despite a decrease between 1980 and 1984 in the degree of industrial development (which has recovered somewhat since 1984), both the extent of specialization and the degree of technological complexity have increased. As will be seen below, these factors determined a spectacular rise in the contribution of exports of manufactured items to total exports.

In Chilean industry, meanwhile, new elements have favored the hypothesis of significant restructuring, even though this restructuring is regressive in nature. In fact, we find that the considerable increase in degree of specialization and contribution of the manufacturing sector to total exports has occurred simultaneously with a fall in the degree of both industrial development and technological complexity.

The foregoing is associated with the particular characteristics of Chilean industrial exports. Essentially, these exports involve little processing of a reduced number of natural resources, most significantly fish and lumber. As Table 5.5 shows, the items derived from these resources account for 63 percent of Chile's industrial exports.

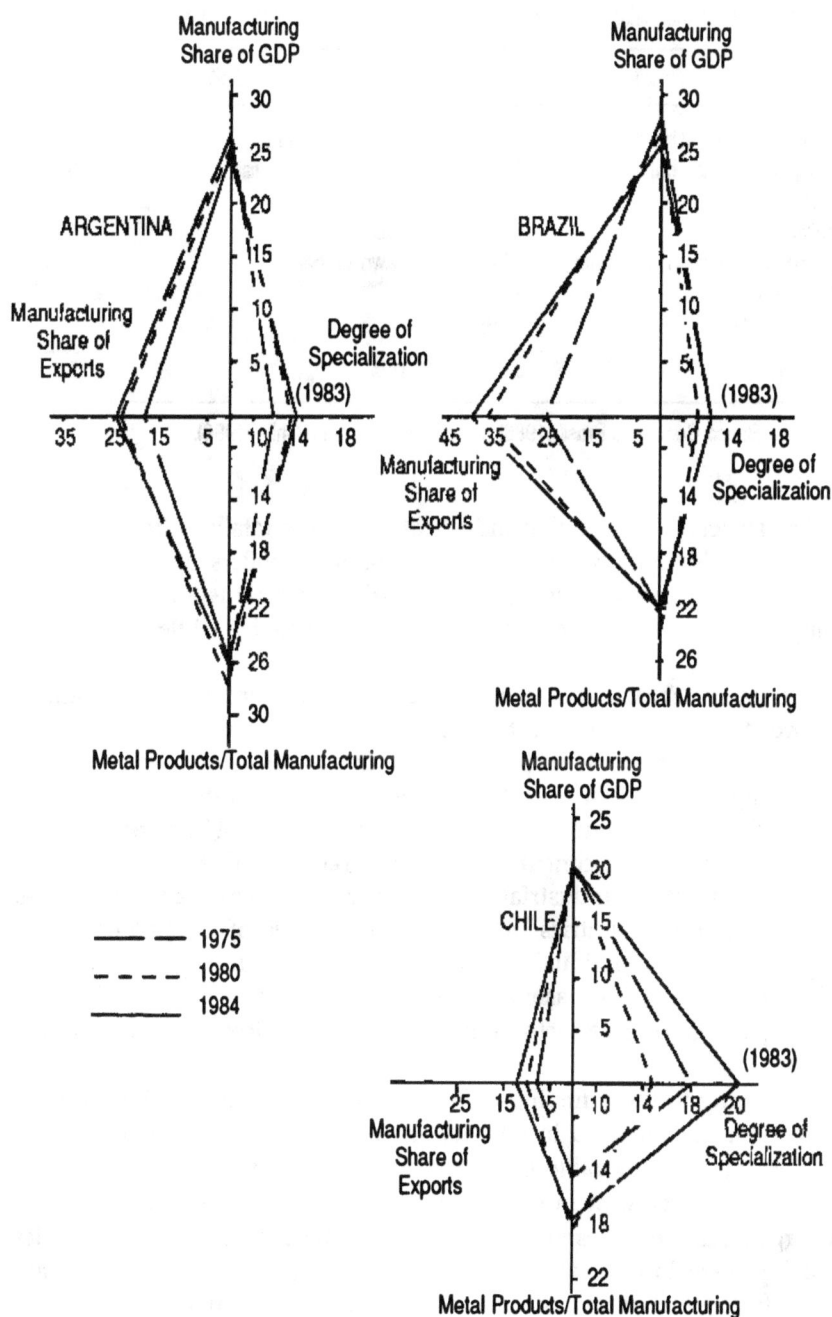

FIGURE 5.1 Industrial Profiles. *Sources:* CEPAL (1986, 1987) and ONUDI (1987).

TABLE 5.5   Main Industrial Export Products (1985) (percentages of total industrial exports)

Brazil		Chile	
Boilers, mechanical instruments	(11.7)	Oils and fishmeal	(32.2)
Transportation material	(12.4)	Fresh and frozen fish	(6.0)
Steel	(10.0)	Pulp	(14.4)
Footwear	(7.1)	Paper	(5.4)
Electric apparatus and machinery	(4.2)	Sawn lumber	(5.3)
Chemicals	(4.7)		
Plastic goods	(2.9)		
Total	53.0	Total	63.3

Sources: Banco Central do Brasil (1986) and Banco Central de Chile (1986).

The structure of Brazilian industrial exports is totally different. These goods—predominantly transportation material, boilers and mechanical instruments, steel, machinery, and electrical apparatus—are technologically much more elaborate than those exported by Chile (see Figure 5.1).

Ultimately, these differences in export breakdown are manifestations of broader divergences in the configurations of industrial structure. Substantial investments in previously defined sectors assured Brazil the leadership of the *chemical* and *metalworking* sectors in the 1970s. Indeed, both industries continued to take the lead in subsequent industrial growth and made significant contributions to the recovery that began in 1984.

With respect to industrial inputs, there are significant differences among the three countries in terms of the degree of dependence upon imports in each individual industrial apparatus. Although current data are unavailable, some basic conclusions may be drawn on the basis of a comparison of intersectoral input-output matrices compiled in the 1970s.[9]

According to these findings, Chilean industry appears to be the most dependent on imported inputs. Its share in total imports is as high as 10 percent in nondurable consumer goods, 19 percent in intermediate goods, and 17 percent in capital goods (Aceituno and Casanova, 1986). In Argentina, the corresponding percentages are 2 percent in nondurables and 7 percent in intermediate and capital goods. (As the figures pertain to 1970, the effects of the opening of the economy that took place in the 1970s are not accounted for in these percentages.) In the case of Brazil, the input-output matrix reveals import coefficients on the order of 1 percent for numerous industrial consumption branches (e.g., textiles, clothing, furniture, and leather) and 3 to 5 percent for machinery

TABLE 5.6   Structure of Sales of the Fifty Largest Industrial Firms (1983) (in percentages)

	Public Enterprises	Domestic Private Firms	Foreign Firms
Argentina	9.3	39.4	51.4
Brazil	21.8	16.5	61.7
Chile	14.4	54.2	31.4

Source: CEPAL/ONUDI (1985b).

construction, transport equipment, and metal products; only in two branches—chemicals and pharmaceuticals—are the import coefficients higher than 10 percent (Bear and Da Phonetic, 1987).

Under such conditions, the superior performance of Brazilian industry is not hard to understand. In comparison to the other two countries discussed, Brazil has had the advantage of a more integrated industry, given the development of a capital goods sector in the 1970s; clear sectoral leadership founded on the ascendancy of the chemical and metalworking sectors; a degree of excellence in certain branches, such as transport material and armament, that allowed it to conquer new foreign markets; and relatively less dependence on imported inputs.

These factors did not apply to either Argentina or Chile. The open-economy policies adopted in the 1970s had a severely negative effect, especially on domestic production of the capital goods that Argentina, and to a lesser degree Chile, had managed to develop. In addition, the general crisis in the region struck the Argentine capital goods industry with particular force.

The Role of Economic Actors in the Industrial Process

Industrial structures and the ways in which they develop are, in the final analysis, the result of actions taken by various agents in the industrial development process—namely, business, government, foreign capital, and workers. Entrepreneurial configurations in the three countries share many features, including the weighty presence of state-owned and foreign corporations, the concentration of sales in a small number of large firms, and the considerable effect of small-scale enterprises on availability of jobs.

The data on participation of the different kinds of firms in the sales of the fifty largest industrial corporations in each country (see Table 5.6) indicate that the most influential actors are foreign corporations (Argentina and Brazil) and domestic private enterprise (Chile). Brazil

TABLE 5.7 International Comparison of Degrees of Concentration[a] (1983) (in percentages)

Number of Firms Share of Total GDP	Argentina 1982	Brazil 1983	Colombia 1983	Chile 1983	Mexico 1983	Uruguay 1983	Venezuela 1983	U.S. 1982
10 L.F./PIB	14.9	9.8	16.1	29.7	16.8	34.0	39.1	16.3
20 L.F./PIB	23.0	13.0	20.8	37.2	19.7	42.2	44.3	23.8
30 L.F./PIB	27.8	15.2	23.8	41.8	21.5	—	47.8	28.3
40 L.F./PIB	31.7	16.9	25.4	45.5	22.8	—	50.1	31.7
50 L.F./PIB	34.3	18.3	26.6	47.8	23.7	—	52.1	34.5

[a]Relative share of the first 10, 20, . . . 50 companies in total gross domestic product (L.F. = largest firms).

Source: CEPAL/ONUDI (1985b).

exhibits a relatively higher importance of public enterprises. Furthermore, the extent of concentration of the Brazilian economy is less than that in Argentina, Chile, and other countries (see Table 5.7). As indicated in a study (CEPAL/ONUDI, 1985b) of sales of the fifty most important companies of each type (public, private domestic, and foreign), public firms account for the largest share of manufacturing industry: 14.2 percent of sales in Brazil compared with 7.8 percent in Chile and Argentina.

Economic policies with respect to the industrial sector have varied among the three countries. In Argentina and Chile the open-economy policies applied in the 1970s had a heavy anti-industry bias. Furthermore, the governments of both countries maintained that the industrial sector developed in previous decades was the source of substantial inefficiencies and that any branches unable to face foreign competition simply had to disappear. Based on this view, policies were enacted that were characterized mainly by tariff liberalization[10] and reduction of sectoral credits. To the negative effects of such measures were added those of a compressed domestic market and an overvalued domestic currency.

The economic policies adopted by the Brazilian government were very different. As noted, far from opening the external sector, the Brazilian economy (and Brazilian industry) reduced its foreign-sector dependence in the 1970s, thanks to government promotion of a policy aimed at strengthening import substitution, particularly by manufacturing intermediate and capital goods. The Brazilian government was persistent in its will to industrialize. Toward this end it took three actions: It organized its industrial sectors, especially intermediate capital goods and power infrastructure; it provided direct incentives to industry to modernize through export promotion; and it established such leading-edge technological sectors as information science, telecommunications, aeronautics, and nuclear applications (Erber, 1986).

The main instruments for executing these policies were the state-enterprises and Banco Nacional de Desarrollo Económico (BNDE), which mobilized the necessary resources to finance an ambitious investment program. Although Brazilian industry still shows some significant gaps (particularly in the case of components for the capital goods industry, intermediate inputs for advanced chemistry, and basic design), its achievements have been significant.

Brazil has developed a domestic minicomputer industry thanks to the decision made in 1977 to reserve this market for domestic suppliers. Similar success has been attained by the aeronauts industry, which is currently capable of producing military training aircraft for export to several countries (including developed ones).

Although Brazilian business has strived to restrict government participation in industrial operations, seeking for this purpose to tighten its links with foreign capital, the technocracy organized around state enterprises and specialized government agencies has thus far withstood such pressures. In any event, there is in Brazil a basic industrial consensus to the effect that direct government action is legitimate in all sectors considered to be crucial for future development.

The situation in Argentina and Chile has been radically different. Industry's loss of drive in the mid-1970s eroded the industrial consensus that had been built in preceding decades. Made worse by the violent social and political tensions of the Perón period in Argentina and the Unidad Popular period in Chile, which led to the military intervention, the economic policies adopted by the military were totally different from those of the preceding course of development. The events associated with the military regimes are well known, of course. But what is remarkable, particularly in Chile, is the lack of resistance by entrepreneurial sectors to policies that have affected their interests severely. In Chile, the major entrepreneurial associations have expressed little if any disagreement with the open-economy policy in force since 1974. Criticism of business has been restricted to relatively specific issues (uniform tariffs, a fixed exchange rate, utilization of governmental purchasing power, etc.) without questioning the anti-industrial essence of the overall model.

Argentine business people during the open-economy period were comparatively more critical. The military government had to dissolve one of the two entrepreneurial associations connected with industry (Confederación General de la Industria) and put the other (Unión Industrial Argentina, or UIA) under intervention. Although most entrepreneurial sectors supported the military action, when Minister Martínez de Hoz took office industrial entrepreneurs emphasized their criticism to the point of a near break with the authorities. In the course of this process, the UIA proposed an industrial policy that vindicated the strategic significance of the industrial sector in the Argentine economy. Owing to the greater resistance of the entrepreneurial circles, and that of the unions, the open-economy policy in Argentina was ultimately less effective than that in Chile. Entrepreneurial action, however, was restricted to lobbying the government, with little in the way of innovative practices. This central element certainly accounts for the sclerosis of Argentine industry.

At the same time, the attitude of Chilean entrepreneurs cannot be understood in the absence of political-economic considerations. The idea held widely by these entrepreneurs that military action was closely linked to defense of private property inhibited their criticism of the government. For this reason, they have gone outside their corporate interests to provide majority support for the economic (and political) actions of the military. Union repression and the leeway left by the open-economy policy for financial or import-related operations has helped to moderate entrepreneurial resistance even more.

Conclusions

The deficiencies of industrial policy stand out even more in the present context, which is dominated by profound transformations of the productive and technological base of all the major economies of the world. To allow the free market to solve all decisions associated with new investment, international specialization, and technological options would be to gamble on the future. Such an option would hardly create the conditions for a sufficiently broad productive reconversion. Rather, the countries that give up any deliberate intervention in this sense run the risk of paralyzing their productive structures or, at most, reproducing subaltern forms of international specialization. It is essential, therefore, that the industrial debate be intensified such that it attains the importance it deserves in the overall context of economic discussion.

Yet to be drawn up are policies that arrive at accurate definitions in such crucial areas as the new role of industry in the economic system as a whole, new lines of international specialization, practical modes of developing regional integration in the industrial field, the policies needed to reduce technological dependence, and the foundations on which to build a new industrial alliance, without which any modernization proposal is doomed.[11] It is safe to say that the economic future of the region will be closely dependent on the speed and quality of the responses given to these issues.

From a purely productive standpoint, the current economic crisis is even more serious for the region than the Depression was. For Latin America the crisis of the 1930s lacked the *paradigmatic* nature of the present situation. In a practical way, the import-substitution strategy referred to the industrial development pattern emerging from the industrial developed world. It is for this reason that Latin American industry was structured in the same sequence as that in developed countries, even though it never reached the same levels of technological self-sufficiency or intra- and intersectoral integration.

Today the problem can be stated in different terms. There is no model to which one might refer to provide specific guidance about each country's own strategies. Therein lies the paradigmatic nature of the present crisis and the resulting impossibility of a purely mimetic development. In such a context, uncertainty and perplexity cannot be avoided. Yet there is still the chance that a new type of Latin American development and industry—not merely a reduced copy of Northern industry—can be built.

In the neoliberal attempt to make a radical break from the economic theory and practice that have prevailed in the region for decades, it was not simply a matter of questioning the role of industry as keystone of the productive apparatus. More essentially, it was *industrialization qua socioeconomic creation* that became the target of numerous attacks— attacks on industry, for its inefficiency and lack of competitiveness; on industrial entrepreneurs, for their inability to innovate and their desire for excessive protection; on government, for committing substantial resources to projects of dubious interest while smothering the drive of private initiative; and, finally, on workers, for turning themselves into "working aristocracies" and exercising a union monopoly that deprived productive processes of flexibility.

In summary, the (partially fulfilled) objective of the neoliberal offensive was to put an end to the historical alliance among the industrial bourgeoisies, government technocracy, and the associated working classes— in other words, to break with the form of overall regulation built on the basis of industrialization processes. In the face of this offensive, industrialism was clearly beaten back. Evidence regarding the limits of industrial development with respect to the original project contributed to a general relaxation of the domestic productive efforts that resulted from favorable international conditions, thus avoiding weighty resistance to the neoliberal attack.

The crisis of the early 1980s alters the scenario significantly. Indeed, recession, trade paralysis, and the foreign-debt problem created a radically different setting. The difficulty for private agents to act in an environment dominated by vast uncertainty tends to reduce the objective base of liberalization and privatization projects. At the same time, adverse international conditions increase mistrust of indiscriminate open-economy policies, as evidence accumulates to the effect that such policies only enhance external vulnerability.

Thus numerous topics, which until recently had been deemed obsolete, began to acquire renewed interest. These topics included endogenous development, selective import substitution, regional integration, active international insertion, and incorporation of new technologies.

Unlike the debates of the 1970s, opposing views today tend to be less clear-cut. Few, indeed, would question the importance of the new themes being discussed by economists. However, the abstract nature of their postulates—together with the difficulty of proposing specific policies oriented in that direction, in a context where the problems caused by the crisis urgently require answers—hinder the progress of the new themes. Economic discussion thus continues to be dominated in most Latin American countries by short-term adjustment problems. In essence, the debate over the new themes retains an academic bias.

Nevertheless, the weakening of the neoliberal offensive has de-ideologized the debate to some extent. Industry has been one of the great beneficiaries insofar as the core of criticism has moved from industrialization per se to specific industrial policies. The reevaluation of industry as a driving force of development and a privileged sector of technological change is one of the significant developments of recent years. It should not be overestimated, however, for the industrial debate is far from attaining the seriousness required to render a source of inspiration for new industrial policies.

Notes

1. To emphasize the strictly industrial elements, the author has omitted all details connected with national specificities in the adjustment processes. See Ominami (1987) for a more extensive treatment of the subject.

2. For a discussion of industrial regression at the global level, see, for example, Errázuriz (1982), García and Gatica (1985), Muñoz (1986), and Pollack (1984); regarding the sectoral level, see Vignolo (1983), Castillo (1986), Donoso and Tampier (1986), Merino and Weinstein (1986), Aninat (1986), and Errázuriz, Leiva, and Tagle (1986).

3. See, for example, Kosacoff (1984), PREALC (1983), Schvarzer (1983), Notchteff (1984), Zimmerman (1985), Chudnovsky (1984), and Katz (1985).

4. This percentage is based on UNDP/ILO estimates.

5. According to ECLAC figures in the *Statistical Yearbook* of 1986, in Argentina the share of exports of manufactures in total exports fell from 24.4 percent in 1975 to 17.1 percent in 1984. In Brazil during the same period the share rose from 24.5 percent to 41.4 percent, and in Chile, from 8.1 percent to 11.9 percent.

6. These percentages were derived from ECLAC estimates based on data in U.S. dollars at constant 1970 prices. In Argentina the degree of opening measured by the imports coefficient grew from 6.3 percent in 1985 to 11.9 percent in 1980, then fell to 6.0 percent in 1984 as a result of adjustment policies. In Chile the degree of opening increased from 13.0 percent in 1975 to 17.5 percent in 1980, then fell to 11.9 percent in 1984.

7. In the United States all three sectors dropped, to the benefit of nonclassified industries.

8. For a similar comparative discussion of industrial structure, the role of capital goods, and development, see Zimbalist and Brundenius (1989).

9. The year was 1970 for Argentina, 1975 for Brazil, and 1977 for Chile.

10. In Argentina the average tariff dropped from 93 percent in 1976 to 35 percent by the end of 1979. In Chile the tariff reduction program was even more accelerated; there the average tariff fell from nearly 94 percent in 1974 to 10 percent in 1979.

11. For an attempt to advance along the subject of industrial alliances, see Bitar and Ominami (1988).

References

Aceituno, G., and E. Casanova (1986), "La crisis actual de las estructuras productivas de las economías latinoamericanas," *Economía de América Latina*, No. 15, Mexico.

Aninat, A. (1986), "Sector textil: Transformaciones y potencialidades." In Centre de Estudios del Desarrollo (CED), *La industria chilena: Cuatro visiones sectoriales.* Santiago: CED.

Bear, W., and M. Da Phonetic (1987), "Structural changes in Brazil's industrial economy, 1960–80," *World Development*, Vol. 15, No. 2, United Kingdom.

Barros de Castro, A., and Pires de Souza (1985), *A economia brasileira en marcha forçda.* Rio de Janeiro: Paz e Terra.

Banco Central de Argentina, *Boletín Mensual*, several issues, Buenos Aires.

Banco Central de Brasil, *Boletín Mensual*, several issues, Brasilia.

Banco Central de Chile, *Boletín Mensual*, several issues, Santiago.

Banco Mundial (1987), *World Debt Tables*, Washington, D.C.

BID (1987), *Progreso Económico y Social en América Latina*, Washington, D.C.

Bitar, S., and C. Ominami (1988), "La política industrial latinoamericana a fines del Siglo XX," *Integración Latinoamericana*, Buenos Aires.

Castillo, M. (1986), "Situación y perspectivas de la industria alimentaria." In CED, *La industria chilena: Cuatro visiones sectoriales.* Santiago: CED.

CEPAL (1986, 1987), *Anuario Estadístico de América Latina y el Caribe* (1985 and 1986), Santiago.

CEPAL/ONUDI (1985b), "Empresas estatales y privadas, nacionales y extranjeras en la estructura industrial de América Latina," *Industrialización y desarrollo tecnológico*, Informe No. 1, Santiago (September).

———— (1986a), "Reflexiones sobre las exportaciones y el comercio de manufacturas de América Latina," *Industrialización y desarrollo tecnológico*, Informe No. 2, Santiago (March).

———— (1986b), "El papel de la pequeña y mediana empresa (PME) en la estructura industrial de América Latina: Una comparación con el caso de Italia," *Industrialización y desarrollo tecnológico*, Informe No. 3, Santiago (September).

Chudnovsky, D. (1984), *La difusión de tecnologías de punta en la Argentina: El caso de las máquinas, herramientas con control numérico, los robots y CAD/CAM*, Centro de Estudios de Transnacionales/Instituto de Planificación para América Latina (CET/IPAL), R/164e, Buenos Aires.

Donoso, R., and J. Tampier (1986), "La industria química chilena: Aportes a una estrategia de desarrollo," in *La industria chilena: Cuatro visiones sectoriales*. Santiago: CED.

Erber, F. (1986), "Innovación tecnológica y política de modernización en Brasil." In C. Ominami (ed.), *La tercera revolución industrial./xit//Buenos Aires: Grupo Editor Latinoamericano (GEL)*.

Errázuriz, E. (1982), *"Industrial development in Chile: The restructuring of industry (1973–1981) and elements for an alternative strategy within a democratic perspective," La Haya, Netherlands, Institute of Social Studies, mimeo.*

Errázuriz, E., A. X. Leiva, and J. Tagle (1986), *Industria eléctrica 1960–1985: Expansión, crisis y efectos económico-sociales*, Programa de Economía del Trabajo (PET), Colección Estudios Sectoriales No. 3, Santiago.

Gárcia, A., and J. Gatica (1985), "Reindustrialización, una condición para el desarrollo," *Chileconómico*, No. 3, VECTOR, Santiago.

Katz, J. (1985), "Reflexiones en torno al problema de la reindustrialización e inserción internacional de la República Argentina," *Boletín Informativo Technit*, No. 238.

Kosacoff, B. (1984), "Industrialización y monetarismo en Argentina," *Economía de América Latina*, No. 12, Centro de Investigaciones y Docencia Económica/ Centro de Estudios de Transnacionales (CIDE/CET), México.

Merino, S., and J. Weinstein (1986), "La industria metalmecánica." In *La industria chilena: Cuatro visiones sectoriales*. Santiago: CED.

Mizala, A. (1985), "Liberalización financiera y quiebra de empresas industriales: Chile 1977–1982," *Notas Técnicas*, No. 67, CIEPLAN, Santiago (January).

Muñoz, O. (1986), *Chile y su industrialización: Pasado, crisis y opciones*. Santiago: Ediciones CIEPLAN.

Notchteff, H. (1984), *Desindustrialización y retroceso tecnológico en Argentina (1976–1982)*. Buenos Aires: Faculta Latinoamericano de Ciencias Sociales (FLACSO)/ GEL.

Ominami, C. (1986), "Tercera revolución industrial y opciones de desarrollo." In C. Ominami (ed.), *La tercera revolución industrial, impactos internacionales del actual viraje tecnológico*. Buenos Aires: GEL.

———— (1987), "Problemas actuales de la industrialización y la política industrial latinoamericana," *Notas Técnicas*, No. 103, CIEPLAN, Santiago (November).

ONUDI (1987), *Industry and development: Global Report 1986*. Vienna.

_____ (1987), *Handbook of industrial statistics 1986.* Vienna.

Pollack, M. (1984), "Monetarismo global y respuesta industrial: El caso de Chile," Programa Regional del Empleo para América Latina y el Caribe (PREALC), Santiago, mimeo.

PREALC (1983), "Monetarismo global y respuesta industrial: El caso de Argentina," Santiago, mimeo.

Schvarzer, J. (1983), *Cambios en el liderazgo industrial argentino en el período de Martínez de Hoz.* Buenos Aires: Centro de Investigaciones Sociales sobre el Estado y la Administración (CISEA).

Secretaria de Industria, Comercio, Ciencia e Tecnologia (1985), "Propuesta para uma política industrial no Brasil," Brasilia, mimeo.

Tavares, M. C., and L. Coutinho (1984), "La industrialización brasileña reciente: Impasse y perspectivas," *Economía de América Latina,* No. 12, CIDE/CET, Mexico.

Vignolo, C. (1983), "El crecimiento exportador y sus perspectivas bajo el modelo neoliberal chileno," *Documento de Trabajo,* No. 2. Santiago: CED.

Zimbalist, A. S., and C. Brundenius (1989), *The Cuban economy: Measurement and analysis of socialist performances.* Baltimore: Johns Hopkins University Press.

Zimmerman, J. B. (1985), "L'informatique en Argentine," *Problèmes de l'Amérique Latine.* Paris: La Documentacion Française.

6

Financial Strategies in Latin America: The Southern Cone Experience

Roberto Zahler

In the mid-1970s the Southern Cone countries of Latin America implemented drastic reforms in the financial sector, within a context of profound political, institutional, and economic changes. These changes stemmed from the collapse of the democratic regimes in Argentina, Chile and Uruguay—and their replacement by authoritarian governments—and from a global criticism of the development strategies that had been prevalent in those countries since the middle of the century. Serious doubts had been raised and increasing criticism had been voiced regarding the efficiency of a growth strategy based on industrialization through import substitution and state intervention in economic activities; the questioning of this style of economic development led to the establishment of new anti-inflationary programs, widespread price liberalization, and radical reforms in the structure and functioning of the external, government, labor, and financial sectors.

The financial reforms originated from a diagnosis that had become quite widespread toward the beginning of the 1970s regarding the limitations and drawbacks of "financial repression." This latter situation, which has characterized economic policies in the financial sector since the 1950s, consisted of a combination of the following elements:

1. ceilings on interest rates, generally at lower levels than inflation, with detrimental effects on financial savings; the need for credit rationing; and the creation of distortions that affected the efficiency of investment decisions;
2. quantitative control and selective allocation of credit at preferential interest rates, aimed at promoting the development of sectors, regions, groups, and activities considered to be of top priority;
3. high minimum legal-reserve requirements with frequently differentiated rates, depending on the length of term and type of currency

of deposits, and on the (regional) geographical location and nationality of the financial institutions;

4. barriers to entry of new financial intermediaries;
5. tax policies that discriminated against financial and saving intermediation;
6. compulsory loans granted to the government by commercial banks
7. exchange control on capital movement with the aim of avoiding capital flight; and
8. direct or indirect state control on an important part of the banking system, guided more by political considerations than by efficiency criteria.

The interpretation of the Southern Cone economic authorities was that financial repression contributed decisively to the depression of private savings and investment, the reduction of the size of the formal financial system, and the constriction of the volume and variety of financial assets. In addition, it promoted the self-financing of economic agents and discouraged financial intermediation, which would have led not only to a corresponding decline in the average profitability of investment projects but also to credit market segmentation between those agents who had access to the formal subsidized market and those who had to seek out financing in the informal markets, at a much higher cost and risk.

In short, state intervention in the financial system—and the number of controls, restrictions, and distortions this involved—was responsible for generating low volumes of saving and capital accumulation, and for stimulating inefficient and unprofitable allocation of investments, with a corresponding effect on the possibilities for expanding productive capacity. According to the official interpretation, financial repression also had an adverse effect on income and assets distribution—on the one hand, by encouraging self-financing and privileged access to subsidized credit by already existing, large, capital-intensive corporations with abundant collaterals and, on the other, through a reduction in the net worth of savers in the formal financial system, who were mostly economically weak and inadequately informed agents with no means of placing their savings in other instruments or institutions.

The financial reforms in the Southern Cone were intended to provoke a radical change in the above-described situation. They were aimed at liberalizing[1] and privatizing credit markets and institutions, encouraging competition between financial intermediaries, and promoting the integration of domestic capital markets with international ones.

The Financial Reforms: Formulation
and Main Results

Overview

The financial reforms were implemented in the Southern Cone soon after the advent of the military regimes: in 1975 in Chile, 1976 in Uruguay, and 1977 in Argentina. The end, or at least temporary halt, of the process of financial liberalization correlates closely with the collapse of the exchange-rate policy—cornerstone of the stabilization programs in all three countries—and with direct or indirect state intervention (through the purchase of nonperforming loans, interest-rate control, etc.) in the financial system. These developments took place in 1980–1981 in Argentina and in 1982 in Chile and Uruguay.

The analysis and evaluation of Southern Cone financial liberalization is hindered by a series of factors.

1. At the beginning of the neoconservative process, the three countries were facing acute inflation: in Chile it was close to 400 percent in 1974; annual price increases in Uruguay accelerated to more than 80 percent in 1975; and inflation in Argentina rose to almost 450 percent in 1976. It is therefore not surprising that the financial deregulation policies were implemented together with price stabilization programs, and that the financial system should have responded to the reforms of the sector as well as to the impact of anti-inflationary policies.

2. In more general terms, it is difficult to evaluate the financial strategies of the Southern Cone, initially because of significative macroeconomic disequilibria, and subsequently because of severe external shocks. With regard to the former, it is necessary to consider the impact of macroeconomic disequilibria on the evolution of the financial sector, which leads us to the fundamental question of whether measures to correct macroeconomic imbalance should be put into effect before, during, or after implementing financial reforms. Regarding the latter, discussions about the greater or lesser vulnerability of freer financial markets in the face of drastic and uncontrollable changes in international interest rates or in the availability of external financing, and the relative efficacy of rigid regulations vis-à-vis discretionary policies, acquire renewed relevance.

3. Together with domestic financial liberalization, other reforms such as general price liberalization, commercial opening-up (mainly in Chile), financial opening-up (especially in Uruguay), fiscal reform, changes in labor legislation, and even (particularly in Chile) the privatization of

government-held companies were undertaken. Given the importance of these other components of the reform "package," it is difficult to isolate and identify the specific elements of the new financial strategy and to link them unequivocally with the observed results.

4. It has been argued that the outcome observed in the financial sector was due more to the speed with which these reforms were implemented (shock versus gradualism in the context of financial deregulation) than to possible flaws in the sector itself. In terms of the sequence of the different policies and reforms, it is relevant to discuss which process should be implemented first—stabilization or reform. It is generally agreed that the answer depends on the magnitude of the initial macroeconomic imbalance and, especially, on the rate of inflation. In addition, the global result of liberalization policies depends on the sequence in which foreign trade and financial reforms are implemented and, in the latter case, on the sequence in which financial openings-up vis-à-vis domestic financial reforms are undertaken.

The Financial Reforms

The main policies that affected the internal financial system of the Southern Cone countries were as follows:

1. Liberalization of interest rates, as a key measure directed toward increasing financial saving and financial deepening, and improving efficiency in the use of loanable funds.
2. Dismantling of quantitative and selective credit controls. (The aim here was to grant greater freedom to financial institutions to allocate credit on the basis of market and competitive considerations.)
3. Homogenization, reduction, and/or remuneration of legal bank reserve requirements, in order to reduce interest-rate spread. (This policy would contribute to lowering the costs of financial intermediation, increase the size of the formal financial sector [in particular, the volume and variety of financial instruments], and reduce the cost of funds for capital accumulation.)
4. Reduction of barriers on the entry of new financial institutions and domestic and foreign banks, especially in Argentina and Chile.
5. Deregulation,[2] which also brought about a slackening of the regulation, supervision, and control of the financial system. (This policy created serious deficiencies, especially in three principal areas: the evaluation of the risks involved in the credit portfolio, the rules governing the concentration of the ownership of financial institutions, and the links between the shareholders and managers

of these institutions and those of the companies indebted to the financial system.)

Financial opening-up rested on the expectation that international capital inflows would complement internal saving, thus contributing to an even further increase in investment; in the process, domestic interest rates would be forced to settle somewhere around the value of international rates. In general terms, financial opening-up included two main components: on the one hand, a reduction on the restrictions regarding the minimum period required to repatriate capital and an increase in the maximum amounts of financial capital inflow allowed; on the other, the authorization of deposits and transactions in foreign currency.

Unlike domestic financial reform, financial opening-up was put into practice at different rates in the three countries. In Uruguay it was implemented right from the start (although tariff reform was deferred and never reached a significant level), whereas in Chile barriers to trade were liberalized initially but it was only toward 1979 that a more decisive move toward financial opening-up was made. Throughout almost the entire period (up to mid-1982) Chile maintained the ban on bringing in capital for periods under two years, owing to the fear that the huge difference between local and international interest rates could provoke a massive capital inflow that might have jeopardized the stabilization program.[3] Argentina controlled capital inflows during the first two years and started to liberalize them gradually, once the price-stabilization program began to revolve increasingly around the exchange-rate policy.

Main Results

The financial reforms in the three countries produced results quite different from those expected, thus suggesting that the global effect of these policies was negative on many fronts. In the three countries the private financial system ended up practically bankrupt and largely intervened by the economic authorities. The specific causes of the failure of the Southern Cone financial reforms are still under discussion and will be analyzed in greater detail later in the chapter. For now, however, we shall turn to a brief review of the main effects of the new financial strategies.

First, as a consequence of the elimination or drastic reduction of the control on interest rates and the distortions affecting the formal financial system, financial deepening—principally in the form of time and savings deposits—increased substantially. In effect, near-money as a proportion of GDP, which was 6–7 percent in 1974–1976 in the three countries, increased systematically and significantly until, in 1981–1983, it reached

TABLE 6.1 Financial Deepening (in percentages of GDP)

	Argentina		Chile		Uruguay	
	Near-Money	M_2^a	Near-Money	M_2^a	Near-Money	M_2^a
1975	6	15	7	11	3	12
1976	2	12	4	8	10	21
1977	7	17	7	11	14	24
1978	12	22	8	13	18	28
1979	12	20	10	14	23	33
1980	14	20	11	17	22	29
1981	15	19	17	23	30	38
1982	12	17	23	29	38	45
1983	10	14	18	24	40	46
1984	—	—	19	25	30	35
1985	—	—	22	26	30	35

[a]Measured at the end of June of each year.

Sources: IMF, *International Financial Statistics* (1986 and 1987).

15 percent in Argentina, 23 percent in Chile, and 40 percent in Uruguay (see Table 6.1). It should be stressed, however, that the majority of financial assets were extremely short term—in general, not more than thirty days. Therefore, Southern Cone financial reforms—in a context of great uncertainty and high and erratic inflation—promoted the development of a money market rather than what is usually understood to be a capital market.

As financial intermediation grew, so did the financial sector in terms of institutions, number of offices and subsidiaries, personnel, and salaries (the latter as compared with both other economic sectors and the salaries paid, for similar jobs and qualifications, in the financial system of industrialized countries). The size of the financial sector increased from approximately 4 percent of GDP in Argentina, 14 percent of GDP in Chile, and 5.5 percent of GDP in Uruguay during 1974–1976, to more than 8 percent, 16 percent, and 10 percent of GDP, respectively, in 1980–1982.

Second, despite the quite impressive growth of "financial saving," national saving decreased slightly in Argentina, dropped sharply in Chile, and increased in Uruguay (see Table 6.2). The implication is that although financial saving was sensitive to shifts in real interest rates, the same did not hold true for saving in a global (national accounts) sense. The evolution of national saving was strongly influenced by the use given by the financial system to deposits, the incentives toward consumption

TABLE 6.2 Savings and Investment[a] (in percentages of GDP)

	Argentina			Chile			Uruguay		
	Savings Domestic	Savings Foreign	Invest-ment	Savings Domestic	Savings Foreign	Invest-ment	Savings Domestic	Savings Foreign	Invest-ment
1970	20.7	0.4	21.1	18.9	1.6	20.4	7.7	2.3	10.0
1971	21.5	0.9	22.5	15.3	2.9	18.2	7.6	3.0	10.6
1972	21.7	0.5	22.2	6.7	6.6	13.3	10.8	-1.8	9.0
1973	21.9	-1.3	20.6	8.8	3.7	12.5	9.1	-0.6	8.5
1974	19.9	-0.2	19.7	19.5	2.8	22.3	5.2	3.4	8.6
1975	18.7	1.4	20.1	7.8	4.3	12.1	6.3	4.0	10.3
1976	22.4	-0.8	21.6	12.8	-1.2	11.6	10.4	1.5	12.0
1977	25.3	-0.1	24.2	8.7	3.8	12.5	10.7	3.1	13.8
1978	23.0	-1.7	21.3	7.5	6.8	14.3	12.8	2.2	15.0
1979	21.1	0.4	21.5	11.7	5.5	17.2	13.0	4.4	17.4
1980	19.6	3.1	22.7	13.7	7.3	21.0	10.2	7.1	17.3
1981	15.5	3.2	18.7	8.0	16.3	24.3	11.6	4.0	15.6
1982	15.0	1.7	16.7	0.3	9.4	9.7	11.7	2.4	14.1
1983	13.6	1.8	15.4	3.1	4.9	8.0	8.8	0.7	9.6
1984	11.4	1.8	13.2	4.9	8.4	13.3	7.2	1.7	8.9
1985	10.8	0.7	11.5	7.0	5.1	12.1	6.6	1.4	8.0

[a]Computed using 1980 dollars data.

Sources: CEPAL (1986, 1988).

and savings derived from macroeconomic policies, and the degree of substitution between internal and foreign saving.

Third, foreign saving grew strongly in Chile and Uruguay, and to a lesser extent in Argentina. This growth was due partly to the considerable domestic demand for external financing stimulated by the policies of financial opening-up and the differences between domestic and international interest rates. The greater availability of international liquidity to the region seems to have been a decisive factor as well.[4]

Fourth, foreign saving replaced internal saving in Chile and Argentina, as largely reflected by the drop in the investment rate in both countries. The investment rate grew in Uruguay, but this outcome was apparently due more to public-sector investment than to the effects of the financial reform.

Fifth, the increase in financial intermediation had a counterpart in the strong growth of internal credit, particularly credit directed toward the private sector. This credit represented 10 percent of GDP in Argentina, 4 percent in Chile, and 14 percent in Uruguay in 1974–1976, and it experienced extraordinary growth until 1981–1982, when it reached 24

TABLE 6.3 Private Domestic Debt[a] (in percentages of GDP)

	Argentina	Chile	Uruguay
1970	16	7	12
1971	16	7	14
1972	14	6	16
1973	14	2	14
1974	17	2	12
1975	8	5	14
1976	6	5	16
1977	10	9	18
1978	12	16	21
1979	15	19	23
1980	22	25	27
1981	26	39	33
1982	22	60	39
1983	18	57	46
1984	n.a.[b]	53	40
1985	n.a.[b]	52	38

[a]Credit from the monetary system to the private sector (June of each year).
[b]Not available

Sources: IMF, *International Financial Statistics* (1986 and 1987).

percent, 50 percent, and 36 percent of GDP in the three countries, respectively (see Table 6.3). From another angle, the greater financial deepening gave rise to a spectacular increase in internal indebtedness, on the part of both the financial institutions and corporations, smaller firms, and families. As indebtedness increased in relation to other forms of financing, domestic debtors became increasingly vulnerable to rises in interest rates, to drops in activity levels, to retractions in financial flows, and, in general, to shifts in variables that had a negative effect on the profitability of the "real" sector of the economy and/or on the debt-service capacity of debtors. Indebtedness in foreign currency generated additional currency risks, which—when the exchange-rate policy collapsed—contributed decisively to the outcome of the entire economic policy and the extremely weakened position in which the financial system was left.

Sixth, the extraordinary capital inflow—which was provoked by the spectacular difference between domestic and international interest rates and, especially in Uruguay and Argentina, by an accelerated financial opening-up—contributed to an appreciation of the domestic currencies. (see Table 6.4). The monetization of capital inflows allowed asset prices—

TABLE 6.4 Evolution of Real Exchange Rates[a] (Index: 1980 = 100)

	Argentina	Chile	Uruguay
1975		131	
1976		115	118
1977	166	111	116
1978	149	127	112
1979	111	114	98
1980	100	100	100
1981	143	93	96
1982	170	112	102
1983	167	118	132
1984	163	118	122
1985	190	138	118

[a]Weighted average with respect to main import countries' structure.

Sources: CEPAL (1986, 1988).

TABLE 6.5 Price Bubble[a] (Index: 1980 = 100)

	Argentina	Chile
1975	—	12
1976	—	16
1977	66[b]	26
1978	70	49
1979	127	55
1980	100	100
1981	48	78
1982	46	59
1983	59	38

[a] Average real price of stock market.
[b] Second semester.

Sources: Argentina, Ramos (1986); Chile, Zahler (1985).

especially nontradable assets—to increase out of all proportion (see Table 6.5), thus generating an apparent (and transitory) increase in wealth, stimulating consumption, and discouraging saving. In addition, the asset-price "bubble" overshot the value of guarantees received by the financial system, thereby giving rise to an excessive and risky supply of credit and leaving financial intermediaries vulnerable—because they

TABLE 6.6 Interest Rates for Loans (in annual percentages)

	Argentina	Chile		Uruguay
	Real [a]	Real [b]	Dollar [c]	Real [b]
1975		114.8[d]	86.6[d]	
1976		51.3	118.3	
1977	26.7[d]	39.2	58.2	5.3
1978	11.9	35.1	51.1	10.1
1979	2.6	16.6	40.5	−9.6
1980	25.9	11.9	46.9	16.7
1981	−1.5	38.7	51.9	23.9
1982	−13.5	35.1	−12.1	34.0
1983		15.9	18.6	28.3

[a]Short-run nominal interest rate deflated by the wholesale price index.
[b]Short-run nominal interest rate deflated by the consumer price index.
[c]Nominal rates adjusted by the exchange rate.
[d]Second semester.

Sources: Argentina and Uruguay, Ramos (1986); Chile, Zahler (1985).

were granting loans on the basis of collateral valuation, which could not hold up once the influx of external financing ceased.

Seventh, foreseeable financial liberalization brought about an increase in interest rates in the formal financial markets. However, annual active real interest rates expanded to extremely high levels for many years (see Table 6.6) and reached 43 percent in Chile, 17 percent in Argentina, and 15 percent in Uruguay during the period between the deregulation of interest rates and the collapse of the exchange-rate policy; in dollar terms, the annual active rate was even higher. Another feature of the real interest rate in the financial markets of the Southern Cone was its extreme variability, in which the rate of inflation appears to have played an important role.

Companies with access to bank credit prior to the financial liberalization found themselves in an impaired situation as a consequence of the abrupt increase in their financial burden. Agents that were previously marginated from the formal financial market—particularly the consumers—were relatively benefited by the new interest rates, because no matter how high the rates went, they rarely reached the extraordinarily real levels that characterized the informal credit market prior to deregulation.

Eighth, passive interest rates in the formal financial sector also grew with regard to the strongly negative levels recorded prior to deregulation.

TABLE 6.7   Interest Rates for Deposits (in annual percentages)

	Argentina		Chile		Uruguay		
	Real[a]	Dollar[b]	Real[a]	Dollar[b]	Real[a]	Dollar[b]	LIBOR[c]
1975			18.6[d]	3.1[d]			7.73
1976			0.0	44.3			6.12
1977	−6.3[d]	16.1[d]	5.1	19.6	−12.1	2.2	6.42
1978	−14.6	37.2	18.7	32.7	0.8	12.9	9.35
1979	−9.4	34.6	4.4	25.9	−21.7	19.5	11.98
1980	−4.4	45.7	4.7	37.4	5.1	26.8	14.08
1981	9.3	−30.5	28.5	40.8	12.8	26.3	16.51
1982	−19.7	−62.9	22.4	−20.4	27.2	−30.0	13.22
1983	−30.2	−22.2	3.9	6.4	12.3	32.8	9.79

[a]Short-run nominal interest rate deflated by the consumer price index.
[b]Nominal rates adjusted by the exchange rate.
[c]Annual average of monthly LIBOR for dollars for 180 days.
[d]Second semester.

Sources: Argentina and Uruguay, Ramos (1986); Chile and LIBOR, Zahler (1985).

In Chile the annual real passive rate for the period averaged 13 percent; in Uruguay it was lower (2 percent per year); and in Argentina it was negative (−7 per year) though higher than the levels that prevailed prior to the financial reforms (see Table 6.7).

The passive interest rate expressed in dollars, however, reached an annual average of 23 percent, 17 percent, and 33 percent in Chile, Uruguay and Argentina, respectively. These figures reflect the fact that, in spite of the strong financial opening-up of Uruguay and Argentina and the extraordinary capital inflows to Chile, domestic interest rates converged very slowly toward international levels.

Ninth, the spread between active and passive short-term rates in local currency was, on the average, extraordinarily high in the three countries: The gross margin in 1975–1981 was more than 20 percent in Chile, and it was 13 percent in Argentina and Uruguay between 1977 and 1981. This situation, especially at the beginning of the deregulation, can be explained by the important cost derived from the high rates of legal reserve requirements, the lack of remuneration of the latter, and the high rate of inflation; moreover, the presence of oligopolies in banking activities, together with the high costs of intermediation due to the absence of capitalization and technological innovation in the sector, appear to be important contributing factors. The gradually increasing number of financial institutions, as well as the more efficient structure and lower costs of intermediation of the new banks that started to operate in the sector, suggests that increasing competition was an important factor in the progressively diminishing margin between active and passive interest rates.

Tenth, the financial strategies of the Southern Cone did not fully take into account the facts that the private financial sector was unaccustomed to working in a liberalized context, and that there was no prior experience in the public sector that could serve to reorient and reformulate the legislation and supervision of the financial sector on the basis of the new conditions and circumstances. The latter was reflected in a financial permissiveness that, by deed or neglect, propitiated or tolerated behaviors that were frequently destabilizing and inefficient. On the one hand, excessive concentration of stockholding in the financial system and its loan portfolio was allowed. In Chile and Argentina there was a significant concentration of credit accumulated through companies belonging to the bank owners themselves; in general, the concentration of credit in the three countries—and the consequent adverse effects on loan portfolio risk and resource allocation—arose from an inadequate control of bank assets. On the other hand, accustomed as the banks were to acting within the framework that prevailed prior to the reforms, the risk and solvency analyses conducted by the banks were based more on the past history of the repayment performance of clients[5] and their real guarantees[6] than on the quality of the projects evaluated technically according to the expected net flows of future benefits, all of which contributed to the imprudent expansion of bank loans.

Eleventh, the extremely high active real interest rates started to erode the borrowers' ability to pay their debts. The pace of investment, economic growth, and salaries was very much smaller than would have been necessary to service the domestic debt, especially considering that the deregulated interest rates were applied not only to new loans but also to accumulated debts. Bank clients started to refinance interest payments and to accumulate arrears (thus multiplying their debts in order to avoid incurring losses, selling assets, or going bankrupt) in the hope that they would be able to survive over a period that was expected to be only temporarily difficult. As the problem became more widespread, the possibility that the state might intervene in order to bail out the banks, alleviate the debt burden, and "remedy" the situation became more plausible. Throughout this process, the pressure on credit demand and rates of interest increased.

At the beginning of the 1980s, the impaired situation of debtors was reflected in a sustained increase in default and a high number of bankruptcies, which unveiled the weakness and fragility of the bank's assets, thus making explicit the vulnerability of the financial system.

This effect had particularly adverse consequences on the economy of the Southern Cone countries, in which the financial sector and the global debt-equity ratio had expanded strongly. The recession aggravated the debtors' already weak ability to service their debts; it also affected the ability of the financial system to face the lesser recovery of their loans. With the general weakening of the economy, the reduced foreign capital inflows, and the need to devalue local currencies, the price bubble of nontradable assets burst;[7] as a result, the value of the real guarantees of the debtors of the financial system deteriorated, making their situation even worse. The expectation of devaluation, which was generalized at the beginning of the 1980s, caused interest rates in local currency to increase further, thereby aggravating the problem of internal indebtedness; the effective depreciation of domestic currencies, which affected almost the entire region, multiplied the problems of domestic debtors, whose debt was denominated in foreign currency.

The magnitude and duration of the recession of the 1980s generalized the situation of local debtors and rendered it much more difficult; this situation in turn led to persistent postponement of the "solution" to the domestic debt problem. The deterioration in the real value of assets made the already serious liquidity and solvency problems of the financial system even worse. To avoid an additional deterioration, many financial institutions were forced to merge, to enter into liquidation, or to be intervened by the government, and controls and other administrative regulations were reimposed. By then it had become clear that the financial systems of the Southern Cone had passed from financial "repression" to financial "bankruptcy" in a period of fewer than six years, and it was necessary to slow down, stop, and even revert the reforms oriented toward financial deregulation in those countries.

Conceptual Issues and Main Questions that Arise Regarding Financial Strategies in the Southern Cone

The financial reforms in the Southern Cone were discontinued owing to the foreign debt crisis that affected Latin America from 1982 on. However, serious economic problems had been accumulating since before that date, and there is evidence that the financial reforms themselves were partly responsible for this situation. As noted in the previous section, many of the problems experienced by the financial sector arose because of errors in macroeconomic policies—particularly as a result of the detrimental effects derived from using the exchange-rate policy as a key instrument in the stabilization programs. An extensive and rigorous analysis of the recent financial strategies of the Southern Cone is beyond the scope of this chapter. But an outline of the questions connected with the formulation and implementation of those strategies is possible—and to this outline we now turn. Indeed, an interpretation of these strategies will enrich our discussion of the design of a financial system that could be functional to economic development.

Financial Deregulation and Interest Rates

One of the most interesting results of the Southern Cone financial liberalization was the extremely high level recorded, during five consecutive years, by the domestic real interest rates in the formal markets, both in absolute terms and in comparison with international rates. A fundamental question arises with regard to the correct meaning of those especially active interest rates. Were they effective, "paid" interest rates, or simply observed, "reference," or "accrued" rates? The continual practice of loan refinancing, along with increasing default and the size of the related and nonperforming loans of the banking system, suggests that caution should be exercised when attempting to interpret the active interest rates of the financial systems of the Southern Cone during that period.

Some of the factors typically noted to explain the gap between domestic and international interest rates are expected devaluation, insufficient financial international integration, and "country-risk." Although these three factors undoubtedly explain part of the interest rate differential, for several years the Southern Cone countries experienced a combination of an extraordinary inflow of foreign credit, growing financial opening-up, ample availability of international reserves, and exchange-rate stability. Thus it is necessary to seek out other complementary elements in order to explain this situation.

Interest Rate Parity. In addition to the prospect of devaluation and country-risk, three elements help to explain the discrepancy between domestic and international interest rates in spite of growing international financial integration. First, the segmentation, differentiated access, and imperfections or inherent features of the international capital market help to create a gap between the two rates of interest. Second, as the degree of "tradability" of the different domestic financial assets is not homogeneous, it is not correct to expect their returns to converge quickly or at a level equal to that of international interest rates. Third, the presence of highly diversified (financial and real) assets makes it necessary to give careful consideration to the links between the expectation of reduced domestic interest rates (on financial assets) and the transmission mechanisms of monetary policy.

If, as a consequence of growing international financial integration, the rate of domestic interest in the financial sector were to drop rapidly to international levels, demand for local currency would increase. The dynamics for reestablishing the equilibrium of the portfolio require an increase not only in the demand for money but also in the demand for all other forms of holding wealth among these capital stock. In other words, the eventual financial-sector equilibrium is only a partial equilibrium; and, unless there are changes in the prices of other assets, in the goods produced by those assets, or in the amount of capital goods (or consumer durables) available, the market of nonfinancial assets, at the international rate of interest, will be in disequilibrium.

Consequently, in order for the domestic interest rate to approach international levels, overall portfolio equilibrium requires the price of nontradable assets to increase over a certain period of time—particularly the price of those assets related to the production of nontradable goods. This point is particularly important: In order for the increase in the price of assets to be sustainable over time, it must be linked in some "real" way—for example, through changes in technology, productivity, consumer preferences, or other determinants of production and spending—to the type of goods produced by the sector that is experiencing price increases. If these changes do not take place, or do so only slowly, interest rates will be unable to converge rapidly, and the increase in the price of assets would have a strong transitory or speculative component. This happened in the Southern Cone in the form of a bubble in the price of assets, which helped increase the valuation of wealth, spending, and demand for credit. In addition, the increase in the price of nontradable goods and assets contributed to a deterioration in the value of the real exchange rate, thereby slowing it down, stimulating foreign indebtedness, and later creating expectations of devaluation that caused a direct increase in domestic interest rates.

The Spread of Interest Rates in the Domestic Financial System. The passive rate imposes a floor—based on international interest rates, expectations of devaluation, and country-risk—on the active rate. The margin between the active and passive domestic rates, though on the decline, was extraordinarily high[8] and helps to explain the high interest rates on loans. A study of the determinants of such a wedge in a sector that was subject to increasingly competitive pressure is a little-explored area and one of the important issues yet to be resolved.

The Stabilization Policies. The attempts to curb the rate of inflation also affected the interest rate. The contractive fiscal and monetary policy—especially in Chile and Uruguay—contributed to an increase in the cost of credit, particularly during the initial years of the reforms. More important was the effect of the exchange-rate policy on interest rates. Widespread in the three countries was the idea that the rise in domestic prices was closely linked to the future time-path of the nominal exchange rate. Considering that the expected exchange rate is strongly influenced by its actual and/or projected evolution, in practice there was a tendency to slow down its time-path vis-à-vis that of other prices and key variables (such as the evolution of wages, money supply and the fiscal budget) on the expectation that these variables would adapt passively to the lesser inflation implicit in the exchange-rate time-path.

One important consequence of an overvalued exchange rate is that the prospect of devaluation tends to raise the domestic interest rate in local currency. Furthermore, an overvaluation of the exchange rate together with financial opening-up, in the absence of compensatory macroeconomic policies or an adequate control or supervision of debts contracted abroad, tend to produce a mutually reinforcing effect. Thus an increase is induced in the relative price of nontradable goods and in real and financial assets, resulting in the above-mentioned effects on spending, greater demand for credit, and increased interest rates.

Domestic Overindebtedness and the Interest Rate. The increasing financial burden of debtors, together with the permissiveness and inadequate supervision and regulation of the financial system, generated an unstable dynamism in the behavior of this sector. On the one hand, the widespread perception that, because of the particular nature of the financial activities, a state guarantee would be *de facto* established on deposits, encouraged depositors to disregard risk considerations when deciding their asset portfolio composition. Thus, banks in difficulties could raise the passive rate in order to attract deposits, thereby forcing the rest of the system to behave in a similar fashion so as not to lose their participation in the market. On the other hand, toward the end of the period, due to the high and generalized domestic overindebtedness and in order not to realize capital losses through the liquidation of assets, debtors and the banks continued in the process of refinancing doubtful and even nonperforming loans, keeping pressure on the credit market and the interest rate while waiting for a "rescue mission" or "solution" on the part of the state.[9] This situation was particularly manifest in Argentina and in Chile, owing to the importance of the economic conglomerates in those countries, but it was also present in Uruguay.

Expansion in Credit Demand. A fundamental element explaining the high level of the active interest rate was the expansion experienced by the demand for credit. This expansion originated from a series of conditions or policies, the most relevant of which were the following: (1) the incentive toward the purchase of consumer durables (especially in Argentina and Chile), due to the reduction in the cost of credit in comparison with its price in the informal sector prior to liberalization, and to the relative drop in prices of consumer goods vis à vis capital goods as a consequence of commercial opening-up; (2) the significant and rapid capital inflows, in combination with the exchange-rate policy, generated by the aforementioned asset-price bubble, which helped (by means of the wealth effect) to strongly encourage the demand for credit; (3) the exaggerated expectations of economic growth, induced by the dynamism of certain sectors (especially the commerce and financial services); (4) strong expectations of capital gains, derived from specific policies such as the temporary price control in 1977 in Argentina and, in the case of Chile, the privatization of companies belonging to the public sector, in a context and at prices of economic recession; and (5) the short term of financial transactions. As the majority of debts were contracted for periods of less than 90 days, the expectation of a reduction in the interest rate due to the growing financial opening-up contributed to the maintenance of a considerable demand for credit, in spite of its extremely high cost, in the hope that it would soon drop to much lower levels.

Financial Reform, Saving, and Investment

A second fundamental question that arises from analysis of the Southern Cone experience refers, on the one hand, to the lack of correlation between the marked increase in financial savings and the behavior of national savings and, on the other, to the inefficiencies observed in the allocation of resources secured by the liberalized financial system.

Financial Savings and National Savings. In the first place, it is inaccurate to liken the increase of financial asset holdings to the concept of saving. The strong growth of financial assets, as a consequence of financial deregulation, occurred in the formal sector and appears to have resulted mainly from the substitution of other forms of holding wealth and from the reduction of the informal financial sector, more than from a significant change in consumption and saving patterns. In other words, financial deepening—especially in Chile and Argentina—reflected a change in the composition of wealth or the stock of assets rather than a deferment of current consumption or an increase in productive capacity. Another situation observed was the financial system allocation of resources to economic agents who were spending beyond their means and preferred to do so in consumer goods rather than capital goods.

Experience shows that financial asset holding is sensitive to shifts in the real interest rate. However, if the interest rate policy is not coordinated with the rest of the macroeconomic policy, there is nothing to guarantee that an increase in financial savings will be translated into greater saving and investment. In the case of Chile and Uruguay, both of which have high passive real interest rates, the increase in financial savings did not occur together with an increase in global savings. Private savings were even less affected. This outcome can be explained, in part, by the strong incentive toward widespread consumption (including consumer durables) derived from the perception of greater wealth. In Uruguay the price of farmland and real estate rose considerably, and in Chile, there was also an increase in the price of industrial property.

External saving showed a negative correlation with internal saving. In other words, the inflow of foreign currency generated by abundant international liquidity, and stimulated by financial opening-up, contributed to the financing of higher levels of consumption. This situation was related to the lack of adequate supervision regarding the use of foreign financing as well as to the wealth effect and the appreciation of the exchange rate linked to the capital inflow.

Financial Intermediation and the Allocation of Loanable Funds. The allocation of funds by the more liberalized financial systems of the Southern Cone showed some interesting traits. The dismantling of quantitative and selective control on credit opened wider possibilities for consumer credit, due to the previously existing bias in favor of investment. To this was added the greater demand for consumer financing, which had previously been concentrated in the informal credit markets.

In more general terms, macroeconomic policy and its (explicit or implicit) orientation in favor of consumption and nontradable activities acquired renewed importance. When, as in the case of the Southern Cone countries, there is a bubble in the price of assets stimulating consumption, and a lag in the real exchange rate, the result is encouraged demand for loanable funds to be used in (mainly imported) consumption goods and the expansion of nontradable activities, such as building. An insufficiently (or inefficiently) controlled financial system contributed to this situation, which generated serious macroeconomic imbalances: increasing foreign debt but without a corresponding capital accumulation in the tradable goods sector.

From the Southern Cone experience one could hardly say that there was much efficiency in the allocation of resources by the deregulated financial system. The best indicator of insufficient allocation is the growing burden of the bank's assets portfolio, the amount of bad loans marked by high default indices, recurrent refinancing of interest on risky loans, and so on—all of which ultimately undermined the solvency of a considerable number of banks and required the direct or indirect intervention of the state.[10]

Among the factors that help to explain this situation, the more relevant (especially regarding Chile and Argentina) is the presence of large and influential economic conglomerates linked to bank ownership. The dealings of those groups, through the creation of "paper-companies" and the use of financial techniques that were opposed to normal banking practices pertaining to risk evaluation and credit concentration, decisively helped to increase the magnitude of the risky, related, and past-due portfolio of the banking system. In more general terms, the changes in the rules of the game as a result of liberalization rendered obsolete many of the criteria that had traditionally been used to evaluate loans in the regulated system. In effect, the drastic change in relative prices and the growing commercial and financial opening-up should have indicated that the size and value of guarantees, and the past repayment performance of bank debtors, were no longer sufficient indicators as to the quality of loans and their expected recovery. Conversely, under the new conditions, systematic errors in judgment[11] were made owing to inexperience and the desire of the financial institutions to increase their market participation—all of which caused the level and composition of the credit portfolio to become riskier, thus weakening the soundness of the financial intermediaries.

Imperfection, and especially the segmentation of the capital market, also had a negative impact on investment efficiency. The difference between domestic and foreign interest rates, and the differentiated and discriminated access to foreign credit, promoted external indebtedness. Furthermore, the "import quotas" of financial capital—in the absence of adequate tax or reserve requirement policies tending to socialize profits arising from the interest rate spread—were allowed to be assigned to projects with very low rates of return and/or to companies whose major merit was their link with the bank owners. As a result, an additional regressive effect on the distribution of income and assets was provoked. Thus, ironically, the Southern Cone experience reproduced—in "financially liberalized" and increasingly privatized economies, and in a general context of freer markets—what the supporters of financial liberalization have traditionally criticized with respect to "financial repression": an inefficient allocation of resources and a regressive redistribution of income.

Conclusions and Main Lessons

The experience of the Southern Cone countries tends to confirm that the financial system and credit markets present inherent peculiarities that justify giving that sector special treatment. A fundamental conclusion is that a "free" interest rate does not necessarily equal a rate of "equilibrium," nor is it possible to infer that financial markets can achieve self-regulation merely through interest-rate movements. Neither can it be concluded that a free interest rate, no matter how high it may rise, contributes, on its own, to an increase in savings and/or to promotion of an efficient allocation of investment. Furthermore, mere financial deregulation does not ensure the development of sources of medium- and long-term financing. Likewise, an explosive growth of financial deepening—without an adequate regulation of the financial sector—can lead to domestic overindebtedness, thus increasing the vulnerability of the entire economy in the face of changes in interest rates and/or economic activity. This last conclusion is particularly valid when flexible interest rates prevail, affecting both new and preexisting debts.

The financial experience of the Southern Cone leaves open the question of whether a well-conceived program of financial liberalization, in an appropriate regulatory context, could contribute favorably to capital accumulation and an efficient allocation of investment resources. In order for reforms oriented toward greater financial liberalization not to present the serious disadvantages observed in the Southern Cone, action must be taken in four main areas.

Control of Initial Macroeconomic Disequilibria

When initial economic conditions show deep imbalances, such as high inflation, balance-of-payments crises, heavy fiscal deficit, and so on, it is convenient to deal with those imbalances first and only later, once they are clearly on their way to recovery, to implement financial reform. Otherwise, the level and variability of inflation, the temptation to use the exchange-rate policy for stabilization purposes, or the indiscriminate acceptance of foreign credit, can neutralize—through a reduction in the term of financial transactions, an exaggerated growth of interest rates due to expectations of devaluation, or overindebtedness and increasing vulnerability of the financial system—any favorable effects that financial liberalization might have had in a more stable macroeconomic framework.

The Role of the State in Connection with the Financial System

In relatively small economies, such as those of the Southern Cone, the important economies of scale of financial activities made it easier for the self-regulated financial sector to be controlled by a few economic groups, thus provoking negative effects on the allocation of credit, income distribution, and even the stability and solvency of the financial system itself. Experience shows that the ownership of large corporations in the real sector of the economy should be delinked from the ownership of financial institutions, thereby diversifying stockholding in the banking system, decentralizing its management, and, in more general terms, safeguarding an adequate transparency in the operations of the sector. In addition, it is fundamentally the case that there should be an efficient legislation to ensure the effective compliance of the rules of credit diversification, thus reducing risk and discouraging speculative and potentially destabilizing maneuvers in the financial sector.

The type of regulation, supervision, and control that should be enforced in a more liberalized financial system represents an important professional challenge, due to the scant knowledge and experience that have accumulated in this regard in countries traditionally accustomed to more controlled financial systems. This situation is even more complicated today, given the growing internationalization of the financial network and, especially during periods of change and innovation, the fact that the dividing line between banking and nonbanking activities and institutions has become very hazy.

The experience of the Southern Cone countries suggests that an efficient financial regulation is one that possesses qualitative and preventive characteristics, which will signal a danger warning in time and identify problems before they become manifest. Conversely, it is not very likely that the authorities will abstain from intervening whenever a financial institution presents serious liquidity or solvency problems. Therefore, in the absence of drastic legal-institutional reforms—such as, for example, elimination of the fractional reserve requirements system, or creation of a system whereby the nominal value of banks assets and liabilities are not guaranteed, thus allowing their value to fluctuate— the policy in this field should include three main components: state backing on certain types and amounts of deposits; regulation of the passive interest rate at positive but low real levels, thus affording liquidity and protection to deposits, discouraging capital flight, and avoiding disproportionate increases in the deposit rate as a consequence of cash requirements of banks having difficulties; and the appropriate supervision and control of the loan portfolio of the banking system, so as to reduce its risk while maintaining the efficiency of the system. Instead of verifying with an accounting criterion the compliance of regulations, or discovering *ex post facto* that irregularities have been committed, supervision should be oriented toward classifying the credit portfolio according to its diversification and risk, reducing the size of the related portfolio to a minimum, requiring the provisions that are considered necessary (based on the evaluation of potential losses and an early identification of doubtful loans), and encouraging the allocation of certain minimum amounts of credit capital accumulation.

Another lesson is that the state should intervene directly (via state-owned banks) or indirectly in the financial system, with the aim of trying to correct its imperfections and main limitations, which do not necessarily disappear (at least during the initial years) in a more liberated atmosphere. On the one hand, it is necessary to mitigate the segmentation that usually occurs between those who have access to foreign credit and those who do not; this could be achieved through reserve requirements or tax policies oriented toward lessening the gap between the internal and external cost of credit and, in this way, reducing its undesirable effects on resource allocation and income distribution. On the other hand, the state should promote the granting of credit to sectors and groups that do not normally have access to the domestic financial system, or can attain it only at a very high cost—as with novel investment projects that have positive technical evaluations based on the future flow of net benefits but, because of their size, labor intensiveness, scant guarantees, and so on, have difficulty gaining access to financing. Another similar case is the demand for financing to improve and flexibilize the productivity of workers, owing to the difficulties of using market mechanisms to reduce the risk of this type of loan. The state could also encourage petty investors, who contribute capital without concentrating property, and stimulate the development of sources of longer-term financing for investments—for example, by modifying the operation of the social security system.

Macroeconomic Policies

First, the need for a coherent macroeconomic policy design derives from the fact that many analysts attribute the failure of the financial reforms in the Southern Cone countries mainly to serious macroeconomic errors, which led to a global economic crisis and to the crisis of the financial system in particular.

Second, and more important, is the sensitivity of the credit market to disequilibria in other markets. Thus, for example, the aforementioned identification of the "free" interest rate with the equilibrium interest rate would be valid only if the other markets—assets, foreign currency, labor, and goods—were in balance. If that is not the case, the "free" interest rate observed in the credit market, even though it might be the result of the interaction of the forces of supply and demand in that market, would be the rate required to absorb the imbalances of the other markets. In more general terms, outliers—that is, key prices that deviate clearly and significantly from reasonable values over a substantial period of time, although they might temporarily "equilibrate" a partial market— are likely to be signaling the presence of strong imbalances in other markets.

During a major part of the Southern Cone experience under review, the interest rate reflected the strong distortions that existed in other markets, especially the assets market with its price bubble, the foreign currency market with its tendency to overvaluation, and the goods market, due to inflation. Furthermore, whereas the foreign exchange and labor markets adjusted mainly through changes in quantities (i.e., through the balance-of-trade and current-account deficit, and employment and unemployment, respectively), the financial sector attained a faster but more distorted "equilibrium" through variations in its "price" (i.e., the interest rate).

Although extremely high interest rates—in comparison with international interest rates, the productivity of capital, or trend values of economic growth—may "balance" the credit market, they erode the financial situation of debtors and increase the vulnerability of financial intermediaries. Moreover, excessive capital inflows—stimulated by the difference between domestic and international interest rates—deteriorate the real value of the exchange rate, thus inhibiting the activity of tradable goods, and creates, or promotes, first a strong trade deficit and then a current-account deficit. These balance-of-payments disequilibria tend to provoke abrupt interruptions in foreign financing, leading to sharp devaluations and greater increases in interest rates, which especially affect domestic debtors in foreign currency and, in the end, the financial system as a whole. Similarly, when the exchange rate "equilibrates" the foreign currency market, but at the cost of growing and cumbersome foreign indebtedness and without an equivalent counterpart in domestic productive investment, a deep imbalance is likely to be generated, because the "equilibrium" value of that exchange rate is based on neither increased productivity nor structural changes in production or trade.

Consequently, the handling of some key macroeconomic prices such as the exchange rate, the interest rate, and salaries should be conducted in a flexible manner and coordinated with the evolution of other fundamental macroeconomic variables, such as the fiscal budget, the monetary base and domestic credit. In particular, the presence of outliers should be quickly corrected, so that no key price is allowed to become excessively rigid. Hence several markets can absorb the impact of the shocks and imbalances affecting the economy and avoid them by concentrating on one or just a few markets. For example, the sudden reduction of foreign financing should be reflected not only in a rise in the interest rate—which occurred in the Southern Cone in 1980 and 1981—but also in speedier devaluation, so as to encourage production and discourage spending in tradable goods.

Third, Southern Cone financial reforms were oriented toward increasing financial deepening. The experience of those countries suggests the need to stimulate investment more directly and to discourage consumption. Fiscal and price policies can play an important role, promoting savings and increasing the demand price for consumer goods relative to that of capital goods. These measures also tend to make foreign savings, generated by greater international financial integration, complement domestic savings.

Fourth, the massive capital inflows were not enough to provoke a rapid and sustained fall in the domestic interest rate. The increase of the country-risk element and the expectations of devaluation—in association with growing foreign debt and exchange-rate overvaluation, respectively—tended to widen the gap between domestic and international interest rates. The speedy and abundant inflow of capital—in the presence of segmented markets, differentiated access to foreign credit, unequal degrees of substitution between different domestic and international assets, and an overvalued exchange rate—contributed more to the generation of a bubble in the price of assets than to the reduction of the domestic interest rate. The wealth effect thus produced tended to stimulate consumption rather than saving, in spite of the fact that a simultaneous increase in financial asset holding was observed.

The lack of correspondence between the massive flow of foreign capital and domestic investment, as well as the impact of financial opening-up on the exchange rate, helped generate serious imbalances in the financial system and in the economy as a whole. Accordingly, another lesson to be learned from the experience of the Southern Cone is that macroeconomic policy must look closely at and if necessary regulate the amount, speed, and cost—as well as orient the use—of foreign financing.

Fifth, a fundamental element in any reform is its credibility. Due to the fact that the reallocation of resources takes time and depends on expected prices, the speed at which the financial reform is implemented must be sustainable and credible over time. Macroeconomic policy can help to minimize difficulties that may arise in the transition toward more liberalized markets. At this point it is important that the real exchange rate should be kept stable, especially if the economy opens up commercially and financially to foreign markets. Likewise, monetary programming should be consistent with that of the balance of payments and of fiscal policy, and the pressure for greater public-sector financing should not crowd out activities in expansion. In turn, credit policy should ensure financing at reasonable costs to sectors in expansion, principally those with export potential, while foreclosing it to sectors that should contract their level of activity.

Speed and Sequence of Reforms

The liberalization of the financial system can generate serious difficulties not only because of possible initial imbalances but also because of the speed and sequence at which deregulation is implemented. Accelerated domestic liberalization can tend to increase consumption more than savings, as occurred in the Southern Cone. When credit is scarce, there is a tendency to spend now and save later, especially if a sharp drop in interest rates and an equally sharp rise in the price of assets are anticipated. In the transition toward more liberalized markets, it seems to be more convenient to implement financial deregulation gradually, first by increasing active rates—though keeping them within reasonable levels—and then, little by little, by increasing passive rates. Otherwise the existing financial intermediaries would be forced to increase deposit rates, thereby sustaining heavy losses in the process.

Financial opening-up can also have undesirable effects, depending on the sequential time-path of active- and passive-rate deregulation. If internal passive rates are very low, external financial liberalization can stimulate capital flight; if domestic active rates are very high, excessive foreign indebtedness and exchange-rate appreciation may be encouraged. For these reasons it is necessary to plan carefully the speed and characteristics of financial opening-up, so as to keep the short-run costs involved in the process of transition down to a minimum. The Southern Cone experience suggests that domestic financial reform should precede financial opening-up as long as the profits deriving from the differential between domestic and foreign rates of interest are socialized. Greater integration with international financing could then be implemented gradually, thus helping to avoid the appearance of equivocal signals, such as occurred in the Southern Cone. These signals, because of the expectation of a sharp drop in the interest rate and a boom in the price of nontradable assets, ended up by stimulating more consumption rather than investment, imports rather than exports, and speculation rather than production.

Notes

The author is grateful for the helpful comments and suggestions made by Günther Held. Needless to say, the opinions expressed in this chapter are the sole responsibility of the author and do not necessarily reflect those of the institutions with which he is affiliated.

1. The use of certain terms can lead to confusion. Strictly speaking, the *liberalization* of the financial sector affected only the more visible variables, whereas in other sectors market imperfections, oligopolies, lack of transparency, and open segmentation accumulated. The lack of information to the public regarding the risks involved in the portfolio of the financial institutions, the deliberate formation—or at least tolerance—of economic groups linked to the financial sector, and even the sporadic intervention of banks and/or financial corporations also suggest that *liberalization* is a term that should be used cautiously.

2. When speaking of a "deregulated" financial system, one may mistakenly give the impression that there was an evolution from a previously controlled system to a self-regulated one. Strictly speaking, such a transition would require appropriate regulatory and supervisory financial institutions, including self-regulating mechanisms, which, in practice, did not exist at the time of the transition. In fact, what occurred in the Southern Cone was the presence of a (basically former) regulation that became inefficient and even contradictory in the context of the process of financial liberalization.

3. However, a gradual integration with international financial markets was allowed, by authorizing banks to increasingly contract debt abroad.

4. In effect, Chile was the country in which there was less financial opening-up and in which the public sector practically marginated itself from external indebtedness. Of the three countries, however, it was the one that recorded the greatest capital inflows, both in absolute terms and as a proportion of the GDP.

5. Traditional bank customers, when faced by tariff, price, tax, and other reforms, could and in fact usually did experience a series of unexpected changes and shifts in the economic conditions within which they operated, thus drastically modifying their ability to service their debt with the financial system.

6. These can be overvalued as a result of speculative maneuvers in some asset markets and/or because of policies that contributed to exchange-rate overvaluation, thus inflating collaterals with no fundamentals to back this situation.

7. The increasing trend in the price of these assets had stimulated an expansion in bank credit supply and in the internal debt of some sectors, despite the high interest rates.

8. In a fashion similar to the case of the active interest rates, the spread may respond more to a criterion of observed (or, in a sense, "accrued") spread than to one of "effective" spread.

9. Once companies and persons reach high levels of indebtedness, their demand for credit becomes very inelastic with regard to interest rates, because the alternative is to liquidate assets. This inelastic demand for credit occurs with special force in both recessions and depressions, situations in which the liquidation of assets involves substantial losses. Under these conditions there is a tendency to capitalize interest payments (especially if there is a lack of transparency with regard to the risk involved in the banks loan portfolio) and to increase passive interest rates, in order to attract the deposits required to finance this process.

10. Moreover, in Uruguay, the only country with an important growth of productive capacity, this situation seems to have responded principally to the elimination of restrictions on capital goods imports and to a reduction of profit taxes rather than to greater financial liberalization.

11. Some of these errors of judgment were due to false signals conveyed by the economic policy.

References

Arellano, J. P. (1984), "De la liberalización a la intervención: el mercado de capitales en Chile 1974–1983," *Colección Estudios CIEPLAN*, Vol. 1, Santiago (June).

CEPAL (1986), "Balance preliminar de la economica latinoamericano." Santiago: CEPAL.

———— (1988), *Annario Estadistístico de América Latine y el Caribe*. Santiago: CEPAL.

Corbo, V., and J. de Melo (1986), "Lessons from the Southern Cone policy reforms," Banco Mundial, (October), mimeo.

Diaz-Alejandro, C. (1985), "Good-bye financial repression, hello financial crash," *Journal of Development Economics*, No. 19.

Fernandez, R. (1983), "La crisis financiera Argentina: 1980–1982." Paper presented at the VI Jornadas de Economía Monetaria y Sector Externo, Banco Central de la República Argentina (May).

Gaba, E. (1982), "La reforma financiera argentina," *Monetaria*, Vol. 5, No. 3 (July).

Hanson, J., and J. de Melo (1985), "External shocks, financial reforms and stabilization attempts in Uruguay: 1974–1983," *World Development*, Vol. 13, No. 8 (August).

Larrain, F. (1987), "La reforma financiera uruguaya de los setenta: De la liberalizaciún a la crisis," *Documento de Trabajo*, No. 109, Universidad Católica de Chile, Instituto de Economía (April).

Larrain, M. (1983), "Incidencia de la crisis financiera en las políticas de supervisión bancaria en América Latina." In *Información financiera*, Santiago: Superintendencia de Bancos e Instituciones Financieras (July).

Massad, C., and R. Zahler (1987), "Otro ángulo de la crisis latinoamericana: La deuda interna," *Revista de la CEPAL*, No. 32 (April).

Ramos, J. (1986), *Neoconservative economics in the Southern Cone of Latin America, 1973–1983*. Baltimore: Johns Hopkins University Press.

Zahler, R. (1980), "Repercusiones monetarias y reales de la apertura financiera al exterior. El caso chileno: 1975–1978," *Revista de la CEPAL*, No. 10 (April).

———— (1983), "Recent Southern Cone liberalization reforms and stabilization policies: The Chilean case, 1974–1978," *Journal of Interamerican Studies and World Affairs*, Vol. 25, No. 4 (November).

———— (1985), "Las tasas de interés en Chile: 1975–1982." In *El desarrollo finaciero de América Latina y el Caribe, 1985*. Caracas, Venezuela: Instituto Interamericano de Mercados de Capital.

———— (1986), "Política monetaria y financiera." In R. Cortźar (ed.), *Políticas macroeconómicas, una perspectiva latinoamericana*. Santiago: Ediciones CIEPLAN.

Zahler, R., and V. Valdivia (1987), "Asimetrías de la liberalización financiera y el problema de las deudas interna y externa." In C. Massad and R. Zahler (eds.), *Deuda interna y estabilidad financiera*, Vol. 1: *Aspectos analíticos*. Buenos Aires: Grupo Editor Latinoamericano.

7

Structural Adjustment Reforms and the External Debt Crisis in Latin America

Sebastián Edwards

Mexico's announcement, in August 1982, that it could no longer meet its international financial obligations took most of the world by surprise. That month marked the beginning of the worst international financial crisis since the Great Depression. What was initially thought to be an isolated case of temporary illiquidity soon spread to most of the developing world, placing the stability of the international financial system in serious jeopardy.

Now, several years after the eruption of the debt crisis, most of the developing world is still struggling to get back on its feet. Although the collapse of the world financial system predicted by some overly pessimistic observers has not materialized, the debt crisis is far from over. In fact, when traditional credit-worthiness indicators, such as debt-exports or debt-service ratios are analyzed, the highly indebted countries are now in an even weaker position than they were in 1982 (see Table 7.1). It has now been generally accepted that a long-term resolution of the debt problems will be a painful and protracted process—one that will require major additional adjustment efforts by the indebted countries as well as extensive negotiations among debtor governments, creditor governments, the multilateral institutions, and the banks.

The adjustment approaches followed until 1988 by most of the highly indebted countries can best be described as *emergency stabilization programs* geared toward generating very large trade balance surpluses in very short periods of time. These countries had little choice but to use every possible tool at their disposal to achieve the needed turnaround in their current accounts. As a result, the adjustment has been costly, in that it has generated declines in real income and important increases

TABLE 7.1   Credit-Worthiness Indicators for Developing Countries (1979–1988)

	1979	1980	1981	1982	1983	1984	1985	1986	1987	1988
Ratio of External Debt to Exports of Goods and Services (in percentages)										
All developing countries	90.8	81.6	94.6	120.1	133.3	133.7	147.8	167.5	168.6	160.7
15 highly indebted[a]	182.3	167.1	201.3	269.8	289.6	272.1	284.2	337.9	349.6	324.7
Western Hemisphere	197.7	183.5	210.3	273.8	290.3	277.1	295.5	354.7	367.6	342.2
Debt Service Ratios to Exports of Goods and Services (in percentages)										
All LDCs	14.1	12.9	16.2	19.5	18.9	20.1	20.5	22.4	20.7	20.0
15 highly indebted[a]	34.7	29.6	39.0	49.4	42.5	41.1	38.7	43.9	40.7	39.5
Western Hemisphere	39.6	33.4	41.9	51.0	43.9	41.7	38.7	45.6	44.9	40.9

[a]Argentina, Bolivia, Brazil, Chile, Colombia, Côte d'Ivoire, Ecuador, Mexico, Morocco, Nigeria, Peru, Philippines, Uruguay, Venezuela, and Yugoslavia.

Source: International Monetary Fund (1987).

in unemployment. In fact, real per capita GDP in a number of Latin American countries in 1987 was below 1970 levels.

A long-run solution to the debt crisis would entail the resumption of sustained growth as well as the regaining of credit-worthiness by these countries, and thus the resumption of voluntary lending by the international financial community.[1] Much of the recent policy literature on the debt crisis has focused on these issues, with some of the discussion dealing with the type of long-run structural reforms the debt-troubled countries should implement in order to attain the dual objective of improved credit-worthiness and growth. Most of this literature has recommended very conventional measures, including trade liberalization, financial reform, major devaluations, and a reduced role for the government.[2] This policy package is indeed at the core of the conditionality contemplated by the Baker and Brady plans. Surprisingly, there have been very few attempts to evaluate whether the design of these traditional policies—in particular, their speed and sequencing—should be altered in the presence of a major debt problem and, in some cases, still significant macroeconomic disequilibria.

The purpose of this chapter is to analyze a number of issues related to structural adjustment in the highly indebted developing countries, with special emphasis on Latin America.

Origins of the Crisis

During the second half of the 1970s and in the early 1980s a large number of Latin American countries, as well as other developing nations, became indebted at extremely high interest rates. Between 1975 and 1982 the Latin American long-term foreign debt more than tripled. Naturally, this huge increase in indebtedness was made possible by the liberal way in which the international financial community, particularly the banks, provided funds to these countries after the first oil shock in 1973. There is no doubt that the pace at which the developing countries were accumulating debt in the late 1970s and early 1980s—at a rate exceeding 20 percent per year—was not sustainable in the medium to long run; some type of adjustment was bound to take place. The world, however, was shocked by the severity of the crisis; instead of an orderly and slow reduction of the flow of borrowing, a major crisis that brought capital flows to a virtual halt took place.

It is difficult to generalize about the origins of the crisis. Although there were some elements in common, an understanding of each country's specific conditions is crucially important. In Brazil, for example, the growth in foreign debt responded to a deliberate development strategy adopted after the 1973 oil shock. This policy was based on import substitution supplemented with a heavy reliance on foreign borrowing to finance major investment projects. In Mexico, the populist policies of the Echeverría and Lopez-Portillo administrations, with spectacular growth in the public sector and in the fiscal deficit, lay behind the crisis. The discovery of additional oil reserves generated a wave of optimism that greatly influenced the magnitude, composition, and allocation of public expenditure. It has been argued that approximately one-half of the Mexican debt accumulated during the Lopez-Portillo administration went to finance capital flight (Buffie and Sanguines, 1987). In Chile, conversely, fiscal policies played no role in the unleashing of the crisis; most of the huge increase in Chile's foreign debt was contracted by the private sector with no government guarantees. The opening up of the Chilean economy, as part of the overall project of economic liberalization of the Pinochet government, allowed the private sector to finance huge increases in consumption—especially of durables—by borrowing from abroad.[3]

In spite of their different experiences during the 1970s, in late 1982 all of these countries faced severe cuts in foreign financing; they had come to share the harsh reality of the debt crisis. It is important that we establish the role of both external and internal factors in the unleashing of this phenomenon.

External Factors

The behavior of the world economy during the early 1980s—especially the increase of interest rates, the decline in commodity prices, and the sluggish growth of the industrial countries—played an important role in determining the magnitude and timing of the crisis.[4] The United

Nations Economic Commission for Latin America (ECLA) has estimated that for the Latin American nations the deterioration of unit prices of non-oil exports and the hike in world interest rates "explain" almost 50 percent of the increase in the region's current-account deficit during 1981 and 1982.[5]

The magnitude of external shocks can be better understood by analyzing the evolution of the *real* interest rate "relevant" to these countries, computed as nominal LIBOR deflated by the rate of inflation of their exports. For Latin America, this measure of the real interest rate jumped from an average of −3.4 percent during 1970–1980 to 19.9 percent in 1981, 27.5 percent in 1982, and 17.4 percent in 1983.

Internal Factors

Among the internal factors the adoption of inadequate exchange-rate policies constitutes one of the most important causes of the crisis; most of the countries that eventually experienced payments difficulties allowed their real exchange rates to become highly overvalued during the late 1970s and early 1980s.[6] The countries of the Southern Cone of South America constitute a primary example of inadequate exchange-rate policies. In Chile, for instance, after a period with a passive crawling peg, and as a way to bring down a stubborn inflationary process, the currency was fixed to the U.S. dollar in June 1979, at the same time as wages were indexed to past inflation and capital controls were relaxed. As a result, the real exchange rate appreciated by more than 30 percent between 1979 and mid-1982, provoking a major deprotection of the domestic tradables sector and a gigantic current-account deficit that exceeded 14 percent of GDP in 1981.[7]

Argentina and Uruguay adopted a declining preannounced rate of devaluation, also as a way to reduce inflation. However, contrary to the case of Chile, in Argentina and Uruguay the predetermined rate of devaluation was clearly inconsistent with the magnitude of their fiscal deficit. This resulted not only in a substantial real appreciation but also in a steady loss of credibility in the sustainability of the stabilization and liberalization programs, and in major capital flight.[8]

In Mexico, as a result of a highly expansive fiscal policy, which was coupled with a quasi-fixed nominal exchange rate, the effective real exchange rate experienced a real appreciation that exceeded 40 percent between 1976 and February 1982. In 1976–1977, in an effort to put an end to an acute situation of real exchange-rate overvaluation, the Mexican government devalued the peso by almost 80 percent relative to the U.S. dollar. By 1981, however, the real value of the peso was already below its 1976 level; in less than five years, more than 100 percent of the real effect of the devaluation had fully eroded. This case is particularly interesting because it clearly illustrates the difficulties that developing nations have faced many times when trying to engineer a real devaluation (see Edwards, 1987c).

Colombia, however, was an exception to the mismanagement of exchange rates. In that country the adoption of an active exchange-rate management, including periodic devaluations (crawling peg), was an important component in the overall strategy aimed at reducing the domestic effects of world economic fluctuations. This pragmatic approach toward exchange-rate management allowed the country to avoid the deprotection effects of the coffee boom of 1975–1979 and to maintain a reasonable macroeconomic equilibrium.[9]

Perhaps one of the most devastating effects of the generalized tendency toward overvaluation is that it fueled massive capital flight. In country after country, as it became increasingly apparent that the overvaluation was unsustainable in the long run, the public began to heavily speculate against the Central Bank by acquiring foreign exchange and moving it abroad. Moreover, in some countries such as Chile and Argentina, the overvaluation cast doubts on the continuity of the overall development strategy based on commercial and financial liberalization. In Chile, for example, the public started to expect a hike in import tariffs and tried to anticipate it by acquiring imported durables in record quantities (Edwards and Cox-Edwards, 1987).

Owing to the semi-illegal nature of capital flight, it is not easy to find official data on this subject. Most available estimates, however, concur in their suggestion that in most of the Latin American countries there was a significant increase in capital flight in the years surrounding the debt crisis. In a recent empirical study, Cuddington (1986) has found that there is a significant relation between overvaluation and capital flight. Table 7.2 contains estimates on capital flight for four Latin American countries. There is an interesting contrast between the Latin American and the Asian nations; for example, in Korea, a country that largely avoided the temptation of real exchange-rate overvaluation, capital flight between 1979 and 1984 was, on average, *negative*.

The Crisis and Macroeconomic Adjustment

In August 1982 the international financial community greatly reduced the amount of funds intermediated to the developing world. Even some countries (such as Colombia) that did not face payments problems, that did not have serious macroeconomic disequilibria, and that had not accumulated debt at a very fast pace were affected by this reduction in

TABLE 7.2 Estimates of Capital Flight in Selected Latin American Countries[a] (in billions of US$)

	1979	1980	1981	1982	1983	1984
Argentina	2.2	3.5	4.5	7.6	1.3	-3.4
Brazil	1.3	2.0	-1.4	1.8	0.5	4.0
Mexico	-1.1	2.2	2.6	4.7	9.3	2.6
Venezuela	3.0	4.8	5.4	3.2	3.1	4.0

[a]These estimates use Cline's definition of capital flight as computed by Cumby and Levich (1987).

Source: Cumby and Levich (1987).

foreign lending. For the developing world as a whole, external financing was reduced by almost 40 percent between 1981 and 1983. Moreover, the fifteen major debtors of the International Monetary Fund (IMF) were forced, in less than three years, to fully close a current-account deficit that in 1982 exceeded $50 billion.[10] By 1985 the aggregate of these countries' current accounts had reached virtual equilibrium ($-0.1 billion). In order to achieve such a significant adjustment, these countries had to engineer a major turnaround in their trade balance, which went from an aggregate deficit of almost $7 billion in 1981 to a surplus of more than $40 billion in 1984.

Latin America was hit by the sudden drying up of loans in a particularly severe way. Table 7.3 contains data on the net transfer of resources to the region from 1976 to 1986. As can be seen, starting in 1982 the net transfer of resources became significantly negative. Between 1982 and 1986 the annual net transfer averaged $-26.4 billion, compared to a positive yearly average net transfer of more than $12 billion between 1976 and 1981. In real terms the net turnaround of resource transfers exceeded $70 billion in the short period of three years between 1980 and 1983!

These adjustments in the current account and trade balance were achieved through major reductions in imports and investment. In the IMF's highly indebted countries the *nominal* dollar value of exports was lower in 1986 than in 1980, with the magnitude of this decline exceeding 15 percent. This drop was basically the result of a decline in the prices of these countries' exports of almost 25 percent between 1980 and 1986. In Latin America the deterioration of the terms of trade was so severe (see Table 7.4) that, in spite of an increase in the *quantum* of exports of 30 percent between 1980 and 1986, more than 100 percent of the net adjustment of the trade balance improvement was achieved via a reduction of imports.

TABLE 7.3 Capital Inflows and Net Transfer of Resources in Latin America (1976–1986) (in billions of US$)

Year	Net Capital Inflows	Net Interest Payments	Net Transfer of Resources
1976	17.9	6.8	11.1
1977	17.2	8.2	9.0
1978	26.2	10.2	16.0
1979	29.1	13.6	15.5
1980	29.4	17.9	11.5
1981	37.5	27.1	10.4
1982	20.0	38.7	−18.7
1983	3.2	34.3	−31.2
1984	9.2	36.2	−27.0
1985	2.4	35.3	−32.9
1986	8.6	30.7	−22.1

Source: CEPAL (1986b).

Table 7.5 contains data on investment ratios for a selected group of Latin American countries. With the exception of Chile, which started from an exceedingly weak position, in all of these countries the gross investment ratio declined significantly after the crisis—particularly in Venezuela. In most cases, public investment and investment in the construction sector were the components most severely curtailed. With respect to public investment these reductions were a result of restrictive aggregate demand policies implemented immediately after the crisis. Naturally, this decline in investment has had serious consequences for the prospects of renewed growth. The adjustment has been costly not only in terms of current output and employment but also in terms of future income.

In most cases the selection of policy packages used to attain adjustment was based on their perceived "effectiveness." The efforts to implement rapidly effective policies gave priority to certain objectives (such as the current account) over others (namely, inflation).

Expenditure-Reducing Policies

In most countries expenditure-reducing policies have been centered on efforts to cut public expenditure. According to CEPAL, in Argentina, Ecuador, Mexico, Uruguay, and Venezuela, government expenditure was cut by more than 20 percent in real terms following the crisis.[11]

In spite of the relatively successful efforts to reduce public expenditures, fiscal deficits increased in relation to the pre-crisis period among the

TABLE 7.4 Terms of Trade in Latin America Between 1981 and 1986 (Index: 1980 = 100)

	Index				Rate of Change (percent)					Cumulative Rate of Change (percent)
	1983	1984	1985	1986	1982	1983	1984	1985	1986	1981–1986
Latin America	87	92	88	80	-9.0	1.1	6.5	-5.0	-8.7	-20.0
Oil Exporters	95	97	93	63	-10.3	5.0	2.0	-3.4	-32.2	-36.9
Bolivia	97	112	110	86	4.0	2.7	16.4	-2.2	-21.5	-13.8
Ecuador	82	96	85	58	-1.3	-17.7	17.0	-10.8	-31.9	-41.9
Mexico	93	86	84	62	-13.9	6.7	-7.2	-2.3	-26.4	-38.1
Peru	96	94	89	77	-9.5	19.7	-2.8	-5.1	-12.8	-22.6
Venezuela	104	116	114	62	-7.9	8.9	12.1	-1.9	-45.5	-38.0
Oil Importers	82	89	83	94	-8.3	-0.1	9.4	-6.6	12.8	-6.0
Argentina	82	99	87	75	-11.7	-4.6	21.0	-12.1	-13.3	-24.9
Brazil	78	86	83	102	-6.0	-2.5	10.1	-3.4	22.6	1.6
Chile	84	78	72	79	-13.2	9.6	-6.3	-8.0	9.3	-21.3
Colombia	94	101	97	114	2.2	8.3	6.9	-3.9	17.6	13.9
Costa Rica	86	90	88	107	-2.0	2.8	5.2	-2.8	21.2	6.5
El Salvador	83	73	69	87	2.2	-11.8	-12.0	-5.0	26.6	-12.9
Guatemala	85	88	83	95	-5.5	3.4	3.4	-6.0	14.3	-5.5
Haiti	66	83	85	104	3.8	-10.7	26.1	2.7	22.5	4.4
Honduras	93	96	76	95	3.6	0.9	3.2	-20.9	24.8	-5.4
Nicaragua	83	105	97	119	-5.3	-3.3	26.9	-7.8	23.1	19.4
Panama	91	95	97	105	-10.3	9.7	4.6	2.2	8.2	5.0
Paraguay	90	134	110	102	-12.6	-3.9	49.8	-17.9	-7.2	2.3
Dominican Republic	77	85	72	83	-31.3	-5.5	9.7	-14.8	15.2	-16.9
Uruguay	99	99	93	96	6.9	6.9	0.4	-5.6	2.6	-4.0

Source: CEPAL (1986b).

major debtors as a group. This was the case mainly because total tax revenues in many of these countries were negatively affected by the recessions that followed the crisis. The steep increase in interest rates that took place in most countries also negatively affected the fiscal accounts, through the increase of the public-sector domestic debt. Moreover, in most cases the sources of fiscal deficit financing were affected by the crisis. Until 1982 most public-sector deficits were financed by foreign borrowing. The drying up of this source of funds forced the local governments to turn to the inflationary tax and to issue additional domestic public debt.

TABLE 7.5 Gross Investment as a Percentage of GDP in Selected Latin American Countries (in percentages)

	Average (1975–1980)	1984
Argentina	25.2	17.8
Bolivia	29.5	28.5
Brazil	25.9	17.0[a]
Chile	13.2	13.7
Mexico	24.4	20.3[a]
Peru	16.6	16.0
Venezuela	34.3	16.0

[a]1983.

Source: International Monetary Fund (1987).

In a number of countries—most notably Argentina and Chile—the exchange-rate policies followed during this period also became an important source of government expenditures. In Argentina, for example, the need to cover the exchange-rate guarantee after the abandonment of the "tablita" generated staggering fiscal outlays. Similarly, the adoption of a preferential (lower) exchange rate for foreign currency debtors in Chile resulted in an implicit subsidy that absorbed large amounts of foreign resources.[12]

The need to use inflationary financing placed pressure on the monetary and domestic credit policies, which became significantly more expansive than the IMF, the World Bank, and the private bank officials felt they should have been. Table 7.6 contains summary data on monetary policy, the fiscal deficit, and the average rate of inflation in these countries. These data quite clearly illustrate some of the most interesting features of the emergency phase of the adjustment process. As pointed out in more detail below, in contrast to IMF-sponsored programs, these stabilization programs have featured acceleration in monetary expansion, persistent high fiscal deficits that largely exceed the levels that prevailed before the crisis, and very high inflation.

In most countries the adjustment also relied on higher real interest rates, which helped keep expenditure—particularly investment—in check. In some cases, however, the rise in real interest rates began some time before the "official" unleashing of the debt crisis in August 1982. For example, in the Southern Cone countries real interest rates began to climb quickly in mid-1981, as these economies were clearly becoming overheated; higher interest rates were in fact an early sign that in these countries the need for adjustment was quickly approaching.

TABLE 7.6 Monetary Policy, Fiscal Policy, and Inflation in Highly Indebted Countries

Year	Annual Percentage Change of Broad Money	Central Government Fiscal Deficits as Percentage of GDP	Average Percentage Change of CPI [a]
1979	51.8	0.8	40.8
1980	55.2	0.8	47.4
1981	64.0	3.7	53.2
1982	69.3	5.4	57.7
1983	86.7	5.2	90.8
1984	117.7	3.1	116.4
1985	125.4	2.7	126.9
1986	73.9	4.5	76.2
1987	n.a.	3.6	86.3
1988	n.a.	n.a.	87.2

[a] Average annual inflation for 1969–1978 was 28.5 percent.

Source: International Monetary Fund (1987).

The debt crisis further shocked the already weakened financial sector of these countries. Especially in Chile, the halt of capital inflows was partially responsible for the timing and magnitude of the financial debacle of late 1982 and 1983. By the end of 1982 the foreign debt of the Chilean banking system exceeded US$6.6 billion, a remarkable figure when compared to the mere US$0.6 billion of debt in 1978! These funds had been obtained without any government guarantee and had been used primarily to finance the operations of the large private conglomerates—the so-called *groups*. By mid-1982 a large proportion of these loans were in fact bad loans: Owing to a number of factors, including the real overvaluation of the peso, the *groups* were facing a very difficult financial situation. During 1982 the amount of foreign funds available to the Chilean banks was reduced by more than 75 percent, generating a fatal blow to the troubled financial sector. As a result of these difficulties, the government stepped in and, in January 1983, liquidated two banks and nationalized others. Responding to pressures by the international banks, the Chilean government decided to take over these banks' foreign debt and to guarantee foreign debt payment. Paradoxically, at the end of 1983 the Chilean financial sector was in some senses at the same juncture as it had been ten years before, in the midst of the Allende socialist government. In other words, it had been nationalized and was tightly controlled by the state (see Díaz-Alejandro, 1984; Edwards and Cox-Edwards, 1987).

TABLE 7.7 Real Effective Exchange-Rate Indexes: 1980 = 100 (trade weight at 1980)

	Argentina	Bolivia	Brazil	Chile	Mexico	Peru	Venezuela
1980	100.00	100.00	100.00	100.00	100.00	100.00	100.00
1981	99.11	79.75	84.06	85.52	87.97	85.77	89.00
1982	177.98	58.21	77.60	92.00	112.34	81.15	80.66
1983	188.62	71.15	91.10	115.91	132.97	85.59	75.51
1984	139.35	28.42	102.65	118.12	114.66	87.91	105.67
1985	173.78	9.50	103.85	145.52	106.22	101.91	104.81
1986	203.71	103.93	111.68	162.39	135.61	84.98	100.81

Note: An increase of this index indicates real devaluation, whereas a decline indicates a real appreciation. These real effective exchange-rate indexes have been computed as trade weighted geometric averages of the bilateral exchange rates, adjusted by the ratio of domestic consumer price index to the corresponding trade partner wholesale price index.

Source: Edwards (1987c).

Expenditure-Switching Policies

As a consequence of the debt crisis, most countries also made use of expenditure-switching policies. These consisted in most cases of a combination of nominal devaluations and, at least initially, of a major escalation in the degree of trade restrictions. The extent of the devaluations varied from country to country. In an effort to ensure that the effects of the nominal devaluations on the real exchange rate did not erode via inflation, most countries adopted some kind of active exchange-rate management whereby the exchange rate continued to be adjusted after the initial parity change. In fact, as of July 1986, twelve of the fifteen major debtors had some sort of crawling-peg regime consisting of periodic adjustments of the nominal rate somewhat related to the differential between internal and external inflation. In general, as can be seen from Table 7.7, most Latin American countries were able to generate important real devaluations between 1982 and 1986, which in some cases more than corrected the overvaluation that preceded the crisis.

As a result of these large nominal devaluations, most countries experienced important increases in their price levels. As noted earlier, in an effort to avoid the erosive effects of these price increases the Central Bank authorities resorted to further devaluations as a means of maintaining a high real exchange rate. Naturally this practice added fuel to the already accelerated rates of inflation.

Immediately following the crisis, in many (but not all) of the major debtors the devaluation policies were supplemented by the imposition of trade restrictions. Table 7.8 presents data on some of the policies implemented by Argentina, Chile, Mexico, and Venezuela in an effort to improve their external position.

An important question is whether the use of quantitative restrictions (QRs) instead of tariffs or more substantial devaluations during the initial phases of the adjustment has introduced unduly high costs in terms of growth and efficiency. A well-known proposition in the theory of commercial policy is that, in terms of welfare and income distribution, tariffs are generally superior to quotas as a means of restricting trade.[13] Although there is some justification for the (very) short-term use of QRs in the first phase of the adjustment, there are no good reasons for continuing their use for long periods of time. From the perspective of efficiency and fiscal as well as income distribution, the maintenance of QRs over a long period have undesirable effects that are well known. For example, Buffie and Sanguines (1987) have argued that the generalized use of QRs in Mexico in 1982–1984 resulted in an unnecessary reduction of imports of intermediate inputs, with concomitant recessionary effects on the Mexican economy.

In some countries the extent of trade restrictions has recently been somewhat relaxed, whereas other countries have announced the prospect of some easing up in the near future. In Chile, for example, tariffs were reduced to a uniform level of 15 percent. Mexico has taken some steps as well, by reducing the coverage of licenses and the average rate of protection almost across the board. In Bolivia, conversely, the stabilization program of 1985 called for the abolition of quotas and the reduction of tariffs.

Another important characteristic of the crisis period is that, in spite of the significant efforts to adjust made by most of these countries, their trade surpluses have systematically fallen short of their interest payments. In Latin America, for example, the interest bill in 1986 amounted to 5.3 percent of GDP, whereas the trade surplus reached 2.3 percent of GDP. In most countries this financing gap has been closed, usually after long and protracted negotiations, through packages of funds provided by the banks and multilateral institutions. It is important to note, however, that the banks have been able to significantly reduce their exposure to the major debtors in spite of the fact that they have made some contributions to the financing of these funds shortfalls.[14] A still-unresolved question is whether the banks will make a serious commitment to providing additional financing to the indebted countries in the next few years.

Crisis Adjustment and Traditional Stabilization Programs

The preceding discussion indicates that, in spite of the active involvement of the International Monetary Fund, the programs followed by most of the major debtors between 1982 and 1986 differed in a number of key respects from the typical IMF-sponsored programs of the pre-1982 era. These differences involve mainly the selection of policy packages as well as the availability of additional financing. In addition, the behavior of the exogenous variables, including the international environment, has tended to differ from that observed in previous years.

According to Khan and Knight (1985), in the typical IMF program we can distinguish both a macroeconomic and a structural adjustment component. The macro, or demand management, package is based mainly on restrictive monetary, fiscal, and domestic credit policies aimed at eliminating the disequilibrium between aggregate demand and aggregate supply, improving the current account, and reducing inflation. Special emphasis is usually placed on the control of fiscal deficits. Conversely, the structural adjustment (or resource reallocation) package usually includes three main policy blocks: (1) trade liberalization; (2) financial reform; and (3) major devaluation, including exchange-rate unification in the case of multiple rates.[15] The objectives of this structural adjustment component are to increase efficiency, raise investment, and enhance growth opportunities.

Historically, however, the implementation of IMF-sponsored programs in most of the countries has not taken place at the same time as a substantial foreign debt is being serviced. On the contrary, it has usually been assumed that, while implementing structural reforms, these countries can command significant additional net funds from abroad (see Khan and Knight, 1985). Although external funds were available in the past, they were not available during the adjustment of the 1980s, when the highly indebted countries had to generate a significant net transfer of resources to the rest of the world.

In terms of outcome, a historically "successful" IMF program can be described in terms of a reduced fiscal deficit, lower inflation, more liberalized trade, and an improvement in the current account and balance of payments. In many ways the 1982–1986 adjustment looks very different from this IMF blueprint, which involves an inflationary adjustment process with high and persistent fiscal deficits (see Table 7.6). In addition, an escalation in the degree of distortions of the external sectors has occurred, along with a profusion of QRs and multiple exchange rates.

Another difference between previous years and the current crisis-adjustment period pertains to the behavior of investment. In a detailed study of thirty-nine historical episodes of structural adjustment programs between 1962 and 1982, Edwards (1989) found that, for the group as a whole, the investment ratio did not experience a significant decline in any of the four years following the implementation of the programs.

Moreover, according to this study, it is not possible to detect, as in the current case, significant declines in real output in past years.

To a large extent the "unorthodoxy" of these new stabilization and adjustment programs can be attributed to three main factors: (1) the magnitude of the adjustment required; (2) the urgency with which it had to be implemented; and (3) the global nature of the crisis. In a sense, when faced with the trade-offs among current-account corrections, efficiency of the adjustment, and inflation, these countries opted—or were forced to opt—for current-account improvements that placed little priority on inflation, efficiency, or costs of the process, at least during the initial phases of the process. Implicitly, the IMF endorsed or encouraged these adjustment programs, at least during the initial phases of the process, in spite of the fact that they departed from the traditional view of the IMF.

Debt-Reduction Schemes

An important development of the highly indebted countries' adjustment during recent years has been their attempt to convert their outstanding liabilities with foreign commercial banks into other types of obligations. The main objective of this strategy has been to capture part of the discount that the secondary market has established for this kind of debt. One country that has been more successful in its development of this type of debt conversion schemes is Chile. In fact, one of the most interesting—and hotly debated—features of the Chilean recovery of the second half of the 1980s is related to the various debt-conversion schemes implemented by the authorities.

As of February 1989 the Chilean debt had been reduced by more than US$6.5 billion through the use of diverse mechanisms based on the secondary market (see Table 7.8). In this section I evaluate the two most important mechanisms—the debt-conversion program (Chapter 18) and the debt equity–swaps program (Chapter 19).[16] The Chapter 18 mechanism allows domestic debtors to (indirectly) buy their own foreign liabilities in the secondary market. The Central Bank does not provide foreign exchange at the official rate for these operations; those institutions that participate in this scheme have to obtain the required foreign exchange in the domestic parallel market. Until September 1985 the Central Bank of Chile allocated a monthly quota to private banks, thus allowing them to acquire up to that amount of its debt in the secondary market. Starting in October 1985 the Central Bank has auctioned the quotas instead of allocating them. In March 1988 the Chapter 18 operations were suspended. Although the Chilean authorities have pointed out that this is a temporary measure, it is unclear when (and whether) Chapter 18 conversions will be allowed to resume.

TABLE 7.8 Examples of Additional Trade Restrictions (1982–1986)

Mexico	1982: QRs imposed on all imports. (From 1970 to 1980 QRs affected only 60 percent of imports.)
Argentina	1984: Decree 4070: All imports require a permit and all imports competing with local production are subject to authorization (with consultations to domestic producers' associations). 1985: Tariff surcharge of 10 percent over imports and 9 percent for exports.
Venezuela	1983: Foreign exchange controls and a two-tier official exchange-rate system. QRs on 70 percent of final consumption goods.
Chile	1982: Import surcharges ranging from 4 to 28 percent imposed on more than thirty items. Also, two-tier exchange rate established. 1983: Import tariffs raised from 10 percent to uniform 20 percent. 1984: Import tariffs temporarily hiked to 35 percent. 1985: The uniform import duty system is stabilized at 20 percent (from the earlier uniform level of 10 percent).

Source: Edwards (1989).

The actual mechanics of debt conversions are rather complicated. A typical Chapter 18 debt operation can be described as follows: A Chilean institution—a private bank, say—decides to rescue some of its outstanding foreign liabilities. As a first step it buys a quota in the Central Bank auction. Next it locates, through an international broker, a holder of its debt that is willing to sell it. At that point the Chilean bank will have to obtain foreign exchange in the local parallel market. This involves two further steps: (1) Pesos have to be obtained to buy the foreign exchange; for this purpose the bank issues domestic debt, which it sells in Chile. (2) It then contacts an intermediary who buys the foreign exchange in the parallel market. Once the foreign exchange is on hand, the debt is actually bought and the liability is extinguished.

The institutions of the public sector, most notably the Central Bank and the state-owned Banco del Estado, have also used Chapter 18 to reduce some of their debt. In this case, however, the payment has not been made with foreign exchange. Instead, the public-sector foreign liabilities are exchanged for long-term bonds denominated in domestic currency. The value of these peso bonds has fluctuated in the Chilean secondary market at around 88 percent of par value. A variant of the Chapter 18 program is the so-called Annex 4 of Chapter 18. This scheme amounts to exchanging liabilities in foreign currency for newly issued stock shares in a Chilean corporation. These operations are directly monitored by the Central Bank and are not subject to the quota allocation. A key aspect of this scheme is that it has been financed not with reserves or other official funds but, rather, with reversed capital flight. This factor turns out to be very important in determining the benefits of the scheme.

An important aspect of Chapter 18 operations is that Chilean residents capture most of the secondary market discount. In fact, three agents have shared the discount: (1) the Central Bank, (2) the suppliers of foreign exchange in the parallel market, and (3) the various intermediaries. Larraín (1988) has recently calculated that in 1987 the average discount on Chapter 18 operations amounted to 35.7 percent. Of this, the Central Bank captured 20.5 points, the suppliers to the parallel market for foreign exchange got 3.3 percentage points, and the remainder were related to different fees.[17]

Chapter 18 conversion schemes have several macroeconomic effects. First, pressure is applied on the black market for foreign exchange. It is for this reason that the government established the quota system in 1986. It was expected that, as a result, the spread in this market would not become "excessive." This outcome was basically brought about. In the first half of 1988, however, the parallel market premium started to increase; for primarily political reasons, and as a way to avoid additional pressures on this market, Chapter 18 operations were temporarily suspended. An important question is whether the funds currently used to finance this scheme in the parallel market—funds corresponding to previous capital flight—could have been lured to the country in a more efficient way. If the answer to this question is affirmative, the desirability of the program becomes more dubious.

The second macroeconomic effect is related to the scheme's effect on interest rates. The domestic counterpart of the rescue of foreign liabilities is the creation of internal debt. This, of course, puts pressure on the domestic capital market, as a result of which domestic interest rates tend to rise. It is important to note, however, that contrary to some popular accounts the Chapter 18 program has no short-run effects on the creation of money by the Central Bank.

It is difficult to quantify exactly the costs associated with these macroeconomic effects. It is generally agreed, however, that these are relatively minor.[18] The desirability of the scheme, then, basically depends on whether it is beneficial for the country to capture a discount that fluctuates around 32 percent. The answer depends partially on whether Chile expects to pay its debt in full or expects to have a large proportion of its debt forgiven (or, alternatively, if it expects to repudiate the debt). If, as the Chilean authorities have pointed out recently, the government expects to pay all of its debt in full, the opportunity to buy some of it at a discount is a good deal. If, however, the expectation is that the country will not pay all of its debt and that a large fraction of it will be forgiven, it is not clearly beneficial to buy the debt in the secondary market, even if it carries a sizeable discount. This has been the view of prominent opposition economists who have openly called for putting an end to these programs once the Pinochet government is replaced by a new democratic administration.[19]

The Chapter 19 program corresponds to debt-equity swaps—that is, to a debt capitalization scheme. A typical operation can be described in the following way: A foreign investor buys Chilean private debt at a discount in the secondary market and converts it into internal debt. This debt is then sold in the domestic secondary market and the proceeds are used to acquire domestic (productive) assets or to finance domestic investment projects. Participants in this scheme cannot repatriate profits for the first four years, and the principal can be repatriated only after ten years. Chapter 19 operations are not subject to quota allocation and are approved on a case-by-case basis by the Central Bank; it is expected that this case-by-case approach will allow the screening of *bona fide* investors and avoid "round tripping" operations. No Central Bank commission has been established to discuss these operations. Most participants in Chapter 19 schemes have invested in mining and other natural resources sectors (e.g., forestry).

In contrast to Chapter 18 operations, Chapter 19 operations do not result in the extinction of a foreign liability. They constitute merely the replacement of one type of liability for another. However, to the extent that profits repatriation is delayed for four years, there is a beneficial liquidity effect. During the operations approved through Chapter 18, Chilean residents have captured most of the secondary market discount; in the case of Chapter 19, however, most of the discount has been captured by foreign investors. This arrangement, of course, is equivalent to providing a major subsidy to foreign investment. Larraín (1988) has recently estimated that this subsidy amounted to approximately 35 percent in 1987. But it is unlikely that provision of such a sizable subsidy is the most efficient way to attract additional foreign investment.

Another important element in evaluating the Chapter 19 program refers to its crowding-out or additionality effects on foreign investment. The question is whether those participants in the program would have invested in Chile anyway. If this is the case, the program has crowded out other investments. Alternatively, the program may have attracted new investors, in which case additionality would be present. It is not easy to quantify this issue, and opinions appear to be divided. Whereas Ffrench-Davis (1987) questions the existence of additionality, Fontaine (1989) argues that there is a significant proportion of new funds; Larraín (1988), meanwhile, takes a somewhat intermediate position, arguing that the fact that foreign banks have opted to participate, even though equity investment is not their main line of business, is a sign that at least some additionality is present.[20].

Overall, then, in at least one dimension Chile was tremendously successful in its use of the secondary market to reduce its debt in the late 1980s. Approximately 25 percent of Chile's long-term debt to banks has been converted in the last few years. The two main mechanisms used for these purpose are fundamentally different. Chapter 18 consists of debt conversions or debt-rescue schemes whereby Chilean residents have captured most of the secondary market discount. Moreover, after the access quota allocation system was implemented, it was the Central Bank that captured most of this discount. By and large, given the fact that it has been financed with reversed capital flight, Chapter 18 has been an innovative program that seems to have resulted in positive net benefits to the country. Chapter 19, conversely, is a debt capitalization program. It has provided an implicit subsidy to foreign investors of approximately 30 percent, and it has resulted in very little, if any, additionality.

Trade Liberalization and Adjustment with Growth

The emergency packages implemented after the eruption of the debt crisis succeeded in averting what some considered to be an almost certain collapse of the world financial system. This success was achieved, however, at a significant cost to the major debtors in terms of declines in employment, income, and standard of living. The key question now is how to move from that situation toward what we can call phase two of the adjustment process—a phase characterized by adjustment *with* growth. At a more concrete level, the Baker and the Brady plans, among other initiatives, clearly reflect the preoccupation of politicians with this issue.

A number of authors—and, indeed, the supporters of the Baker and Brady plans, as well as of the IMF—believe that a rapid trade liberalization, coupled with devaluation, privatization, and financial reform, is the most reasonable strategy to achieve these objectives.[21] For example, Balassa et al. (1986, p. 88) have recommended that, among other things, the developing nations should eliminate all QRs and, over a period of five years, reduce import tariffs to a uniform 15 to 20 percent level; and that these tariff reforms should be coupled with significant devaluations, in order not to "deprotect" the tradable goods sector.[22] To a large extent these recommendations are very similar to what many economists have been advocating for many years for the developing countries. However, the new proposals are more drastic, in the sense that they argue for a bolder movement toward free trade. The current proposals on significant trade liberalizations have not taken into account the important issues related to strategy, including the appropriate speed and sequencing of reform. Also, there has been little consideration of the possible short-run trade-offs between these liberalization reforms aimed at improving efficiency and other objectives of the overall programs.

Most of the traditional literature on trade liberalization has assumed that these reforms take place in the absence of a foreign-debt overhang problem. Moreover, many writers have assumed that during the trade reform process countries would be able to attract substantial voluntary lending. McKinnon (1973, 1982), for example, has forcefully warned of the dangers related to excessive capital *inflows* during a trade liberalization episode. However, it is currently clear that, in the vast majority of LDCs, there is very little danger of trade liberalization attracting excessive (or indeed any) voluntary capital inflows. Today, the problem is quite the opposite: Countries have to generate a positive resource transfer *to* the rest of the world.

Outward Orientation, Export Promotion, and Trade Liberalization

There is by now an impressive amount of empirical evidence suggesting that countries that have adopted outward-oriented development policies that emphasize export promotion have outperformed those countries that have followed inward-oriented strategies based on import substitution. Even CEPAL—which is not exactly known for its endorsement of outward policies—has recognized that the excesses of import substitution have been very costly for Latin America; some of CEPAL's senior staff members have recommended that export promotion should play a more central role in that region's development policies in the future.[23]

There seems to be relatively less agreement, however, on whether "trade liberalization" packages have played an important role in the performance of the outward-oriented economies. For example, Sachs (1987) questioned the idea that trade liberalizations are indeed a required component of successful outward-oriented strategies. Making reference to the experiences of the East Asian countries—Japan, Korea, Singapore, Taiwan, and Hong Kong—Sachs argues that these countries' success was to a large extent due to the active role of government in promoting exports in an environment where imports had not yet been fully liberalized, and where macroeconomic (and especially fiscal) equilibrium was fostered. Whether one agrees with Sachs depends on how outward orientation, export promotion, and trade liberalization are defined. Recently some confusion has emerged regarding these concepts, as it is not clear what people mean by them.

In the more traditional policy literature of the 1960s and 1970s, trade liberalization was defined in a very general way; what economists usually meant was *some* relaxation of trade and exchange controls. In fact, in the by-now classic National Bureau of Economic Research (NBER) study on trade regimes directed by Bhagwati and Krueger, a liberalization episode was defined as a more extensive use of the price mechanism that would reduce the anti-export bias of the trade regime.[24] In her 1985 review article on the problems of liberalization, Krueger went so far as to say that even a (real) devaluation in the presence of QRs constituted a liberalization episode. These are indeed very mild and imprecise definitions of liberalization. In fact very few people today would raise an eyebrow at them. Only recently has "trade liberalization" acquired a more drastic connotation, meaning (for many people) an elimination of QRs coupled with a severe reduction of import tariffs to a unifom level of around 10 percent. Moreover, trade liberalization has, in many ways, become synonymous with free market-oriented policies with minimum or no *government intervention* at any level.[25]

The difference between the old and new definitions of "trade liberalization" is, to a large extent, one of degree or intensity. Whereas a devaluation in the presence of QRs, or the replacement of QRs by (quasi) equivalent tariffs is a mild form of liberalization, the reduction of tariffs (with no QRs) to a uniform 10 percent, or, for that matter, the complete elimination of tariffs, is a very drastic liberalization. In order to elucidate the different issues involved in policy discussions it is crucial that we specify the *intensity* of liberalization we are referring to. Unfortunately, this is not always done; the policy literature on the subject is plagued with imprecisions and ambiguities.

There is little doubt that a successful export promotion policy requires *some* kind of trade liberalization. In fact, the historical evidence clearly shows that those countries that have successfully embarked on this kind of strategy have had a more "liberal" trade regime than those countries following indiscriminatory import substitution. The successful outward-oriented countries have generally had lower coverage of prior licenses systems, lower average tariffs, less dispersion in their tariffs, and fewer episodes of real exchange-rate overvaluation.[26]

A recent major multicountry study by the World Bank found that there was a clear relation between movements toward more liberal trade systems—although most countries still retained a number of controls—and a better economic performance (Michaely, Papageorgiou, and Choksi,

1986). In that regard, the case of Korea—certainly one of the most successful of the export-oriented countries—is very illustrative. In 1985, 90 percent of Korean imports were subject to automatic approval (i.e., were not subject to any form of QRs) and the average tariff rate was only 26 percent. Moreover, the tariff structure was characterized by higher tariffs concentrated on final goods, with capital equipment and intermediate inputs having relatively low levels of protection.[27] This degree of import protection was significantly below that of most of the developing nations and also below the degree of Korean protection in 1965, before the outward-oriented policy was embraced. The Korean experience of export promotion coupled with trade liberalization can be contrasted with the Chilean case. Between 1975 and 1979 Chile implemented a drastic trade liberalization that eliminated all QRs and reduced tariffs to a uniform 10 percent in four years; in addition, as part of a massive move toward free market orientation, this period's policies almost completely eliminated the government's role in defining external sector strategies. By allowing the real exchange rate to appreciate by approximately 30 percent between 1979 and 1982, the Chilean experience of that period became one of "ultra" trade liberalization *without* export promotion (see Edwards and Cox-Edwards, 1987).

Within the Latin American context, Colombia after 1967 provides another educational example of successful export promotion cum partial trade liberalization. Until that year Colombia's external sector was highly distorted and had been subject to deep and recurrent balance-of-payments crises. Coffee exports provided most foreign exchange, and the Colombian economy was subject to the vagaries of the world coffee market. In 1967 three major measures were taken. First, every attempt to fix the exchange rate was abandoned, and a crawling-peg system aimed at avoiding real exchange-rate overvaluation was adopted. Second, an aggressive export-promotion program was enacted. Here a subsidies scheme—the so-called CATs—and the government export-promotion office (Proexpo) played an important role. And, third, imports were greatly liberalized; in 1983 the average tariff in Colombia was only 29 percent, whereas the proportion of imports subject to QRs had greatly declined since 1967. As a consequence of these policies the Colombian non-coffee-exports sector has performed quite well, thereby helping Colombia sustain a vigorous growth rate since 1970.[28]. In fact, Colombia stands alone among the Latin American nations as a country that escaped the traumatic experience of the debt crisis while being able to maintain a reasonable rate of growth.

Although the evidence supporting the merits of outward orientation is abundant, there is no well-developed theoretical model—or empirical evidence for that matter—linking very low (or zero) import tariffs to higher *growth*.[29] Nor is there evidence suggesting that a completely "hands-off" policy on behalf of the government is the most desirable alternative. In fact, the success of the East Asian countries with export-led growth suggests that some selectively determined degree of inter- vention—aimed at supporting exports—played a key role.[30] In this section no attempt will be made to solve the important question of the optimal degree of government intervention, or of the optimal level and structure of import tariffs. This, indeed, is one of the most difficult questions of economic policy, and its answer (even at the pure abstract and theoretical level) will depend on the existence of other distortions, the completeness of markets, and the availability of other policy tools, among other things. Instead, we shall proceed under the assumption that in most of the highly indebted countries the current structure of imports protection is higher than the (unknown) optimal level and that, in the long run, these countries will gain from engaging in *some* trade liberalization aimed at reducing and uniforming import tariffs.

Trade Liberalization with a Government Budget Constraint

An important policy question is whether the trade liberalization com- ponent of an outward-oriented strategy should be attempted at the same time as a country is embarked on a severe stabilization and anti- inflationary program. Not surprisingly, the answer depends on the intensity of the trade reform and of the ongoing rate of inflation.

Historically, there has been a close link between *mild* trade liberal- izations and stabilization programs.[31] Consider the following typical scenario leading to a stabilization program coupled with a mild to medium trade liberalization effort:[32] At some point in time the authorities of a particular country decide to pursue a fiscal policy that is inconsistent with the chosen nominal exchange-rate regime—usually a pegged rate. Given the underdeveloped nature of the domestic capital market, the fiscal expansion is basically financed with domestic credit creation. As a result, a loss of international reserves will occur; domestic inflation will exceed world inflation; and the real exchange rate will become increasingly overvalued. In an effort to stop the drainage of reserves, the authorities will usually respond by imposing exchange controls and by increasing the degree of restrictiveness of the existing trade imped- iments: Tariffs will be hiked and QRs will be imposed. Naturally, as long as the fundamental causes of the macroeconomic disequilibrium— that is, the inconsistent credit and fiscal policies—are not tackled, all the authorities will gain by imposing new trade restrictions is post- ponement of the need for corrective macroeconomic measures. The real exchange rate will become more overvalued, international reserves will continue to decline, and a black market for foreign exchange will emerge. At some point this disequilibrium situation will become unsustainable, and a stabilization program—usually under the aegis of the IMF—will be enacted. This program will usually consist of (1) a significant nominal devaluation geared toward correcting the overvaluation developed in the previous period, (2) a contractionary macroeconomic policy, and (3) a liberalization of trade restrictions aimed at dismantling those controls imposed during the expansionary phase of the process. These types of trade liberalization have historically been mild and have seldom consisted of complete elimination of QRs and major tariff reductions of the kind now recommended for the indebted countries.[33]

Perhaps Chile during 1975–1981 constitutes the most notable case of a major liberalization undertaken in conjunction with a major stabilization effort. In this case, the trade liberalization that eventually eliminated all QRs and reduced tariffs to a uniform 10 percent level was pursued at the same time as inflation was being reduced from 400 percent to 10 percent.[34] The Chilean episode illustrates very vividly one of the most serious trade-offs that emerges when a major liberalization is undertaken at the same time as a major anti-inflationary program. As in most successful stabilization programs, during the last phase of the Chilean stabilization effort—when inflation was reduced from 40 percent to 9 percent per annum—there was a significant real exchange-rate appreciation that reduced the degree of competitiveness of the tradable goods sector at a time when the *equilibrium* real exchange rate had significantly depreciated owing to the trade reform. This real appreciation was, in part, the result of the active use of exchange-rate management to bring down inflation since 1978. As is well known by now, this real appreciation played an important role in the disappointing outcome of the Chilean episode: It seriously deprotected the tradable goods sector; it generated perverse expectations of devaluation; and, ultimately, it conspired with the high real interest rates to provoke the worst financial debacle of Chilean history (Edwards and Cox-Edwards, 1987).

A crucial objective of any stabilization program—and, as pointed out in the second section of this chapter, particularly of those undertaken by the major debtors—is to reduce the magnitude of the fiscal deficit. Often there will be an important trade-off between a trade liberalization that reduces import tariffs and the achievement of this fiscal objective. Surprisingly, much of the policy and theoretical literature on trade liberalization policies has tended to ignore the fiscal role of tariffs in the developing nations. Most theoretical and policy discussions on trade liberalization assume, along the lines of traditional trade theory, that tariff proceeds are handed back to the public. In reality, however, things are very different, with governments using tariff proceeds to finance

TABLE 7.9 Taxes on International Trade as a Percentage of Government Revenue: Selected Latin American Countries (1984) (in percentages)

	Import Tariffs[a] / Total Tax Revenue	Taxes on Trade[a] / Total Revenue
Argentina	4.9	13.3
Bolivia	25.6	30.0
Chile	13.4	10.8
Peru	10.2	n.a.
Mexico	3.0	2.7

[a]Refers to central government.

Source: Constructed from raw data from the International Monetary Fund's *Government Finances Statistics Yearbook* (1985).

their expenditure. This is particularly the case in many of the poorer developing countries, where, for varying institutional reasons, taxes on international trade represent a high percentage of government revenue. Table 7.9 contains data on the fiscal importance of taxes on international trade in five countries. Indeed, taxes on trade could be as high as one-third of the total revenue of the central government.

As long as tariff rates are below the maximum revenue tariff, there will be a trade-off between trade liberalization and the generation of the government surplus required to finance debt servicing. The reduction of tariffs will generally reduce distortions, but it will also have a negative effect on government finances. What is required, then, is to replace trade restrictions by less distortive taxes that can generate the same (or a higher) amount of revenue. The implication, of course, is that major reforms of the tax system would be required in most countries. As long as this tax reform effort also focuses on efficiency aspects, it will tend to be based on the imposition of a value added tax (VAT). But this is not an easy task, and it takes time, as a number of efforts to implement sweeping tax reforms have recently shown. Tax reforms are not only politically difficult to get approved but, from an administrative perspective, also difficult to implement. This is particularly true for poorer countries. However, in middle-income countries where an operating tax system of some sophistication already exists, a major tax reform can be implemented with some speed. The Chilean tax reform of 1975 is, in that sense, a good example; in little over a year a major tax overhaul that introduced a VAT, full indexation, and unification of corporate and noncorporate tax rates was successfully implemented (Corbo, 1985).

Although in most cases the implementation of a major tax reform will take a substantial amount of time, there are some policies conducive to both improved efficiency and higher revenues in the short run. The most obvious one is the replacement of QRs (i.e., licenses, prohibitions, and so on) by import tariffs. By replacing the QR by a tariff, the government can regain the revenue previously captured by those favored by the restrictions.

The replacement of QRs by tariffs has two other potentially desirable effects. First, there is the potential for a positive effect on income distribution. This is the case because large (or even multinational) firms or large established merchants usually get the import licenses and, thus, the rents. By replacing the QRs with tariffs, these rents are passed on to the government, allowing it to reduce other taxes or even increasing expenditure on social programs. Second, the replacement of tariffs by QRs will generally increase the effectiveness of devaluations. The reason is that the effects of devaluations are significantly different under quantity rationing (i.e., import quotas or licenses) than under import tariffs. In the latter case, a (real) devaluation will result in a higher price of both importables and exportables relative to nontradables. Under QRs, however, although the domestic price of exportables will still increase, that of importables will usually not be affected. All the devaluation will do is reduce the rents received by the party that got the license.

Nevertheless, a potential problem with the replacements of QRs by tariffs is that it is not easy to decide on the tariff level that should be imposed instead of the QR, since under a number of plausible conditions (domestic monopoly being perhaps the most common) tariffs and quotas will not be equivalent. In this case, there is *no* tariff that will exactly replicate both the domestic price and the quantity resulting from the QR. One possible alternative policy that has been used with some success in a few countries is to auction the quotas rather than allocating them in an arbitrary way.[35] Some of the attractive features of this option are the fact that it is possible to maintain the certainty on the volume imported, while at the same time the government captures back the rent associated with the quota allocation.

To sum up, in many countries—especially the poorer ones, with their rudimentary tax systems—taxes on trade are a very important source of government revenue. Thus introduced is a relevant trade-off between trade liberalization reforms and the maintenance (or achievement) of fiscal balance. In terms of the sequencing of reform, then, an important principle is to make sure that tariff-reduction reforms should be undertaken only after the fiscal sector has been reformed and other sources of revenue have been found.[36] Also, when the fiscal imbalance has been solved, the possibility of real exchange-rate overvaluation is reduced.

Structural Adjustment and Devaluation

Nominal devaluations are an important component of most stabilization programs and, as discussed in the second section, they have played a central role in the adjustment efforts following the debt crisis. The purpose of these nominal devaluations is to generate a *real* exchange-rate adjustment, which would reverse the real appreciation that most often precedes the balance-of-payments crisis. By improving the degree of domestic competitiveness and raising the domestic price of tradables, the real devaluations are supposed to improve the external sector accounts of the country in question. Historically, however, when implementing stepwise discrete nominal devaluations, many developing nations have found it difficult to sustain the real devaluations for a long period; in a large number of cases, after some time—usually ranging from one to two years—the real exchange-rate effect of the nominal discrete devaluation was fully eroded. In almost every instance this erosion can be traced back to the failure to implement consistent macroeconomic policies alongside the devaluations (see Edwards, 1989).

Devaluations have also played a key role in the trade reform component of structural adjustment programs. It is generally accepted in policy circles that in order for a tariff reform to be successful, it has to be accompanied—if not preceded—by a real devaluation. The argument usually given is based on a partial-equilibrium interpretation of the elasticities approach to exchange-rate determination, and it runs along the following lines: A lower tariff will reduce the domestic price of importables and consequently increase the demand for imports. This, in turn, will generate an external imbalance (i.e., a trade account deficit) that, assuming the Marshall-Lerner condition holds, will require a (real) devaluation to restore equilibrium. It is along these lines, then, that the proponents of major liberalizations by the debt-ridden countries have insisted that these tariff reductions should be accompanied by significant nominal devaluations (Balassa et al., 1986).

The "required" amount of devaluation will depend on a number of factors, including the initial conditions, the extent of the trade reform, the magnitude of the disequilibrium gap to be closed, and the accompanying macroeconomic policies.[37] In addition, and perhaps more important, the required devaluation will depend on the speed at which the trade reform is implemented. For a number of reasons, including the short-run fixity of capital, short-run supply elasticities are much lower than long-run elasticities; thus, under most circumstances a rapid trade reform will necessitate a higher real devaluation to maintain external equilibrium.[38] However, it has to be kept in mind that the effects of the devaluation will also depend on the exchange regime adopted by the country.

Until quite recently, most traditional structural adjustment programs in the developing nations have contemplated discrete nominal devaluations whereby the official nominal exchange rate is abruptly adjusted by a fairly large percentage. Even more recently, however, an increasing number of countries are opting for the adoption of some sort of crawling peg after the devaluation. In a recent study on eighteen devaluation episodes in Latin America, Edwards (1987c) found that those countries that had adopted a crawling peg were significantly more successful in sustaining a real depreciation than the discrete devaluers. Yet this is not surprising in itself, as the crawlers maintained their real devaluation targets by "fighting off" the real exchange-rate erosion with additional nominal devaluations in the following years. Typically, under this type of regime, after the initial exchange-rate adjustment the authorities further devalue the currency in magnitudes approximately equal to the domestic rate of inflation. Of course, a potential problem with this policy is that it can lead to an explosive (nonconvergent) process, whereby the devaluation generates inflation, which partially erodes the real effect of the devaluation; this in turn leads to a higher devaluation, an even higher inflation, and so on *ad infinitum*. This possible instability could happen in those countries where the structural macroeconomic disequilibrium—particularly the fiscal deficit—has not been corrected to a significant extent, and where a trade reform is therefore unsustainable.

In spite of the prominent role of devaluations in conventional adjustment programs, very little research has empirically investigated the effects of devaluations on the real level of economic activity or on income distribution. A recently revived strand of literature has argued that although devaluations may have a positive effect on the external accounts, they will achieve this effect at the cost of significant reductions in real activity. This is the so-called contractionary devaluation hypothesis. Edwards (1989) has analyzed in detail the behavior of numerous key economic variables, including real output during thirty-nine devaluation episodes in developing countries. In this study the evolution of these key variables during the period from three years prior to the devaluation to three years after the devaluation was analyzed and compared to the behavior of the same variables for a control group of twenty-four nondevaluing countries. Table 7.10 provides a summary of the distribution of the rate of growth of real GDP for the devaluing countries and the control group. Notice that, three years prior to the devaluation, this distribution was very similar to that of the control group. In fact, using a Chi-square test for homogeneity, we are unable to reject the null hypothesis that these data came from the same distribution ($X^2(2) = 0.046$). Matters are very different as we approach the devaluation, however. During the two years prior to the devaluation we can see a

TABLE 7.10 Growth of Real GDP in Devaluing and Nondevaluing Countries (in percentages)

	First Quartile	Median	Third Quartile
39 devaluation countries			
3 years before	7.4	6.0	4.7
2 years before	8.4	6.1	3.6
1 year before	7.3	5.4	2.3
Year of devaluation	6.1	4.2	1.2
1 year after	6.4	4.7	3.1
2 years after	6.4	4.7	3.1
3 years after	9.2	5.8	3.2
Control group of 24 nondevaluing countries	7.4	6.4	4.5

Source: Edwards (1989).

significant difference between the devaluing and control groups, with the former exhibiting substantially lower levels of growth in every quartile. The Chi-square test strongly rejects the null hypothesis of homogeneity for the year of the devaluation ($X^2(2) = 7.02$) and all three years following the devaluation. Notice, however, that in the latter years, a fairly fast recovery occurred in the rate of growth of real GDP.

Although the above information is quite revealing, it does not allow us to know whether the behavior of real GDP growth is caused by devaluation or if it is the result of some of the policies preceding the devaluation. This problem can be partially avoided by using regression analysis. The following result was obtained using instrumental variables on a variance component model of twelve countries for 1965–1980:

$$\log y_{tm} = \underset{(1.146)}{0.102} [\log M_t - \log M^*_t] + \underset{(2.331)}{0.210} [\log M_{t-1} - \log M^*_{t1}]$$

$$+ \underset{(3.023)}{0.112} \log(GE/Y)_t - \underset{(2.103)}{0.083} \log e_t + \underset{(2.086)}{0.069} \log e_{t-1}$$

$$+ \underset{(1.431)}{0.044} \log r_t - \underset{(-0.265)}{0.008} \log r_{t-1} \qquad \begin{aligned} R^2 &= 0.998 \\ SEE &= 0.038, \end{aligned}$$

where y is real output, $[\log M - \log M^*]$ is the unexpected rate of growth of money, (GE/Y) is the ratio of government expenditure to GNP, e is the real exchange rate, and r is the terms of trade. According to these results, in the short run devaluations have led to a slight fall in output: A 10 percent depreciation has led to a loss of almost 1 percent

TABLE 7.11 Devaluations and Income Distribution (in percentages of compensation to employees with respect to GDP)

	Year of Devaluation	−4	−3	−2	−1	Devaluation Year 0	+1	+2	+3
Argentina	1970	40	41	40	40	41	42	39	43
Bolivia	1971	37	37	34	36	35	32	30	33
	1979	33	34	35	35	36	36	n.a.	n.a.
	1982	35	36	36	n.a.	n.a.	n.a.	n.a.	n.a.
Chile	1982	39	36	38	40	n.a.	n.a.	n.a.	n.a.
Colombia	1962	n.a.	n.a.	34	36	38	38	36	37
	1964	34	36	38	38	36	37	36	37
	1965	36	38	38	36	37	36	37	36
	1967	38	36	37	36	37	36	38	38
Costa Rica	1974	47	48	48	45	45	46	47	45
Ecuador	1961	n.a.	n.a.	n.a.	28	29	29	29	28
	1970	27	27	28	28	29	30	28	26
	1982	28	28	32	30	29	n.a.	n.a.	n.a.
Mexico	1976	37	36	37	38	40	39	38	38
	1982	38	38	36	37	36	n.a.	n.a.	n.a.
Nicaragua	1979	54	55	54	56	n.a.	n.a.	n.a.	n.a.
Peru	1975	36	38	39	37	37	37	37	32
Venezuela	1964	45	45	42	43	43	43	44	45

Source: United Nations, *Yearbook of National Accounts Statistics.*

of GDP. However, in the second year, the economy returned to its growth trend.[39]

There is little doubt that income distribution considerations enter heavily in the decisions as to what kind of policies should be implemented. However, income distribution data are very scarce in the developing countries. This undoubtedly explains, at least partially, why there are so few studies on the effects of devaluations on this variable. In Table 7.11 we present, as an illustration, some very preliminary data on devaluation and income distribution in ten Latin American nations. This table contains the ratio of labor compensations to GDP for a period that ranges from four years prior to a major devaluation to three years after the devaluations. The first column in the table provides information on the year of the devaluation. Although the ratio of workers compensations is a very rudimentary measure of income distribution, and although this type of "before" and "after" methodology has well-known shortcomings, these data are quite revealing. They confirm that in *some* instances devaluations have been followed by major worsenings in income distribution (as in Peru in 1975). This trend, however, cannot be found in all cases—not even in the majority of episodes. In fact, in many such cases, the ratio of labor compensation increased following the devaluation. Above all, however, these data indicate that in order to have a full understanding of the income distribution consequences of devaluations, we must look at more detailed data and at alternative categories, including the effect of devaluations on the rural-urban distribution of income.

In sum, then, the discussion in this section reveals once again the existence of important trade-offs associated with the different goals of the adjustment program. Although devaluation will generally have a positive effect on the external sector, helping generate the necessary excess supply for tradables and easing the transition following a trade liberalization, it will have a negative impact on the cost of foreign exchange to the government and on the rate of growth of GDP. In addition, devaluation will usually have important effects on income distribution and inflation. As the magnitude of "required" (real) devaluations is closely related to the speed at which structural reforms are implemented, it is desirable to proceed gradually on both the debt repayment and the structural reforms programs.

Credibility, Sustainability, and Reversibility of Trade Reforms

Credibility is a fundamental ingredient of successful structural reforms. If the public attaches a nontrivial probability to policy reversal, it will try to anticipate this event, generally introducing strong destabilizing forces into the structural adjustment process.

Latin America's history is replete with economic reforms that have failed due to the lack of credibility. In this connection, the frustrated Argentinian trade reform during the Martínez de Hoz period is very educational. Due to the lack of credibility on the future of the preannounced trade reform, firms used foreign funds in order to survive in the short run. As Carlos Rodríguez (1983, p. 28) has put it in his evaluation of Argentina's experience of 1978–1982: "As a consequence of the *lack of credibility* on the continuity of the economic program, many firms—which would have disappeared due to the tariff reductions— decided to get into debt in order to remain operating while waiting for a change in the economic strategy" (emphasis in original).

A fundamental aspect of establishing credibility is related to the perception held by the public of the internal consistency of the policies being pursued. In that respect, for example, the inconsistency of the Argentinian fiscal policy—which maintained a very large deficit—with the preannounced exchange-rate regime severely undermined the degree of credibility of the reform process. In the case of Chile the markedly overvalued currency in 1981 was seen by large segments of the public as being inconsistent with the long-run viability of the liberalized economy. In general, if the real exchange rate experiences an unprecedented real appreciation, the public will think that exports will not be able to develop and that there is a nontrivial probability that the reform will be reversed in the future. Under these circumstances it would be optimal for consumers to get into debt today in order to acquire "cheap" importables.

The inability to establish consistency between fiscal and exchange-rate policies has often been at the heart of the trade reform credibility crises in Latin America. For example, in most cases where (mild) trade reforms have been reversed, the public perceived early on that the inflation tax required to finance the fiscal deficit was inconsistent with maintaining a predetermined nominal exchange rate. Under these circumstances, expectations of overvaluation, speculative attacks, exchange controls, and future devaluations developed. In trying to anticipate these events, the optimizing private sector will usually take steps—such as diversifying its portfolio internationally (in an instance of "capital flight")—that will sometimes move the economy in a direction opposite from that intended by the reform. Edwards (1987c) has found that more than 80 percent of reversals of trade liberalizations in Latin America can be traced to inconsistent fiscal policies.

An important question is whether a gradual (i.e., slow) trade reform will be less or more credible than an abrupt one. As theoretical models of credibility of economic policy are only now being developed, they have not yet reached a level that enables us to answer this question with precision.[40] In principle, it is possible to argue that gradualism has characteristics that work in both directions, at the same time enhancing and compromising credibility. On the one hand, by reducing the unemployment effect, and by allowing for a firmer fiscal equilibrium a gradual trade reform will tend to be more credible; on the other hand, a slow reform will allow those groups negatively affected by it (i.e., the import-substitution manufacturing sector) to organize and lobby against the policies. In the end, as is so often the case in economics, the question of whether gradualism will enhance credibility depends on factors specific to each country. What is clear, however, is that policymakers should always pay special attention to the establishment of credibility when important long-term structural changes are being pursued.

As we lack knowledge of the policymaking process and its interaction with the private sector, we cannot derive a precise theorem at this point; but the arguments presented in this section suggest that, in general, it would be more prudent to implement the trade reform component of an outward orientation policy in a gradual way.

Conclusions

The adjustment packages of 1982–1987 in Latin American Countries sought "effectiveness." On some grounds—especially in terms of the turnarounds of the current accounts—the results have been quite impressive. The costs, however, have been high. Not only did real income decline, but real wages fell abruptly in most countries, and unemployment soared. There is little doubt that this outcome does not represent a sustainable adjustment path. A successful adjustment means that debtor countries will have to bring down their debt-to-GDP ratios to a level consistent with the reestablishment of credit-worthiness, while recovering their growth of output and consumption. To fulfill the first objective, a country would have to transfer a given discounted value of resources to the rest of the world. To fulfill the second, the country must increase its rate of capital formation and the efficiency of resource use. The problem faced by the highly indebted nations can be posed as follows: How can these nations minimize the present value of foregone consumption of making a transfer of a specific discounted value? The problem has two dimensions: minimization of the cost of the transfer (including its distributive aspect) at each moment in time, and the intertemporal issue of the flow of transfers over time consistent with a given present value of that flow.

The speed with which the transfer to the rest of the world is made will affect the discounted value of the cost of achieving credit-worthiness. A very fast increase in the trade surplus can be obtained only at a very high cost in terms of nontraded goods and losses in unemployment, both because it takes time for factors to be retrained and to move, and because of wage inflexibility in the short run. It also takes time to implement efficient fiscal instruments to generate the fiscal surplus, particularly if one wants to eliminate the present reliance of taxes on trade and the inflationary finance of the deficit. Finally, improving the allocation of investment and promoting the return of capital flight may involve liberalizing financial markets, which will increase the fiscal cost of servicing internal debt. Thus, improved efficiency and capital accumulation will require important increases in nondistortive taxes and cuts in public expenditures, but this, too, takes time. In sum, there are important trade-offs between the speed of effecting the transfer and minimizing its cost at one moment in time. Instruments that help to improve the trade balance quickly—such as quantitative restrictions—increase the resource cost of achieving the transfer. Instruments that quickly solve the fiscal problem—such as the use of tariffs or QRs instead of a devaluation—also increase that cost.

A slower speed of adjustment can be achieved only if the magnitude of the transfer that countries have to make is reduced during the initial years. One way of achieving this slower speed is by providing these countries with additional lending during the transition. In principle, this action will allow the implementation of slower expenditure-switching policies and of more efficient fiscal instruments to raise public resources. Most important, it will allow the investment rates to be kept up without unduly sacrificing consumption. Thus there is a complementarity between extra lending during the transition and the recovery of growth while transferring abroad a given present value of resources.

A longer-run solution of the debt crisis will clearly require the adoption of policies that rely more heavily than in the past on export growth. Export promotion requires some kind of trade liberalization and tariff reduction—especially with respect to imported inputs and capital goods. Indeed, the historical evidence clearly shows that those countries that have successfully pursued export promotion (i.e., the East Asian nations) have had a trade regime substantially more liberal than those countries that have followed indiscriminatory import substitution based on protectionism. A crucial question, however, is how much trade liberalization is needed. It is argued in this chapter that, although outward orientation requires *some* trade liberalization, there is no reason—either theoretical or empirical—to suggest that the "optimal" degree of liberalization implies zero, or even very low, tariffs coupled with no government intervention in any sphere of the development process. The successful experiences with export-led growth in the East Asian countries support this view; although in these countries the trade regime has been significantly liberal, government intervention has been important and tariffs have never been close to zero or even at a very low (i.e., 10–15 percent) uniform level.

An important policy question is whether the trade liberalization component of an outward-oriented strategy should be attempted at the same time as a country is embarked on a severe stabilization program. It is argued here that, in general, substantial trade reforms should not be undertaken at the same time as a major anti-inflationary program is under way. This is the case for both fiscal and real exchange-rate reasons. However, there are some measures, such as the replacement of quotas for tariffs, that can help both the anti-inflation drive as well as the quest for improved efficiency.

Under the most plausible circumstances a fast trade liberalization will generate short-run unemployment effects. Indeed, the empirical evidence from the Southern Cone tends to confirm this assumption. The implication is that trade liberalization should be a gradual and preannounced process. But this conclusion gives rise to serious credibility issues. Only if the announced gradual trade reform is "credible" will economic agents react as expected by the authorities. The analysis of devaluations presented in the third section of the chapter clearly suggests that, under many circumstances, abrupt devaluations can generate nontrivial short-run costs in the form of output reductions and unemployment. In short, gradual liberalizations will require smaller devaluations, and will possibly reduce the associated costs.

A sustained increase in the indebted countries' exports—which is, of course, a prerequisite for a long-term solution to the crisis—requires an efficient tradable goods sector and a "realistic" real exchange rate; but, more important, it also requires a reversal in the current protectionist trend in the industrial countries, particularly the United States. The data presented in Edwards (1987a) indicate that the extent of nontariff barriers, as a form of protection in the industrial countries, is currently very significant. The data also reveal that these trade impediments are particularly important for goods originating in the developing nations, and that their tariff equivalents are very significant in many cases. Asking the highly indebted developing countries to pay their debts at the same time as their exports are being impeded from reaching the industrialized markets is not only unfair but also politically unwise.

Notes

The author has benefited from discussions with Marcelo Selowsky, to whom he is grateful. He also wishes to thank Alejandra Cox-Edwards, Edgardo Barandiarán, Pari Kasliwal, Miguel Savastano, and Jeff Sachs. In addition, the financial support received from UCLA's Academic Senate and from the National Science Foundation is gratefully acknowledged.

1. Most experts now agree, however, that in some of the poorer countries it would be highly implausible to reduce the debt-export ratio to levels required for access to new voluntary financing. In these cases certain innovative and less orthodox solutions, including debt forgiveness, may be the most efficient way out.

2. See, for example, Balassa et al. (1986) and Krueger (1987).

3. On the Brazilian experience, see Cardoso and Fishlow (1987); on the Mexican experience, see Buffie and Sanguines (1987); and on the Chilean experience, see Edwards and Cox-Edwards (1987).

4. See Dornbusch (1987a) for a discussion of the role of the developed countries' macropolicies on the development of the crisis.

5. See Bianchi, Devlin, and Ramos (1987).

6. Note, however, that it is not completely accurate to talk about overvalued real exchange rates without first analyzing the way in which the equilibrium real exchange rate has evolved (see Edwards, 1988b). In the case of the debtor

countries, however, existing evidence clearly suggests that significant overvaluations have developed.

7. On the Chilean experience, see Edwards (1985) and Edwards and Cox-Edwards (1987).

8. On Argentina, see Calvo (1986a); and for a discussion of the experiences of the three Southern Cone countries, see Corbo, de Melo, and Tybout (1986).

9. On Colombia, see Thomas (1986).

10. The fifteen highly indebted countries of the IMF are Argentina, Bolivia, Brazil, Chile, Colombia, Cote d'Ivoire, Ecuador, Philippines, Morocco, Mexico, Nigeria, Peru, Uruguay, Venezuela, and Yugoslavia.

11. The exact time periods are Argentina, 1982–1985; Ecuador 1982–1983; Mexico, 1983–1984; Uruguay, 1982–1984; and Venezuela, 1982–1983.

12. On the Argentinian exchange-rate guarantees scheme, see Calvo (1986a); on Chile, see Edwards (1985).

13. For a detailed analysis of the nonequivalence between quotas and tariffs, see Bhagwati (1978). See also Hillman, Tower, and Fishelson (1980).

14. See *World Economic Outlook*, April 1987.

15. Note, however, that in spite of Khan and Knight's description in the past not every Fund-sponsored program included exchange-rate actions. It is important to recognize that the IMF has historically exhibited significantly more flexibility than its critics have given it credit for. To some extent, it has taken a case-by-case approach. From the record, however, it seems that the Fund staff considers the vast majority of the cases to be quite similar.

16. These designations stem from the fact that the regulations governing these operations are contained in Chapters 18 and 19 of the *Compendium of Rules on International Exchange* of the Central Bank of Chile.

17. These computations refer to all operations that have used Chapter 18, not just to those of the private sector.

18. See Larraín (1988).

19. See the Opposition Manifesto "El Consenso Político Económico es Posible," *La Epoca*, September 7, 1988.

20. Obviously, when evaluating this program one must also take into account the desirability of foreign investment.

21. Balassa et al. (1987) and Krueger (1987) are good representatives of this view. See also Fischer (1986).

22. The other policies advocated by Balassa et al. (1986) include financial reform, stable real exchange rates, and a much reduced role for the government.

23. For evidence on the performance of outward- versus inward-oriented strategies see, for example, the World Bank's 1987 *World Development Report* and the literature cited therein. On CEPAL see, for example, Bianchi et al. (1987).

24. See Krueger (1978) and Bhagwati (1978). For earlier discussions of liberalization, see Little et al. (1970); and for a recent treatmment of many of these issues, see the volume edited by Choski and Papageorgiou (1986).

25. This was indeed the meaning given by some to the concept of trade liberalization during the Southern Cone experiences with market-oriented policies in the late 1970s and early 1980s. Bhagwati (1986) made an effort to define in

a precise way export promotion, import substitution, and "ultra" trade-promoting trade policies. In the remainder of this chapter, trade liberalization will refer exclusively to trade and commercial policies.

26. An impressive accumulation of empirical evidence supporting the better performance of outward-oriented countries has been compiled in the 1987 *World Development Report.*

27. See, for example, World Bank (1986).

28. On Colombia, see Thomas (1986).

29. Naturally, the welfare effects of trade liberalizations can be observed within second-best economics. Rigorously speaking, if there are other distortions— as invariably there are in the real world—it is not possible to know a priori if a partial trade liberalization will be welfare improving. If there are no other distortions, it is possible to establish a positive relationship between the level of tariffs and the level of *income*. Still, however, there is no traditional growth model that will link no tariffs to higher growth (see Lucas, 1988).

30. Note, however, that even the Koreans made mistakes when they pushed the government's role too far. In that respect, the fiasco of 1974–1979, when the government picked the wrong "winners," is well known. See World Bank (1986).

31. See, for example, Krueger (1981) and Little (1982).

32. See, for example, Edwards (1987a) for a detailed analysis of eighteen stabilization cum mild liberalization episodes in Latin America.

33. Naturally, although this scenario is very common, it is not the only one leading to a stabilization cum structural adjustment program. In an alternative scenario, that fits some countries' experiences during the period leading to the debt crisis, whereby the fiscal expansion is financed with foreign borrowing instead of money creation. In this case the path leading to the need to adjust is not necessarily characterized by a piling up of trade and exchange controls.

34. The recent Bolivian experience is also characterized by a tremendous trade liberalization. However, the fact that this liberalization was part of a package intended to defeat *hyperinflation* sets the Bolivian case apart.

35. A number of countries—such as Jamaica, Sierra Leone, and Uganda— have successfully used foreign exchange auctions, but only a few have implemented generalized auctions for imports of goods. See Krumm (1985) for a discussion of the varying experiences with exchange auctions.

36. Note, however, that from a welfare perspective this is by no means a trivial proposition. Indeed, from a purely theoretical point of view it is not clear that reducing tariffs and increasing other taxes will be welfare improving. Moreover, at least at the theory level, it is not clear that welfare will increase if, as liberalization advocates have sometimes proposed, consumption taxes are raised as tariffs are reduced. This proposal, of course, is a simple application of the second-best theorem.

37. I am referring here to the extent of *real* devaluation. However, since the real exchange rate is not a policy tool, economic authorities face the additional difficulty of deciding the degree to which the *nominal* exchange rate must be adjusted in order to generate a given real devaluation.

38. This statement assumes that a tariff reduction will result in an equilibrium real exchange-rate depreciation. Although this is the more plausible case, theoretically it is not the only possible result. See Edwards (1987c).

39. The countries included in this regression are Brazil, Colombia, El Salvador, Greece, India, Israel, Malaysia, Philippines, South Africa, Sri Lanka, Thailand, and Yugoslavia. For details, see Edwards (1986).

40. Guillermo Calvo, however, has recently made important contributions to this key area of the theory of economic policy (see Calvo 1986b, 1987).

References

Balassa, B. (1982), *Development strategies in semi-industrial countries*. Oxford: Oxford University Press.

Balassa, B., G. M. Bueno, P. P. Kuczynski, and M. H. Simonsen (1986), *Toward renewed economic growth in Latin America*. Washington, D.C.: Institute of International Economics.

Bhagwati, J. (1978), *Anatomy and consequences of exchange control regimes*. Cambridge, Mass.: Ballinger Publishing Co.

―――― (1986), "Export promoting trade strategies: Issues and evidence," World Bank Discussion Paper, Washington, D.C.

Bhagwati, J., and T. N. Srinivasan (1978), "Trade policy and development." In R. Dornbusch and J. Frenkel (eds.), *International economic policy: Theory and evidence*. Baltimore: Johns Hopkins University Press.

Bianchi, A., R. Devlin, and J. Ramos (1987), "The adjustment process in Latin America, 1981–1986." Paper presented at the World Bank–IMF Symposium on Growth Oriented Adjustment Programs, Washington, D.C.

Buffie, E., and A. Sanguines (1987), "Economic policy and foreign debt in Mexico," NBER, mimeo.

Calvo, G. (1986a), "Fractured liberalism: Argentina under Martinez de Hoz," *Economic Development and Cultural Change* (April).

―――― (1986b), "Temporary stabilization predetermined exchange rates," *Journal of Political Economy*, (December).

―――― (1987), "Reform, distortions and credibility," *Working Paper*, University of Pennsylvania.

Cardoso, E., and A. Fishlow (1987), "The macroeconomics of the Brazilian external debt," NBER, mimeo.

Celasun, M., and D. Rodrik (1987), "Debt, adjustment, growth: Turkey 1970–85," NBER, mimeo.

CEPAL (1986a), *Panorama económico de América Latina 1986*. Santiago.

―――― (1986b), *Balance preliminar de la economía Latinoamericana 1986*. Santiago.

Choski, A., and D. Papageorgiou (eds.) (1986), *Economic liberalization in developing countries*. Oxford: Blackwell.

Collins, S., and W. A. Park (1987), "External debt and macroeconomic performance in Korea," NBER, mimeo.

Conrad, R. and M. Gillis (1984), "The Indonesian tax reform of 1983," Harvard Institute for International Development, *Discussion Paper*, No. 162.

Corbo, V. (1985), "Reforms and macroeconomic adjustments in Chile during 1974–84," *World Development*, Vol. 13 (August).

Corbo, V., J. de Melo, and J. Tybout (1986), "What went wrong in the Southern Cone?" *Economic Development and Cultural Change* (April).

Cuddington, J. (1986), *Capital flight: Estimates, issues and explanations.* Princeton, N.J.: Princeton Studies in International Finance.

Cumby, R., and R. Levich (1987), "On the definition and magnitude of recent capital flight," NBER Working Paper No. 2275.

De La Cuadra, S., and D. Hachette (1986), "The timing and sequencing of trade liberalization policy: The case of Chile," Catholic University of Chile, mimeo.

Diaz-Alejandro, C. (1963), *Devaluation in a semi-industrial country.* Cambridge, Mass.: MIT Press.

––––––– (1984),"Good bye financial repression, hello financial crash," *Journal of Development Economics*.

Dornbusch, R. (1987a), "Debt problems and the world macroeconomy," MIT, mimeo.

––––––– (1987b), "Our LDC debts." In M. Feldstein (ed.), *The U.S. in the world economy.* Chicago: University of Chicago Press.

Edwards, S. (1985), "Stabilization with liberalization: An evolution of ten years of Chile's experience with free market policies, 1973–1983," *Economic Development and Cultural Change* (January).

––––––– (1986), "Are devaluations contractionary?" *Review of Economics and Statistics* (August).

––––––– (1987a), "Tariffs, terms of trade and real exchange rate in an intertemporal model of the current account," NBER Working Paper No. 2481.

––––––– (1987b), "The U.S. and foreign competition in Latin America," NBER Working Paper N.2544. In M. Feldstein (ed.), *The U.S. in the world economy.* Chicago: University of Chicago Press.

––––––– (1987c), "Exchange controls, devaluations and real exchange rates: The Latin American experience." Paper presented at the Conference on Exchange Controls, Bogotá, Colombia (June).

––––––– (1988a), "Exchange rate misalignment in developing countries," World Bank Occasional Paper.

––––––– (1988b), "Terms of trade, exchange rates and labor market adjustments in developing countries," *World Bank Economic Review* (September).

––––––– (1989), *Real exchange rates, devaluations and adjustment.* Cambridge, Mass.: MIT Press.

Edwards, S., and A. Cox-Edwards (1987), *Monetarism and liberalization: The Chilean experiment.* Cambridge, Mass.: Ballinger Publishing Co.

Fischer, S. (1986), "Issues in medium term macroeconomic adjustment," *World Bank Research Observer* (July).

Fontaine, J. A. (1989), "The Chilean economy in the eighties: Adjustment and recovery." In S. Edwards and F. Larraín (eds.), *Debt, adjustment and recovery.* Oxford: Blackwell.

Ffrench-Davis, R. (1987), "Conversión de pagerés de la denda extrema en Chile," *Colección Estudios CIEPLAN*, No. 22, Santiago (December).

Hillman, A., E. Tower, and F. Fishelson (1980), "On water in the quota," *Canadian Journal of Economics* (May).

International Monetary Fund (1987), *World economic outlook* (April).

Khan, M., and M. Knight (1985), *Fund supported adjustment programs and economic growth*, IMF Occasional Paper No. 41, Washington, D.C.

Krueger, A. O. (1978), *Foreign trade regimes and economic development: Liberalization attempts and consequences*. Cambridge, Mass.: Ballinger Publishing Co.

———— (1981), "Interaction between inflation and trade regime objectives in stabilization programs." In W. Cline and S. Weintraub (eds.), *Economic stabilization in developing countries*. Washington, D.C.: Brookings Institution.

———— (1983), *Trade and employment in developing countries: Synthesis and conclusions*. Chicago: University of Chicago Press.

———— (1986), "Problems of liberalization." In A. Choksi and D. Papageorgious (eds.), *Economic liberalization in developing countries*. Oxford: Blackwell.

———— (1987), "The problems of LDC debt." Paper presented at the NBER Conference on the U.S. in the World Economy, West Palm Beach.

Krumm, K. (1985), "Experiences with foreign exchange rate auctions," CPO Working Paper. Washington, D.C.: World Bank.

Larraín, F. (1988), "Debt reduction schemes and the management of Chilean debt," World Bank, Washington, D.C., mimeo.

Little, Ian M. D. (1982), *Economic development*. New York: Basic Books.

Little, I., T. Scitovsky, and M. Scott (1970), *Industry and trade in some developing countries*. Oxford: Oxford University Press.

Lucas, R. E. (1988), "The mechanics of economic development," *Journal of Monetary Economics*.

McKinnon, J. (1973), *Money and capital in economic development*. Washington, D.C.: Brookings Institution.

———— (1982), "The order of economic liberalization: Lessons from Chile and Argentina." In K. Brunner and A. Meltzer (eds.), *Economic policy in a world of change*. Amsterdam: North-Holland.

Michaely, M., D. Papageorgiou, and A. Choksi (1986), "The phasing of a trade liberalization policy: Preliminary evidence." Paper presented at the American Economic Association meeting, New Orleans.

Neary, P. (1978), "Dynamic stability and the theory of factor-market distortions," *American Economic Review*.

Ramos, J. (1986), *Neoconservative economics in the Southern Cone of South America*. Baltimore: Johns Hopkins University Press.

Rodriguez, C. A. (1983), "Políticas de estabilización en la economía Argentina 1978–1982," *Cuadernos de Economía* (April).

Sachs, J. (1986), "Managing the LDC debt crisis," *Brookings Papers on Economic Activity*.

———— (1987), "Trade and exchange rate policies in growth oriented adjustment programs," NBER, *Working Paper*, No. 2226.

Selowski, M. and H. Van der Tak (1986), "The debt problem and growth," *World Development* (September).

Thomas, V. (1986), *Linking macroeconomic and agricultural policies for adjustment with growth*. Baltimore: Johns Hopkins University Press.

Woo, W. T., and A. Nasution (1987), "Indonesia economic policies and their relation to external debt management," NBER, mimeo.

World Bank (1976), *World development report 1987*. Oxford: Oxford University Press.

—— (1986), *Korea: Managing the industrial transition*. Washington, D.C.

8

IMF and World Bank Roles in the Latin American Foreign Debt Problem

Patricio Meller

The debt crisis has induced Latin American countries to carry out a long and expensive adjustment process. In the process, Latin America has transferred a considerable amount of real and financial resources abroad; but the problem of foreign indebtedness has not yet been solved. The International Monetary Fund (IMF) has played an important part as a mediator between the debtor countries and the creditor banks; in this role it has served purposes different from the original ones that were laid down in Bretton Woods in 1944. In order to reconcile the problem of foreign indebtedness with the Latin American countries' economic growth, adoption of the strategy of "adjustment with growth" has been suggested. As both the IMF and the World Bank will play an important part in this strategy, a review of the conditionality of both institutions is required.

In the past, Latin American economists have often criticized the IMF conditionality. The "adjustment with growth" strategy will soon result in a double conditionality from the IMF and the World Bank. In this sense, it is convenient that Latin American economists make their proposals and suggestions a priori, instead of criticizing a posteriori the nature and elements of this double conditionality. The possible components of this double conditionality require an examination of the "adjustment with growth" strategy. In particular, there are two reasons why the analysis of this strategy should start with a brief review of the external debt stock accumulated by Latin America (Fishlow, 1987): (1) External debt services absorb an important part of the resources available in the Latin American countries; and (2) so long as the external debt remains high, the international private banks will not be willing to extend new financial credits. In addition, this high debt stock creates distortions in the savings and investment decisions in the debtor countries.

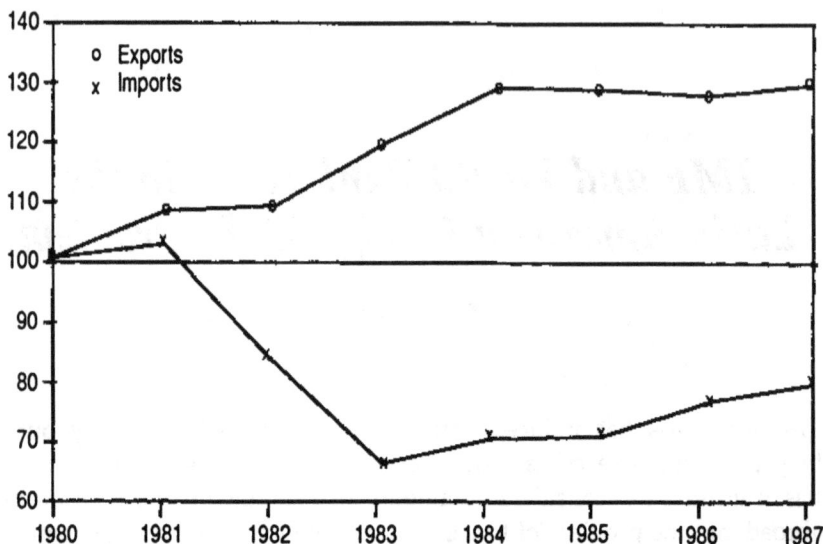

FIGURE 8.1   Latin American Quantum of Exports and Imports (1980 = 100). *Source:* CEPAL (1988).

Latin America's Adjustment Process in the 1980s

In the 1970s Latin America had a rate of economic growth of more than 5 percent annually; between 1981 and 1986 the average annual rate of growth reached only 1 percent. With a given high relative rate of population growth, the worsening of the terms of trade, and the transfer of resources abroad, since 1983 the Latin American per capita income has been 10 percent lower than in 1980. Therefore, the 1980s have been called "a lost decade for Latin America."

If 1980 is taken as the base year, the trade balance measured in current dollars indicates that Latin America's external adjustment was achieved through a contraction of imports. However, the use of a real quantum index for the Latin American exports and imports reveals the following (see Figure 8.1): (1) Although the import quantum index decreased considerably, this fall was less than 30 percent between 1984 and 1986. (2) The export quantum index rose by about 30 percent between 1980 and 1987; thus the annual rate of growth of Latin America's export index amounts to about 4 percent. Still, one can see that the greatest growth was reached in 1983 and 1984 (a rate of growth of about 9 percent), with a period of stagnation afterward.

Figure 8.2 shows Latin America's net flows of capital between 1973 and 1988. On the one hand, we can see that from 1973 onward the

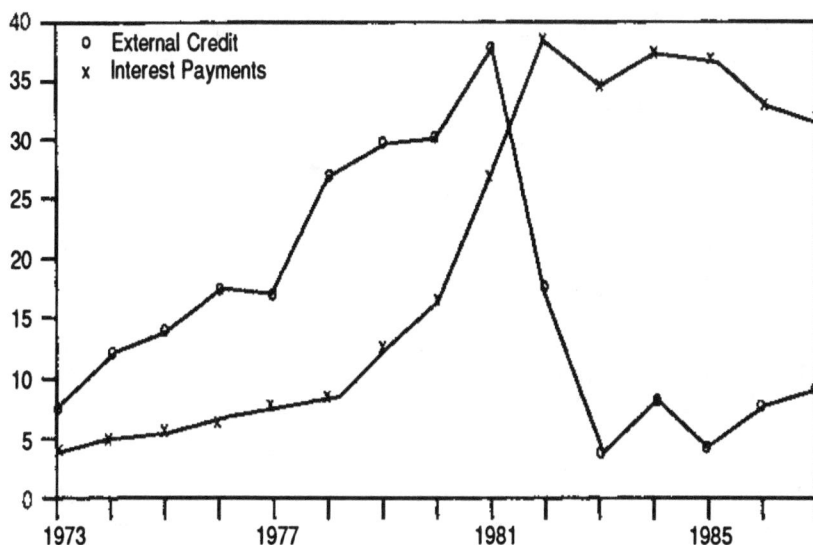

FIGURE 8.2   Latin American Net Flow of Capital (in billions of US$). *Source:* CEPAL (1988).

flow of external net credits (i.e., new credits plus direct investments and minus the redemption of old credits) into Latin America grew steadily to a peak of US$37.5 billion in 1981. From 1983 onward this annual flow was less than US$10 billion. On the other hand, Latin America's annual net interest payments (for its foreign debt) and the flow of profit transfers (for foreign-owned production factors) came to less than US$10 billion in most of the years between 1970 and 1979, whereas in the 1980s the flow of net payments exceeded US$30 billion every year from 1982 onward.

In the 1980s Latin America suffered two different external shocks: the fall in the terms of trade and the rise in the international interest rate. A third shock was the sudden halt in the flow of external credit due to the pro-cyclical behavior of the international private banks (i.e., they lent when it was not needed, and did not lend when it was most needed). This effect will not be dealt with here, but Ffrench-Davis (1986) and Sebastián Edwards (in Chapter 7 of this volume) can be consulted for an examination of the topic.

Latin America's terms of trade decreased from a base level of 100 in 1980 to 85.5 in 1987. Thus, in the 1980s Latin America's terms of trade fell by almost 15 percent. However, the use of 1980 as a base year overstates the deterioration of Latin America's terms of trade.

With respect to the second shock—that is, the rise in the international interest rate in the 1980s—it is important to distinguish between two

TABLE 8.1 Impact of Latin American External Shocks (in billions of US$)

	Current Account Deficit Due to					
	Deterioration in the Terms of Trade with Respect to 1975–1980	Increase in the International Interest Rate with Respect to 1975–1980		Latin American Interest Payments	Current Account Effective Situation	Current Account Hypothetical Situation without External Shocks
		Real Shock	Nominal Shock			
	(1)	(2)	(3)	(4)	(5)	(6)=(5)–(1)–(2)–(3)
1981	0.0	5.4	–1.8	37.3	–40.3	–33.1
1982	8.5	20.8	–6.4	46.6	–41.0	–18.1
1983	12.0	21.2	–15.0	40.1	–7.6	10.6
1984	10.3	24.5	–16.6	43.1	–0.2	18.0
1985	13.3	23.4	–19.3	40.1	–4.0	13.4
1986	18.7	25.4	–27.6	34.8	–14.2	2.3

Sources: CEPAL (1988) and IMF (1987).

different effects (Dornbusch, 1987). The first effect relates to the existence of a higher nominal interest rate due to higher inflation, with the real interest rate assumed to be fixed. In this case, higher (international) nominal interest rates (with a fixed real rate of interest) may produce liquidity problems on the part of the debtors, inasmuch as the payback period for the real value of the debt is shortened; this effect would be the inflationary effect of nominal interest rates. The average nominal interest rate (LIBOR) in the 1970s was 8.8 percent; this figure went up to 11.0 percent between 1980 and 1987. However, it must be noted that the rise in nominal interest rates occurred simultaneous with a fall in the inflation rate of developed countries. The second effect corresponds to the effect of raised real rates of interest on the debtors. The average real rate of interest (LIBOR) in the 1970s was 0.4 percent, and it went up to 4.7 percent between 1980 and 1987.[1]

Bianchi, Devlin, and Ramos (1987) analyze an interesting fictitious case in order to examine the effect of the two shocks—that is, the fall in the terms of trade and the rise in the rate of interest that Latin America had to face in the 1980s. Using the period from 1975 to 1980[2] as a reference base, Table 8.1 reveals the following:

1. In the 1982–1986 period, the combined impact of the fall in the terms of trade and the higher international interest rates (compared to the 1975–1980 period) represents annually more than 42 percent of the interest payments made by Latin America. Therefore, if it were not for these adverse shocks, Latin America would have been able to generate

current-account annual surpluses of more than $10 billion in the 1983–1985 period.

2. The international real interest rate reached high levels at the beginning of the 1980s. This produced the real interest rate shock, which each year quantitatively accounts for more than 50 percent of total interest payments in the 1983–1986 period. The relative drop in the inflation rate of developed countries in the 1980s cushioned the impact of this real shock in that period. Nevertheless, given the important drop in the inflation rate of developed countries during the 1980s, the international nominal interest rate was relatively inflexible downward, thus generating high real interest rates.[3]

3. The fall in the terms of trade of Latin America was practically zero in 1981, and became important only as of 1983, coincident with the expansion of export quantum.

It is interesting to compare the ratio of the gross interest of Latin America's foreign debt to the war compensatory payments of France (1872–1875) and Germany (1925–1932). Bianchi, Devlin, and Ramos (1987) carry out such a comparison; similar comparisons are drawn by Massad (1986), Reisen (1986), and Fraga (1987). Table 8.2 gives an updated synthesis of these comparisons, in which two alternative indicators are used: the gross interest payments (or war compensations) as a percentage of the gross domestic product (GDP) and of the export volume. Generally speaking, the gross interest payments of Latin America's foreign debt as a whole are twice as large (in relative magnitudes) as the war compensations that Germany had to pay after World War I; the percentage is slightly higher than the figure that corresponds to the war compensatory payments of France in the nineteenth century.[4]

Given limited international reserves, the amount of which is small relative to the annual debt service payments, Latin America must necessarily achieve a trade surplus in order to carry out the net transfer of funds, and such a trade surplus implies a real transfer of resources. Figure 8.3 shows the respective real transfers of resources that Latin America made between 1982 and 1986. In fact, the transfer exceeded US$30 billion from 1983 to 1985. In Table 8.2 the real transfers of resources that Latin America made in order to fulfill its foreign debt service are, by means of relative numbers, compared with the transfers that France and Germany carried out in order to make their war compensatory payments. If one compares Latin America's real transfer of resources with respect to national income or its export volume, the results for Latin America are at least twice as high as those for Germany and France. In sum, Latin America carried out a difficult and painful adjustment process and, in so doing, made a real and financial transfer of resources that far exceeded the historical experiences regarding war

TABLE 8.2 Comparison of Payments Related to Latin American Foreign Debt and to War Reparations by Germany and France (in percentages)

	Relative Amounts of Latin American External Debt (Gross) Interest Payments and War Reparations by Germany and France		Relative Amounts of the Real Transfer of Resources	
	Interests or Reparations GDP	Interests or Reparations Exports	Trade Account Surplus National Income	Trade Account Surplus Exports
Latin America 1982–1986	5.7	35.4	4.3[a]	29.3
Germany 1925–1932	2.5	13.4	2.5[b]	13.8[b]
France 1872–1875	5.6	30.0	2.3	12.3

[a]1982–1985.
[b]1929–1932. During 1925–1928 there were trade account deficits.
Sources: Latin America, Bianchi, Devlin, and Ramos (1987); Germany, Machlup (1964).

compensatory payments.[5] Nevertheless, the foreign debt coefficients indicate no improvement. In fact, as Table 8.3 shows, the coefficient that represents the ratio of interest payments to exports went up from 20.2 percent in 1980 to 41 percent in 1982, and since 1983 it has remained slightly above 30 percent. On the other hand, the coefficient representing the foreign debt to exports ratio went up steadily from 2.14 in 1980 to 3.21 in 1982, and it exceeded 3.8 from 1986 on.

General Aspects of the International Monetary Fund and the World Bank

The Relationship Among the IMF, the World Bank, and Latin America

The IMF has repeatedly and over long periods of time been present in Latin America. From 1954 to 1980 the Latin American countries signed 231 programs with the IMF; during this time most of the countries had ten programs, and some of them had as many as fifteen programs (Bolivia and Colombia) or even nineteen programs (Perú and Haití). From 1982 to 1986, the Latin American countries signed with the IMF

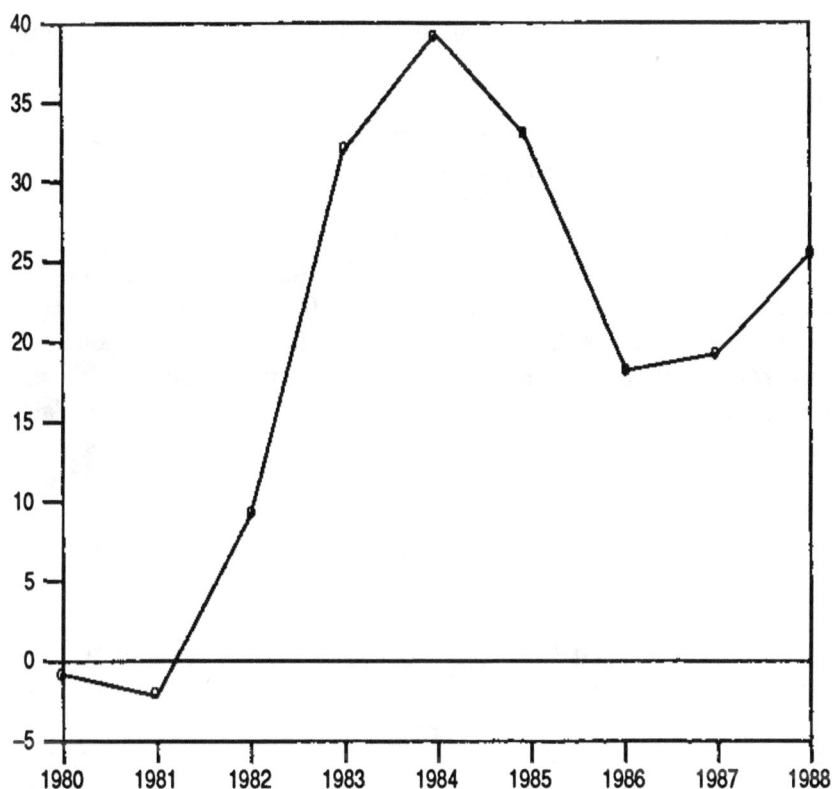

FIGURE 8.3 Latin American Real Transfer (in billions of US$). *Source:* CEPAL (1988).

TABLE 8.3 Latin American Foreign Debt (in percentages)

	1980	*1981*	*1982*	*1983*	*1984*	*1985*	*1986*	*1987*
Interest payments/exports	20.2	28.0	41.0	36.0	35.3	35.2	36.0	30.5
Foreign debt/exports	214	248	321	343	322	342	416	387
Gross foreign debt (in billions of US$)	230.4	287.8	330.7	350.8	366.9	373.2	392.9	409.8

Source: CEPAL (1988).

twenty-nine standby programs and six extended fund facility programs (see Cardoso, 1987).

In these recent agreements between the Latin American countries and the IMF, the following observations were made: (1) Despite the marked improvement in the trade balance, many of the programs were interrupted or even discontinued because some of the quantitative targets that had been laid down in these programs could not be reached (Bacha, 1986). Therefore, in some Latin American countries almost 50 percent of the credits that were recently extended by the IMF could not be used. (2) One of the conclusions drawn from this situation is that the reduction of the external disequilibrium and even a trade surplus can be achieved without reaching certain quantitative targets that were previously laid down in the IMF programs and that refer to internal variables (i.e., government deficit, the expansion of the internal credit volume, and credit to the public sector).

Before the 1980s the credits extended by the World Bank were insignificant with respect to quantity. Nevertheless, the access to loans provided by the World Bank was far easier for Latin America before 1977 than afterward. In fact, from 1958 to 1968 and again from 1968 to 1977, the credits that the World Bank gave to Latin America increased on average by 11.4 percent and 9.6 percent per annum, respectively (the annual rates of growth of the total amount of credits extended by the World Bank came to 1.1 percent from 1958 to 1968 and to 14.1 percent from 1968 to 1977). The situation changed between 1981 and 1984, when the total credits of the World Bank increased by 19.8 percent per annum, whereas the credits to Latin America increased annually by only 3.5 percent on average (SELA, 1986). The explanation for this relative decrease in the amount of credits that the World Bank extended to Latin America (Bacha and Feinberg, 1986) is as follows: The recent adjustment on the part of the Latin American countries caused a decrease in the investment level. Many of the projects that had been approved by the World Bank had to be canceled because the respective country did not have the funds at its disposal in order to make the local financial contribution. In many cases this local financing was not available owing to the restrictive expansion of internal credits imposed by the quantitative targets of the IMF.

The new credits that the World Bank offers now are very often of the structural adjustment lending (SAL)[6] type. Because of their stipulations they are not very attractive to many Latin American countries—especially the larger ones, which are highly sensitive to the loss of national autonomy. Table 8.4 shows that during the period 1983–1987, the World Bank granted to Latin America $5,080 million of credit attached to

TABLE 8.4 World Bank Sectorial and Structural Adjustment Programs in Latin America (1983–1987) (in millions of US$)

	Structural Adjustment Loans (SALs)	Sectorial Adjustment Loans
Argentina		850
Bolivia		102
Brazil		1,155
Chile	750	
Colombia		550
Costa Rica	80	25
Ecuador		100
Jamaica	191[a]	127
Mexico		850
Panama	160	
Uruguay	80	60
TOTAL	1,261	3,819

[a]Includes US$76 million in 1982.

Source: World Bank (1988).

adjustment programs, of which fewer than 25 percent were of the SAL type.[7]

Schematic Characteristics of the IMF and the World Bank

In Bretton Woods (1944), the roles of the IMF and the World Bank were defined as follows: The IMF's main concern was the short-term adjustment of a country having an external disequilibrium. To bring about this adjustment, the IMF granted a loan so that the country in question could correct the disequilibrium in its balance of payments. Indeed, the World Bank generally endeavors to support growth and economic development; to this end it extends loans for specific investment and development projects.

The IMF focuses mainly on macroeconomic matters, and its goals are to stabilize the balance of payments and to control inflation. It tries to achieve these goals through fiscal policy, monetary policy, and foreign exchange policy instruments. The World Bank, by contrast, focuses on microeconomic matters and aims at stimulating savings and investments—and thereby economic growth. In order to achieve this objective, the World Bank concentrates on relative prices and commercial policy. The IMF's methods are directed toward controlling the aggregate demand. To this end the IMF uses a flow analysis of nominal variables, whereas the World Bank attempts to influence aggregate supply. The World Bank's analysis consists of project evaluation; it is based on real variables and makes use of the input-output table, the national accounts, and a consistent analytical framework.

The division of labor between the IMF and the World Bank broke down in the 1980s. Today it is generally known that, on the one hand, the disequilibria in the balance of payments of the Latin American countries (and the developing countries in general) are due to structural factors and therefore require a long-term remedy. On the other hand, short-term macroeconomic adjustment also influences the development of long-term growth. In other words, short-run measures have an effect on long-run outcomes. In addition, the solution of short-run problems requires that these problems be considered from a long-run perspective. This insight caused the IMF to adopt a longer-term point of view; the introduction of extended fund facility (EFF) programs and structural adjustment facility (SAF) programs aims at influencing the aggregate supply. The World Bank, for its part, has introduced macroeconomic analysis and variables for the evaluation of the loans that it extends in order to promote savings, investment, and growth.

To sum up one can say that, on the one hand, it is difficult to distinguish between the IMF's EFF and SAF programs and the World Bank's structural and sectorial adjustment programs. On the other hand, owing to the interdependence of short-run and long-run measures, the economic programs suggested by the IMF and the World Bank must be coordinated. Moreover, the Bank's adjustment programs have generally been applied in those countries where an IMF program was already operating. Therefore, it is difficult to isolate the effects of both programs. All these matters generate the new issue of double conditionality.

The application and enforcement of a double conditionality will eventually turn into a cross-conditionality between the IMF and the World Bank. This cross-conditionality implies that a country that does not fulfill the targets set either by the IMF or the World Bank will have its credits from both institutions suspended. In sum, the cost for a country of not fulfilling part of one of the programs increases notoriously (Lizano and Charpentier, 1986). Today there is a strong relationship, but as yet no cross-conditionality, between the IMF and World Bank programs; indeed, the lack of cross-conditionality should be emphasized.

In my opinion, Latin America's future prospects are as follows: On the one hand, the short- and medium-term access of the Latin American countries to the international capital markets will be limited. Therefore, the credits that the IMF and the World Bank extend will be of great importance. On the other hand, Latin America will be faced with a short- and long-term conditionality because of the double-conditionality on the part of the IMF and the World Bank. On account of previous experiences, especially with the IMF (as will be explained in the following section), Latin America's internal economic policy will, in the future, be determined by outside multilateral institutions.[8]

Latin America's Criticism of the IMF's Conditionality

As early as the 1950s the structuralist economists questioned the monetarist paradigm and approach of the IMF;[9] in this section the discussion will focus only on IMF conditionality. Latin American criticism of the IMF's conditionality is characterized by the following five aspects: (1) The IMF uses the same recipe everywhere. (2) There are problems with the control of the IMF's quantitative targets. (3) The programs of the IMF are unnecessarily recessionary. (4) These programs have a regressive effect on the distribution of income. And (5) there is an international asymmetry in the adjustment costs of external disequilibriums. This last aspect will be dealt with later on; in the meantime, the first four critical arguments will be discussed briefly.

The Standard IMF Program. The analytical framework of the IMF includes the following elements:

1. The external disequilibrium is produced by an internal disequilibrium. When a country tries to spend more than it produces (internal disequilibrium), the resulting gap tends to be filled by a surplus of imports relative to exports (a case of external disequilibrium).
2. Internal disequilibrium is caused mainly by the government (i.e., the central government, the state enterprises, and the Central Bank), and in the end the public deficit (and generally the fiscal deficit, which is its largest component) can be held accountable for the external disequilibrium.
3. Another factor that causes an external disequilibrium is the domestic credit expansion, inasmuch as the external disequilibrium is financed by this means.
4. The economic program of the IMF aims at the reduction of internal expenditure (or the control of the aggregate demand) by means of a fiscal policy that is meant to diminish the fiscal deficit and a monetary policy (credit policy) that is meant to control inflation. In addition, the foreign exchange policy concentrates on changing the composition of expenditure and production.
5. The IMF presupposes these elements and sets quantitative goals, which are connected to changes in the level of international reserves, the level of the fiscal deficit, the rate of growth of domestic credits, and the level of credit to the public sector.

Moreover, instead of analyzing the facts concerning each individual case, the IMF always uses the same analytical approach in order to explain the external disequilibrium. In other words, even before they arrive in a given Latin American country, the experts of the IMF know better than the Latin American economists how to tackle the problem of an external disequilibrium.[10] Dialogues with the IMF always have the same results: "This country spends more than its means"; in other words, "there is an excess demand that must be reduced."

Latin America criticizes this diagnosis as follows: (1) How can a country with an unemployment rate of more than 15 percent and a capacity utilization of less than 75 percent have excess demand? (2) In a given period of time (t_1), a country might have external equilibrium. Then, in the subsequent period of time (t_2), this country might be caught by an unfavorable external shock, such as a dramatic drop in the price of its most important export product, and this shock would diminish the total export volume and thereby cause an external disequilibrium. Therefore, as external and exogenous factors account for the external disequilibrium, it cannot be said that the disequilibrium was produced by a domestic mismanagement of economic policy (Bacha, 1983; Ground, 1984).

The Problem of Monitoring the IMF Programs. The control system of the IMF is scheduled to supervise the economy every three months. This means that every three months the country in question must reach certain targets regarding the indicators that were laid down in the IMF programs (e.g., international reserves and domestic credit). If the country fails to reach these targets, it does not receive the IMF's and international banks' quarterly financial payouts of loans, which enable the country to cover the deficit in its external sector. Therefore, it is the central preoccupation of the ministers of finance to find the means to achieve the quarterly targets set by the IMF, and their efforts are considered to be successful only if they achieve these goals. In sum, the whole economy begins to work on a quarterly basis.[11]

Recessionary IMF Programs The basic principles of the IMF explicitly state that the institution must "promote balance of payments adjustments that do not destroy national or international property" and contribute to the "maintenance of high employment and production levels." Nevertheless, it is empirically clear that the external goals of the IMF are most often met at a considerable internal cost. Thus a kind of overkill occurs.

It is generally agreed that the extremely strict and recessionary character of the IMF programs should be modified. But why are these programs so recessionary? The following elements contribute to their recessionary course: (1) It is difficult to have complete control over the economic instruments by which each program is implemented; the money supply, for instance, is mainly endogenous. This difficulty produces even more restrictive measures whenever the financing is in jeopardy, given the risk of not achieving the quantitative targets that were laid down by the IMF. (2) Instead of lowering the pressure on the economy by laying down a plausible range for the achievement of the respective target, the IMF fixes the target in terms of absolute numbers even for quarterly periods of time; this fixing assumes a degree of exactness and control that economic science cannot assume.

One can argue, from a theoretical perspective, that it is the composition of the IMF programs that accounts for their recessionary nature. This is true for the following reasons: (1) The monetary and domestic credit contraction lowers the level of liquidity in the economy, producing a reduction of the working capital of firms and thus affecting production levels. At the same time, expenditure and aggregate demand fall. This additional factor reduces aggregate supply; in the short-run, that is, changes in aggregate demand, and not relative prices, determine aggregate supply. (2) It has been observed, both theoretically and empirically, that devaluations have a short-run contractionary effect (Krugman and Taylor, 1978). (3) In sum, a restrictive macroeconomic policy (contractionary fiscal and monetary policy) coupled with a devaluation produce a severe short-run contraction of production levels.[12] In fact, the external disequilibrium is reduced in the short run because of the recessionary impact.

The Distributive Effect of the Adjustment Costs. From the point of view of redistribution, the internal adjustment costs of the IMF programs produce generally regressive results; in other words, the greatest part of the adjustment costs is borne by the groups with the lowest relative income. In fact, the currency devaluation, in combination with wage control, results in a real loss of purchasing power of the workers. The reduction of public spending brings about an increase in the rate of unemployment because public investment goes down. Moreover, the cut in subsidies for primary consumer goods (food, public transport, etc.) and the reduction of social expenditure (health, housing, etc.) diminish the welfare of the groups with the lowest income.

When Chile or Brazil want to devise a cost-cutting program, for instance, the question arises as to why the IMF interferes in the preparations for such a program. The prices of bread and milk, and generally the agricultural policy as a whole, "are internal matters, concerning only the respective country." . . . "Why should a cut in the subsidies for wheat solve Brazil's problems regarding its external disequilibrium? Where is the macroeconomic analysis that proves such an assumption?" (Díaz-Alejandro, 1983). The suggestion that food subsidies be eliminated or that public utility prices be raised to international levels has generated political instability in several countries. Even in those cases where important welfare benefits can be foreseen on the basis of better resource allocation, the short-run political and economic costs of a sudden elimination of these subsidies may outweigh the eventual benefits (Taylor, 1985). Moreover, why should a salary cut for teachers at public schools contribute to a rise in international competitiveness? Indeed, why would such a salary cut be taken in cases where the unemployment rate is more than 15 percent?

Yet in many cases governments use the IMF as a scapegoat to implement adjustment programs with a regressive impact. Owing to the confidential nature of IMF agreements, it is difficult to empirically test this proposition. Still, it is clear such scapegoating is neither general nor uniform. Each case is different.

Adjustment and Financing

Despite the harsh criticism of the IMF's role, we should keep in mind that the Fund did not cause the existing economic problems; Latin America's economic disequilibria were already there before the IMF intervened. In fact, the Latin American countries have resorted to the IMF only when there was nothing else left for them to do. Adjustment in the case of an external disequilibrium necessarily entails costs, regardless of whether the IMF is involved.

When a country is faced with an external disequilibrium, it must decide between two options: adjustment or external financing. However, these alternatives are interdependent. Even though a decision in favor of financing implies a postponement of the adjustment, the creditors who supply the money for financing the external disequilibrium will do so only if they observe that the respective country takes measures that guarantee the realization of such an adjustment in the future. To this end, the IMF supplies its financial resources for a limited period of time, provided that the country in question accepts its conditions. These conditions in turn aim at overcoming the existing external disequilibrium.

The IMF has different functions. First, this institution was created for the purpose of lending funds to countries with external liquidity problems. Second, it could be regarded as a sort of "credit club" that applies certain rules in order to preserve the welfare of all its members. Thus the IMF has to reconcile the specific national interest in the period of adjustment with the interests of the other members of the club (especially the interests of those creditor countries that supply the greatest part of the IMF's fund). Among these rules are the free convertibility of currencies, the free access to the foreign exchange market, and the opening of borders for imports. Third, the IMF has a catalytic effect on financings from other sources. Thus the IMF and its programs are the prerequisite that the international private banking industry and the governments demand before they will extend credits to a country with difficulties in its trade balance.[13]

Thus one might say that the Latin American countries turn to the IMF only when the economic authorities are desperate and see no other way. In other words, the Fund is a lender of last resort. This situation has two consequences for Latin America. On the one hand, the IMF is an institution whose credits (and seal of approval to obtain other credits) are needed in order to undertake a less rigorous adjustment process. On the other hand, the bargaining power of the Latin American countries is limited as far as the adjustment policy is concerned.

The central problem in Latin America is not the existence of the IMF; on the contrary, the Latin American countries need the IMF. Rather, the central problem is connected with the adjustment policy, which imposes the IMF's conditionality on these countries. And conditionality is in-dispensable for two reasons: The IMF gives not presents but loans, which have to be paid back; and the credits of the IMF must be used for the express purpose of diminishing the existing external disequilib-rium. Until recently, most of the Latin American countries complied with the two requirements of the IMF's conditionality; however, the internal costs incurred were too high. In sum, Latin America's central problem pertains to the type of conditionality that is connected with the IMF's adjustment programs. It is now time for the Latin American countries to devise and propose an alternative type of conditionality that can be implemented in these programs. Of course, large countries have a better bargaining position from which to achieve a conditionality less detrimental to their national interests. This bargaining position, however, should not depend on the countries' size.

Some Problems with the Eventual Conditionality of the World Bank

In contrast to the IMF, the World Bank is a very heterogeneous institution. Even the central focus guiding its activities has undergone some fun-damental changes.[14] That is why the eventual (or shall we say "tentative," for there is much debate concerning this topic inside the World Bank) conditionality of the World Bank depends on two different, but very interrelated, elements: the role of the World Bank and its view of the less developed countries (LDCs).

During the 1970s perceptions held by the World Bank were as follows: (1) In the LDCs the benefits of higher growth were not reaching the poor; that is, the trickle-down theory was not working. (2) The idea of "redistribution with growth"—which states that it is possible for LDCs to achieve redistributive goals without sacrificing growth—was developed. (3) Therefore, the easing or elimination of poverty became the central conceptual focus of the World Bank. More important, it became a moral objective, to the effect that the World Bank should exert pressure on LDCs in favor of the poor. To carry out this idea credits are granted for investment projects that directly benefit specific groups of the poor (Annis, 1986; Feinberg et al., 1986).

During the 1980s some changes occurred in the focus of the World Bank:

1. A negative attitude has arisen with respect to the economic policies and institutions of the LDCs; it is believed that "poor and unsound policies and weak and corrupt institutions" prevail. Since investment levels depend, in part, on the global economic policy context of each country, in some countries the policies and institutions introduce so many distortions that it is difficult for the World Bank to find viable investment projects to finance.

2. The World Bank creates new credit lines for countries that have to make structural adjustments in order to solve external disequilibrium problems; that is, it creates credit lines that are intended to support not individual investment projects but, rather, specific economic programs.[15]

3. The contents of these economic programs constitute the basis of the new World Bank conditionality. The objective of the programs is to increase the overall efficiency of the economy by establishing adequate incentives, which in turn require changes in commercial and pricing policies, the size and structure of the state, and the role of the government in the economy.

The World Bank currently maintains that the type of distortions commonly found in LDCs are price controls, differentiated incentives between tradable goods, subsidized interest rate and credit control, restrictions in labor force mobility, and real wage adjustments (Michalopoulos, 1987). Increased efficiency in resource allocation and productivity in these kind of economies can be achieved by removing price controls, liberalizing foreign trade, and deregulating factor markets. Deregulating the capital market improves credit allocation and hence investment, whereas eliminating labor market restrictions produces a more efficient allocation of the labor force. In addition, given the critical external disequilibrium it is important for the LDCs to increase the production of tradable goods. In the eyes of the World Bank, such an increase requires a stable macroeconomic environment with an appropriate exchange rate and an incentive structure that is neutral with respect to producing for the domestic or the external market. This last element implies a complete rationalization and liberalization of foreign trade consisting of (1) eliminating quantitative restrictions and nontariff import barriers; (2) tariff reductions; (3) equal (and low) tariffs for all kinds of goods; (4) reduction or, if possible, elimination of all export taxes. With respect to timing, it is convenient to accomplish all of these objectives simultaneously; it is not convenient to liberalize imports after exports have expanded and the country has accumulated sufficient international reserves. In addition, World Bank economists have recommended that incentives be provided to attract international investment, thus avoiding discriminatory treatment between national and international firms. They have also recommended a complete reexamination of the role of the government as owner and operator of public firms and establishment of alternative privatization and destatization measures (Michalopoulos, 1987).

The economic reforms mentioned in the previous paragraph are of great magnitude. Indeed, by comparison the IMF conditionality—even when shown to be strict, inappropriate, or imperfect—intervenes much less in internal matters than does this eventual World Bank conditionality. The IMF conditionality uses a conceptual framework based on budget constraints, in an attempt to reduce external and internal imbalances. In contrast, the eventual World Bank conditionality—which consists of external and internal liberalization, deregulation, and privatization—requires a conceptual framework based on dynamic growth strategies in a "second-best" imperfect world. There is no strong or consistent theoretical or empirical basis for such a framework, however (Helleiner, 1986; Sachs, 1986).

Other reservations concerning the future of World Bank conditionality are as follows: One, the World Bank has a very biased view of LDCs. World Bank economists exhibit a marked hostility toward the government and public enterprises. They consider government and public enterprises to be obstacles to growth and believe that government interventions in the economic process create distortions. By their definition, public enterprises are always inefficient; that is why efficiency and social well-being will increase if such enterprises are privatized. Finally, they deem public bureaucrats to be inept and corrupt, and private entrepreneurs to be efficient and honest. But the empirical evidence in Latin America indicates that matters are not so black and white; rather, they are quite complex.

Two, the SAL programs are very ambitious, and the concomitant policy package implies a clear interference in the developing strategy, in economic policy management, and in the distributive and redistributive patterns of a country; in most Latin American countries this interference is simply unacceptable (Annis, 1986; Feinberg et al., 1986).

In sum, it would be more convenient if the World Bank returned to the views it held in the 1970s—assuming, of course, that it tried to avoid past errors. That is, the World Bank should have the elimination of poverty as its main priority. It is true that LDCs have to make structural changes, but there is much uncertainty as to the timing and velocity for implementing such reforms; also, as each case is different, the timing and velocity depend on the initial conditions as well as on the existence of a consensus that would encourage the structural changes.

Hence it is essential that the local government be the one to decide these matters. During periods of adjustment and structural reform, the costs of transition are usually borne more heavily by the poorer groups of society. To avoid this, compensatory programs should be created, especially in the areas of nutrition and employment, and directed toward the affected groups. The World Bank should help local governments to design alternative adjustment strategies that minimize the social costs and/or contain compensatory mechanisms for the poor.

Issues Relating to Latin America's Foreign Debt

The New Role of the International Monetary Fund

In the settlement of the quasi-crisis of the international financial system, which had been triggered in 1982 by the problem of Latin America's foreign debt, the IMF played an important part as a mediator between the debtor countries and the creditor banks. To this end the Fund organized and coordinated complicated financial packages of very different origins, and in so doing it helped many Latin American countries solve their liquidity problems from 1982 to 1985. Moreover, during this period of time the IMF considerably increased its credit volume regarding its own financial resources.

As a mediator, the IMF imposed conditions on both the debtor countries and the creditors. The debtor countries had to accept an adjustment program that included the complete payment of the external foreign debt service. The creditor banks for their part had to allocate additional financial resources (on a "not very voluntary" basis) to a financial package, in which the funds of the IMF were only one component.

It should be recalled that the original task of the IMF consisted of extending credits to countries with short-term external disequilibria problems. In other words, the IMF's role is short run and concentrated on the flow disequilibrium of the balance of payments. Bacha (1985) points to the fact that the IMF took on a long-term stock problem by taking the part of a mediator regarding Latin America's foreign debt. This way of looking at the problem is based on the opinion that Latin America's foreign debt and the punctual payment of the debt service are not temporary liquidity problems but can be seen as a problem of unbalanced stocks, as will be explained below.

Owing to its new role as a mediator, the IMF is faced with new dilemmas (Bacha, 1986). If a country cannot carry out the adjustment program that it signed with the IMF, two things might happen: (1) the IMF might cancel the program; but such a step would cause an economic crisis in the country in question, for no country can obtain external funds without the IMF's consent. Thus an economic program signed with the IMF gives the required external credibility to the economic program of a country.[16] When an adjustment program that was proposed or even imposed by the IMF is discontinued, the economic crisis thereby caused brings up the question of why the Fund proposed that such an impracticable economic program be implemented. (2) If, on the other hand, the IMF maintains the credit flow, even though the goals of the program were not reached, it might lose some of its external credibility as an international monitoring agent.

Latin America's Point of View

In order to keep up the necessary flows for the foreign debt service, the Latin American countries have undergone a long and painful adjustment process since 1982. This process entailed a fall in per capita income, consumption, and real wages; an increase in unemployment and inflation; and a decrease in investment and economic growth.

Now that this adjustment policy has been in effect for a few years, the question arises as to whether the problem of foreign indebtedness has been solved or at least alleviated. As noted, the majority of indicators regarding foreign indebtedness show that the situation is the same as in 1982—or even worse. What, then, was the purpose of this long and painful adjustment? What would have happened if all the Latin American countries had simultaneously discontinued their foreign debt service as early as 1982?

Latin America's long and costly adjustment process was useful inasmuch as it prevented the collapse of the international financial system. Given that the preservation of the international financial system is a public good of worldwide importance, the question arises as to why Latin America was burdened most heavily with its maintenance.[17]

Since 1985, the institutional financial agreements of 1982, which aimed at managing the problem of Latin America's foreign debt, have begun to collapse. The Baker plan (also known as the Baker initiative) and changes in the top management of the IMF and the World Bank are external indicators of this situation. The long adjustment process has exhausted the debtor countries, and the international banking system is not willing to lend fresh funds to the debtor countries. Moreover, the IMF's available funds have diminished. Besides, there is a negative flow of funds into Latin America. Thus we must ask the following question: Through what kind of pressure can the Latin American countries be made to accept the conditionality of the adjustment programs—a conditionality that implies, among other things, the payment of the whole foreign debt service?

The Problem of Latin America's Debt Overhang

At present, it is obvious that Latin America's foreign indebtedness is not a temporary liquidity problem. It is this foreign indebtedness that accounts for the stock disequilibria in the region, and these disequilibria in turn can be described as a critical a long-term growth problem.

From Latin America's point of view, the role of the IMF and the World Bank should consist in convincing the international creditor banks that the Latin American countries cannot grow and at the same time fulfill their foreign debt service. The Latin American countries have come to the point now where they do not have enough financial resources to pay their debts, although they are quite willing to pay. It is easier for a debtor country with a growing economy to pay off its foreign debt than it is for a country whose economy is stagnating or shrinking.

The following example illustrates this "pay or grow" dilemma. To have an annual rate of growth of 5 percent, a Latin American country needs an average investment rate (in relation to the GDP) of 20 percent (see Table 8.5). Furthermore, it needs a savings rate of 24 percent in order to finance this rate of investment and to meet the interest payments for its foreign debt, which amount to 4 percent of the GDP. Thus, a Latin American country needs a savings rate of 24 percent for a growth of 5 percent and the simultaneous fulfillment of its foreign debt service.[18] At present, the savings rate of the Latin American countries varies between 15 percent and 18 percent. A Latin American country needs an increase of 30 to 50 percent in its domestic savings rate if it wants to pay off its debt and to grow at the same time. But the domestic savings rate cannot increase if the per capita consumption level has fallen by 15 percent. In addition, given the depressed levels of consumption in Latin America, consumption cannot be permanently depressed in order to finance investment and the external debt services.

Table 8.5 shows the conflict in Latin America between "paying and growing." Since 1982 the magnitude of the investment reduction has

TABLE 8.5   Latin American Savings and Investment (in percentages of GDP)

	Gross Investment (1)	National Savings (2)	Transfer of Financial Resources (3)
1980	23.3	21.3	2.2
1981	22.5	20.2	1.8
1982	20.7	20.3	−3.1
1983	17.4	21.7	−5.1
1984	17.5	22.9	−4.1
1985	16.9	21.4	−4.7
1986	17.4	19.6	−3.0
1987	16.6	n.a.	−4.3

Note: The difference between the sum of columns (2) and (3) and column (1) is due to the use of international reserves.

Sources: Feinberg and Bacha (1987); Bianchi, Devlin, and Ramos (1987).

been similar to the amount of external resource transfer. Hence, for an approximately stable savings rate, Latin America has had to transfer overseas part of these savings, which in turn have generated an equivalent fall in investment. Lower investment levels are now generating lower growth rates—a process that will continue in the future.

On the other hand, the level of the external debt overhang is a factor of uncertainty for both national and foreign investors, and thus it generates negative expectations. Therefore, the question arises as to how the rate of investment can increase and thereby produce the necessary growth.

The New Role of the World Bank
in the External Debt Problem

Until 1984 the World Bank maintained a passive attitude with respect to the external debt problem. This was a result of the opinion, held within the developed countries, that external debt was just a transitory liquidity problem. Since the problem persisted and financial alternatives were few, the LDCs began to increase their demand for idle World Bank funds. As of 1985 the World Bank has played a more active role in the debt problem because of the growing awareness that the debt crisis was affecting the LDCs' growth; low growth rates would increase the difficulty of finding viable investment projects for the World Bank to finance. The Baker plan stresses this active role for the World Bank for two basic reasons: The IMF suffered important institutional erosion during the costly 1982–1984 adjustment process, and a new international institution should replace it; and there has been an important change in the perception of the debt problem and a growing preoccupation with the growth performance of debtor countries during the adjustment period. For both reasons, a more active role for the World Bank is necessary.

For some Latin American debtors (Chile, Colombia, México, and Panamá) the World Bank has played an important role in catalyzing or providing collateral for new credits from the international private banks. Indeed, by extending credits and collateral, the World Bank has helped countries attain credits from commercial banks. The international private banks would like to see the World Bank take the additional step of extending its collateral to the already existing debt stock or to any new credits. Obviously the World Bank has resisted such pressures, given its belief that the risks involved in a loan should be assumed by those who are lending the resources (Feinberg and Bacha, 1987).

Adjustment with Growth

The Strategy

The strategy of "adjustment with growth" corresponds to a long-standing Latin American proposal. It is widely agreed that the numerous adjustment programs repeatedly signed by the Latin American countries and the IMF have reduced the external disequilibrium. But they have also brought about two problems: As noted, they entail very high internal costs; and since they do not produce the required structural change, they cannot lead the economy to a stable, high, and feasible growth path.

Today most economists favor "adjustment with growth." Nevertheless, opinions differ widely regarding the set of economic measures required by the implementation of this strategy.

The Potential Conflict Between Adjustment and Growth. A macroeconomic adjustment program might require a considerable reduction of the fiscal deficit and a fall in the rate of growth of domestic credit. A reduction of the fiscal deficit presupposes an increase in the taxation of all the economic participants involved (including the exporters) and a decrease in public spending (including public investment). But a decrease in internal credit has a negative impact on the financing of investments because it diminishes the funds available for it. Accordingly, the macroeconomic program noted earlier, which focused on achieving and implementing the adjustment, would not provide positive incentives to growth; in other words, there would be a trade-off between adjustment and growth.

Nevertheless, one could argue that the macroeconomic adjustment is a prerequisite for long-term and lasting growth. A stable macroeconomic environment without potential disequilibria (external or internal) and stable economic rules encourage the economic agents to take a long-term planning stance.

The Future Double-Conditionality of the IMF and the World Bank. Two elements are implicitly used in the conceptual framework underlying the establishment of a future IMF–World Bank double-conditionality: the "multilateral" view and the successful growth experience of the Asian exporter countries.

The "multilateral" view, prevalent during the pre-1980 period, was based on the belief that international economic cooperation would be an important element in advancing world development and prosperity. But this view, held by developed countries and international organizations, changed during the 1980s (Dadzie, 1987): (1) In the developing countries, inadequate domestic policies are considered to be the cause of the recent economic difficulties. Therefore, the solution seems to be the application of "adequate and correct" (macroeconomic) policies, together with structural changes aimed at making the economy more flexible and thus at improving resource allocation efficiency. (2) Each country has to put "order in the house" and adjust the economy to the exogenous changes in the external variables. (3) From a development perspective, it is not the international commercial and financial relations that have to improve; rather, domestic incentives must be created so as to make the private sector the driving force of development. (4) The world economy has become so interdependent that not even coordinated action by the governments of the developed countries can change the course of events.

In addition, the successful experience of economic growth in the Asian exporting countries suggests that the future double-conditionality of the IMF and the World Bank will support the development strategy—the so-called outward-oriented development—of these countries. Indeed, it is worth mentioning that most Latin American economists (those at CEPAL included) are now convinced that this *should* be the development strategy. The only real difference of opinion concerns the set of economic policy measures required by the implementation of this strategy.

In sum, the economic framework of the future IMF–World Bank double-conditionality will be based on the following principles: responsible, appropriate, and correct macroeconomic policies (i.e., fiscal and monetary policies); promotion and expansion of savings and investment; an increase in the production of tradable goods, especially exports; and creation of a better incentive structure in the domestic economy.

Of course, at this level of generality it is difficult to find an economist who will criticize the principle of "responsible, appropriate, and correct" policies.[19] Then, why don't governments of the LDCs implement such measures? The obvious answer is that in a "second-best" world (given the distortions of political and economic pressures), where governments are trying to achieve many different goals (e.g., growth, inflation, unemployment, income distribution, poverty, and external disequilibrium), the responsible, appropriate, and correct policy is not immediately obvious. This is especially true insofar as the relevant magnitudes of the trade-offs between various economic goals are unknown.

This strategy of adjustment with growth is led by export promotion, to which the double-conditionality of the IMF and the World Bank will implicitly or explicitly point. Its implementation includes the following elements: (1) a liberalization of markets and of the external sector, which corresponds to an import liberalization; (2) a domestic currency devaluation, a stable real exchange rate, and a reduction of export taxes (all of which are aimed at promoting exports); (3) the private sector, domestic or external, is the "engine of economic growth" (an expression sometimes used as a euphemism for the privatization of public enterprises); (4) stable and permanent economic rules, the implicit purpose of which is to reduce the government's interference in the economy; and (5) a reduction in the relative size of the government in the economy (Guitián, 1981 and 1987; Krueger, 1978; Balassa et al., 1986; Michalopoulos, 1987).

The Asian Experience. In the economic literature, opinions vary widely regarding the successful Asian export growth experience. In this context, Sachs's (1987) observation seems noteworthy. From 1950 to 1973 Japan achieved one of the highest average rates of economic growth. During this period of time it used the following set of economic policy measures. (1) *Foreign exchange policy:* The government had total control over the foreign exchange; the exporters gave all the acquired foreign exchange to the government. There was no special rule regarding the distribution of foreign exchange; the government bureaucrats allocated it to the various sectors and enterprises. Between 1950 and 1964 no public foreign exchange was provided for tourism. (2) *Capital accounts:* The government was the only economic agent entitled to engage in foreign borrowing. Foreign investments were rigorously controlled, and multinational enterprises with a foreign majority control were not admitted. (3) *The rate of interest:* The real rate of interest was low and was not allowed to exceed a maximum limit; credits were allocated arbitrarily. (4) *Incentives for exporters:* Exports were promoted not by a liberalization of imports but by special tax benefits, such as subsidies and tax exemptions. This kind of incentive was also granted to exports with natural comparative advantages (Sachs, 1987).

According to Sachs (1987), one can conclude that the Japanese export experience was based neither on free trade, on the unrestricted development of free-market mechanisms, nor on the government's restraint.

Some Latin American countries applied a similar program; the result was not the same, however. Why? One possible answer to this paradox is that there are no economic recipes for achieving certain objectives that are valid everywhere and all the time; thus export promotion—or the same economic prescriptions applied in different regions, in a different world economy, environment and with different timing—could produce different results. Nevertheless, in my opinion, incentives in the majority of the Latin American countries throughout 1950–1970 were biased against exports; overvalued exchange rates and high import barriers were among these disincentives. There were even doubts as to the export capacity of the Latin American economies.

Regarding a successful export strategy for Asian countries other than Japan, the following aspects have been observed: (1) Export promotion is the engine of economic growth. (2) However, export promotion is not equivalent to the liberalization of imports, nor is it a prerequisite for export promotion. (3) A similar observation can be made regarding privatization and the government's role (Sachs, 1987). In Korea, the government promotes the formation of business enterprises and marketing organizations for export products. There is nothing like the Japanese MITI (Ministry of Trade and Industry), which is famous for the layout of its future export sectors; however, the Korean government has direct influence in the big export firms and thus plays an important and active part in the implementation of the export promotion strategy. In sum, the economic policy package that resulted in the successful Asian export promotion strategy and the strategy of "liberalization with deregulation"(which the potential future double-conditionality of the IMF and the World Bank would entail) are not the same.

Some Difficulties with the (Eventual) Double-Conditionality of the IMF and World Bank. The economic program suggested by the eventual double-conditionality of the IMF and World Bank is supposedly going to induce an adjustment with growth and thereby increase the welfare of the country. But if this is so, why haven't the Latin American countries applied the program by themselves? Why does pressure have to be applied through a double-conditionality? (Sachs, 1987). In this connection, one of the conclusions drawn by Killick (1984) is that the IMF adjustment programs have a much better chance of succeeding when the local government in question is convinced of the convenience of the programs.

There are a number of questions regarding the eventual double-conditionality of IMF and World Bank. In the first place, there is a deep disagreement as to the focus of the IMF and World Bank's "adjustment with growth" strategy; the central premise is that in an LDC, external equilibrium has to be made compatible with external debt service flows and with the amount of new credits obtained. Hence, in this scheme, the growth rate is residual. Fishlow (1987) argues that the focus of the new "adjustment with growth" strategy should be different: Given the minimum necessary growth rate allowing an LDC to develop, what is the necessary level of external resources needed? In this case, it is the external credit flows that are residual. Then, the crucial question is: Where are those resources going to come from?

In the second place, there is no theoretical analysis to model the transition from a disequilibrium to an equilibrium situation. This is particularly so when the transition involves the "timing" and sequencing of structural reforms such as external and financial liberalization, economic deregulation, etc. The dynamics of change in disequilibrium markets is very hard to model and there is simply no theoretical model to do it (Helleiner, 1986). Nevertheless, in an imperfect and distorted context, the IMF–World Bank double-conditionality always suggest the use of price incentives and all-around liberalization. Helleiner (1986) points out that this general view can be defended only if it is applied very cautiously and in a very flexible manner; but "as a universal rule it is not politically nor economically valid or acceptable."

In the third place, the eventual IMF–World Bank double-conditionality is going to make the negotiating process more difficult inasmuch as one negotiation will not be finished until all the other ones are (Lizano and Charpentier, 1986). This situation is analogous to solving a simultaneous equation model with variable (and sometimes not clearly convergent) parameters during a period in which the country is in great need of receiving foreign credits. The following argument illustrates the logic of cross-conditionality. As the IMF–World Bank double-conditionality is supposedly a coherent, consistent, and complementary set of policies, its success requires that the whole package be applied. Therefore, to guarantee that the whole program is implemented, it is convenient to establish a cross-conditionality. From the standpoint of the country in question, this cross-conditionality would profoundly affect the socio-political stability of the respective government because *all* resource flows to the country are going to be tied to this cross-conditionality. Therefore, the cross-conditionality between the IMF and the World Bank implies that the LDCs will try to avoid these international organizations as sources of credit; or, if they resort to them, they will be exposing themselves to the prospect of social, political, and economic instability.

Finally, the development strategy and the magnitude and type of economic growth, as well as other socioeconomic goals, are central components of the sometimes vague concept of national sovereignty. A country will be very sensitive to an obvious intromission in crucial economic and political areas, such as liberalization, deregulation, or foreign investment. The exertion of pressure for an economic program focused on balance-of-payments results is a very narrow objective; moreover, the criterion for measuring the success of an economic program cannot be based solely on how well it provides resources to cover the foreign debt service (Miller, 1986). Rather, the central criterion should be the impact of this economic program on growth and other socio-economic goals (especially distributive goals).

The Distributive Problem. From the point of view of a country with an external disequilibrium, the achievement of adjustment is a public good, which is to the advantage of every economic agent in the country in question. Why, then, do economic agents not cooperate to the same extent and make sacrifices to this end? How can the adjustment costs be equally distributed? What kind of economic policy could achieve a fair distribution? The same set of questions applies to the strategy of adjustment with growth. In the latter case one could argue that those who make sacrifices today will gain from a higher rate of growth in the future. Nevertheless, there are some questions to be asked with respect to this train of thought: (1) What measures can guarantee that those who make the greatest sacrifices now will be compensated for them in the future? And will this future compensation be greater for those who make more sacrifices now? (2) How can the present loss of welfare be compared to the potential gain that is expected in the future? Those economic agents who have been unemployed for six months, thus facilitating the adjustment, wonder at what price the future gain should be fixed so as to balance the present economic, psychological, and social costs.

The Financing of the Strategy. Without a doubt, the central problem concerning the strategy of adjustment with growth is the fact that a country needs a greater relative volume of resources for a longer period of time in order to implement the strategy. This is the case because the strategy of adjustment with growth requires that LDCs make very deep economic changes. In particular, aggregate supply (basically tradables) must be increased in the medium and long run. But this measure would require more resources than those needed for the traditional short-run IMF programs aimed at reducing aggregate demand (Sengupta, 1987). Foreign financial resources are especially critical in the first few years of the strategy of adjustment with growth, in order to prevent the decline of per capita consumption in the LDCs. It is very difficult to implement an economic reform package when consumption levels are very low and an additional decrease is required. And such implementation is virtually impossible in a democratic regime.

In view of the current international economic situation and the above-mentioned problems, Latin America's prospects are as follows: First, the international banking system will not grant long- or medium-term loans.

The banking system will probably finance only short-term credits and foreign trade operations. Second, the amount of funds from foreign investment and from possible future aid by the governments of the developed countries is relatively small relative to that required by the implementation of the strategy in question.

There are only two possibilities left. One alternative would be to increase the credit funds available from the IMF and the World Bank. Such an increase could be achieved by means of a greater contribution by the governments that belong to these institutions, more frequent use of the Special Drawing Right (SDR) on the part of the IMF, and an increase in the amount of credits provided by the World Bank in proportion to its assets.[20] As a result, the IMF and the World Bank would have to play a predominant role in the economies of the Latin American countries in the near future. This is why the discussion about double-conditionality is so important.

The remaining alternative is to reduce the negative flow of funds out of Latin America or, in extreme circumstances, even to abolish this flow. In other words, the "adjustment with growth" strategy is impossible to implement so long as the present level of foreign debt service payments are maintained, given the reduced (and rationed) flow of foreign credits. Therefore, the flow of the funds destined for the foreign debt service should be reduced considerably.

The Problem of Asymmetry

The traditional problem of an international asymmetry in the adjustment costs reveals some of the difficulties that the strategy of adjustment with growth might entail. This section deals with various aspects of this problem of asymmetry.

1. Regarding the problem of external disequilibrium, there is an asymmetry between the already developed countries and the developing ones. The IMF is unable to convince the developed countries to carry out a coherent and consistent economic program, which would promote international financial stability and the growth of the world economy.

Moreover, the external disequilibrium and fiscal deficit of the U.S. economy are central to the problematic functioning of the world economy, but the IMF can do nothing about these factors. How would the people and government of the United States react if the IMF suggested a reduction of the U.S. fiscal deficit from 4 percent (of GDP) to 2 percent within a year? Comparable (and in some cases more severe) conditions have been agreed upon in most of the stand-by programs that the Latin American countries have signed with the IMF. The stability of the world financial and economic system today basically depends on the economic policies applied by developed countries. Thus there is an asymmetry in the conditionality of the IMF, in that it is applicable only to LDCs but not to the developed countries; but owing to this asymmetry, the IMF cannot carry out its central task. The new role of the IMF has been reduced to that of a "spectator and commentator of the evolution of the world economy," but it cannot influence or alter its course (Miller, 1986). Therefore, no matter how harsh the conditionality over LDCs may be, elimination of external disequilibria or maintenance of the flow of debt service payments will not produce an orderly evolution of the world economy. LDCs today are only appendages of the world economy, and their economies cyclically amplify what happens in the economies of the developed countries.

2. The economic program that the IMF has traditionally proposed to each country as well as the current strategy of export promotion involve one fundamental difficulty. They are both based on the implicit assumption that each country is able to solve the problem of its external disequilibrium in a one-sided way. In reality, however, the reduction of one country's trade deficit entails the simultaneous reduction of the trade surplus of another country or a group of countries. As has recently been observed, this is not a simple task.

In the case of Latin America, the situation seems to be even more difficult. In order to obtain the financial resources it needs to pay its foreign debt service, Latin America must produce a trade surplus; this trade surplus in turn requires that some countries accept trade deficits. The implication is that those nondebtor countries that achieve a trade surplus should grant special trade advantages to the debtor countries. However, the countries to which the creditor banks belong are not exactly identical with the countries that have a trade surplus; and even if they were, it does not necessarily follow that the developed countries would change the structure of their economic policy in order to guarantee the required greater flow of exports from the debtor countries. The same argument is valid for the implementation of the export promotion strategy in the developing countries.[21]

Some Final Suggestions

The purpose of this chapter has been to analyze some aspects of the current problems and interdependences concerning the conditionality of the IMF and the World Bank, Latin America's foreign indebtedness and its adjustment process, and the strategy of adjustment with growth. But the chapter represents only the initial stage of an investigation of these factors; hence it can do no more than to suggest a possible direction for the analysis to take and to mention critically those directions that it should not take. A subsequent stage of research should concentrate on the special set of measures needed for the implementation of the strategy of adjustment with growth and on the principles that should govern the international organizations' conditionality.

A few suggestions are listed below.

First, the fact that Latin America's transfer of resources to foreign countries amounts to 4 percent of the GDP is incompatible with the implementation of the strategy of adjustment with growth. The Latin American countries cannot sustain a negative flow of resources of this magnitude. And, by the same token, the final solution of the problem of Latin America's foreign indebtedness can no longer be delayed. As Dornbusch (1987) points out, the foreign debt problem is fundamentally a political and not an economic problem; but "today, in contrast to the 20's and 30's it is insisted that the problem is fundamentally economic."[22] It is indeed time to implement some of the suggested solutions (on this topic see Ffrench-Davis and Feinberg, 1986; Massad, 1986; De Carmoy, 1987).

Second, the conditionalities of the IMF and the World Bank must be reviewed and readjusted, so that the Latin American countries are not forced either to agree to excessive adjustment costs or to accept technical and ideological solutions that conflict with most people's wishes and aspirations. For an IMF or World Bank program to be acceptable to a country, it must limit the external disequilibrium reduction objective so as to make possible a minimum growth rate compatible with the country's available resources. Also, the program should consider distributive social objectives. The adjustment process and the structural reforms are implemented at great costs to the poor—but so, too, is the no-adjustment alternative. The real problem is how to distribute fairly the sacrifices involved in the adjustment.

The new IMF and World Bank credits should not be used to prepay debt because they could then not be used to finance the adjustment with growth strategy. Also, during those periods in which countries are undertaking the changes required by the adjustment and structural reforms, the IMF and World Bank should abstain from charging amortization and service payments.

On the other hand, coherent and consistent conditionalities of the IMF and the World Bank are reasonable if both institutions are simultaneously present in a certain country. Even so, the host country should have a chance to give its own opinion and to influence the arrangement of the double-conditionalities that are imposed on it. But in this case it should be explicitly stipulated, in the IMF as well as the World Bank arrangements, that there is no cross-conditionality.

The basic principles suggested for the IMF's conditionality are as follows:[23]

1. *Inverse conditionality.* Each country should be responsible for its own adjustment program, which should take into account the existing external restrictions. In this way the homogeneous and uniform programs of the IMF would be replaced by "home-made" adjustment programs, which could be devised from case to case. This point is probably more relevant to small countries, since large ones have more negotiating power to acquire such programs.
2. *Conditionality with real variables.* In order to set a maximum limit to the internal adjustment costs, an additional increase in external credits should be agreed on in case of either an excessive fall in the rate of growth or an excessive rise in the unemployment rate. The program signed with México in 1985 had a clause of this sort.
3. *Conditionality on two levels.* In this case a distinction is suggested between the external variables measured in terms of foreign currency (i.e., those that are connected with the balance of payments and the international reserves) and the internal variables in terms of domestic currency (fiscal deficit, internal credits, and inflation). The priority conditionality of the IMF should then correspond to the variables that are expressed in foreign currency. Moreover, the IMF should loosen the internal targets after the external targets have been reached.
4. The level chosen for the external variables should be compatible with the minimum growth rate previously discussed (see point 2). The level of the internal variables should consider an adequate expansion of domestic credit (probably within a certain range) so as to maintain an adequate liquidity to sustain the established growth rate. Moreover, the criteria to establish the fiscal deficit target should consider a minimum level of public investment, to meet the growth target, and of social spending, to meet the distributive and poverty eradication targets.
5. The Compensatory Financing Facility (CFF) program should be expanded and should take into account fluctuations in the international interest rates, because the shocks of fluctuations of these rates are very important for the Latin American debtor countries. The CFF program should also consider a higher volume of resources related to the fall in exports. Even more logically, access to the CFF program should be related to the magnitude of the negative external shock faced by a country, and not to the country share.[24]

Helleiner (1986), Feinberg et al. (1986), and Feinberg and Bacha (1987) have suggested that the central elements of World Bank conditionality should be as follows.

First, the World Bank should focus its conditionality on what were its chief objectives in the 1960s and 1970s: equitable growth and the eradication of poverty. With respect to the adjustment program, conditionality should specifically consider the following points: alternative adjustment strategies that minimize social costs, compensatory programs that alleviate the effects of the adjustment on the poor, mechanisms that distribute the adjustment costs fairly, and the distributive impact of different adjustment alternatives.

Obviously, these points have not been resolved either theoretically or empirically. Therefore, it should constitute a priority in the World Bank's research program. The World Bank should also maintain the relative quantitative importance of credits to specific investment projects. Of these projects, those that generate employment—for example, credits to small- and medium-sized firms and credits for construction of houses for low-income groups—should have priority.

With respect to Structural Adjustment Loans (SALs), the World Bank should concentrate on the sectorial type. The SAL credits, from a political perspective, are insufficient to compensate for the costs of the reforms included in its conditionality. In the case of the sectorial-oriented adjustment loans, a macroeconomic program in agreement with the IMF is not always a prerequisite. This is the case with loans oriented toward improving nutritional levels, human capital levels, energy policy, or the country's infrastructure.

Finally, it is commonly agreed that a strategy of export promotion is necessary. In the interdependent modern world, the external sector is very important for small- and medium-sized countries—and all of the Latin American countries can be categorized as such. Some of the measures that could promote exports are the following: (1) A stable exchange rate policy should be maintained whereby the domestic currency is permanently slightly undervalued for a relatively long period of time (i.e., for ten to fifteen years). (2) All import barriers for intermediate goods used in the production of exports should be phased out. Also, for an initial period of at least five years, a direct mechanism for the subsidizing of marginal and/or new exports is required. Afterward, these subsidies should be gradually abolished. Analogous arguments, such as those used in regard to the protection of infant industry, could be used in order to justify these measures. The mechanism of export subsidy is undoubtedly preferable to an unrestricted liberalization of imports. (3) Obviously the private sector will react positively to appropriate economic incentives; from this reaction it can be concluded that, if the above-mentioned measures are introduced, the private sector will be an indispensable agent in the expansion of exports in the Latin American countries. (4) The public sector, too, can play an important part in establishing the appropriate global context, supplying the basic infrastructure, promoting the formation of the human capital needed for development, inducing, or in some cases initiating, certain activities that—owing to externalities or economies of scale—the private sector is not willing to undertake (but once initiated can be transferred to it), promoting active trade policies through bilateral or multilateral agreements and information provided by embassies abroad, and so on. Success in the competitive world of today requires that no economic agent be excluded, and that all economic agents of a country go together in the same direction. The moral of this situation is obviously that the Latin American countries must necessarily have a mixed economy, in which both the private sector and the government play an important part. Polar systems, which attribute a predominant role either to the public sector exclusively or to the private sector exclusively, are doomed to failure. But every country has to determine the appropriate roles and the mix composition for its private and public sectors in its own way.

Notes

The author is grateful for the helpful comments provided by J. A. Fontaine, R. Lawrence, J. Marshall, R. Newfarmer, F. Ossa, J. Rosenblüt, A. Solimano, V. Tokman, R. Zahler, and his colleagues at CIEPLAN.

1. The following example will clarify the effects of the rise in nominal interest rates. For simplicity, second-order effects are omitted. Let us assume that a debtor has liabilities of 400 in the initial period and that there is a fixed real rate of interest of 2 percent. For the first period let us assume two different situations, one with an inflation rate of 3 percent and a resulting nominal interest rate of 5 percent, and the other with an inflation rate of 10 percent and thus a nominal interest rate of 12 percent. In the first case the debtor interest payments are 20, 8 of which correspond to the real rate of interest and 12 to the redemption of the total debt owing to the inflation of 3 percent. In the second case the debtor interest payments are 48, 8 of which correspond to the real rate of interest and 40 to the redemption of the real part of the total debt with an inflation of 10 percent. Let us consider a third case in which the real interest rate rises to 4.5 percent and the inflation rate is 10 percent; therefore, the nominal interest rate is 14.5 percent. In this case the debtor pays 58 in interest, 18 of which correspond to the real interest rate and 40 to the inflation rate of 10 percent.

2. In the article by Bianchi, Devlin, and Ramos (1987), two different reference periods are used: 1950–1970 for the variation in export prices (excluding oil); and 1930–1980 for the real interest rate. In my opinion, to really understand what happened in the 1980s, it is best to use the previous decade as the reference

period. In this case, due to the change in relative prices in 1973–1974, the 1975–1980 period is used. In any case, if the whole 1970 decade was used, the effect of the fall in the terms of trade would practically disappear, whereas the total effect of interest rates would grow.

3. For O'Connell (1986), the principal element that influenced the growth in the external debt in the 1980s was "the exorbitant and unexpected level reached by the international real interest rates."

4. For similar calculations pertaining to individual countries, see Bianchi, Devlin, and Ramos (1987).

5. Many Latin Americans wonder why they have to pay amounts that are twice as high as those that Germany had to pay after its defeat in World War I and that France had to pay after its defeat by Prussia in the nineteenth century. After all, Latin America has not lost any war.

6. The SAL is a World Bank loan linked to policy and institutional reforms in borrowing countries. This type of loan serves to finance imports not related to specific investment projects and therefore can be disbursed quickly.

7. If Chile is omitted from Table 8.4, the SAL programs, established by the World Bank in Latin America from 1983 to 1987, would amount to less than 12 percent of the total credit granted for adjustment programs.

8. Why do Latin American economists neglect to discuss a topic of such great importance to Latin America? The book by the Sistema Economico Latinoamericano (SELA, 1986) and the report by the Group of 24 (see Grupo de los 24, 1987) set an outstanding example of the kind of discussion that Latin America needs.

9. Bibliographic references to this subject include Bacha (1983), Buira (1983), Ground (1984), Killick (1984), and David (1985). For more recent discussions, see SELA (1986), Marshall (1987), Meller (1987), and Pastor (1987).

10. For severe criticism of the professional competence of some IMF economists, as well as examples of the mistakes made, see Taylor (1985).

11. A former Latin American critical argument went as follows: The period of time granted by the IMF for the adjustment to the external disequilibrium varied between twelve and twenty-four months. In general, a country had to carry out a great deal of the adjustment within one year. This was a result of the IMF's role, which was specified to be of a short-run nature. If the existing disequilibria were of a considerable magnitude, the question arose as to whether it was really necessary to make the adjustments of the economy in such a short period of time. That the period of adjustment and the duration of the IMF program had to concur is a completely arbitrary matter. After some time the IMF accepted this argument and created the EFF programs, which have replaced some of the stand-by programs. Also very recently, the quarterly targets have been changed to half-year targets.

12. See Meller and Solimano (1987) for a theoretical formulation of this phenomenon, in which devaluation overshooting produces a contractionary overkill.

13. Recently, this role of the IMF, as an international inspector-supervisor, has been much more important—in terms of the amount of resources lended—than its own credits.

14. Bibliographic references on this topic include Annis (1986), Bacha and Feinberg (1986), Feinberg et al. (1986), Feinberg and Bacha (1987), Helleiner (1986), Michalopoulos (1987), and Miller (1986).

15. In 1980 there were only four sectoral or structural adjustment oriented credit operations, for a total amount of US$370 million. In 1987 there were thirty-one operations of this type, for an amount of more than US$4,100 million.

16. Sometimes an economic program signed with the IMF results in a certain degree of internal credibility. However, this type of program sometimes sets off internal disequilibria.

17. A possible answer to this question is that Latin America has run into foreign debts and therefore has to pay them back. Still, as Keynes has already pointed out, if an individual owes a bank $100,000, this debt is the debtor's problem. However, if he owes $100 billion, then it is the bank's problem. Undoubtedly, the creditor banks and the Latin American countries share some guilt regarding the level reached by Latin America's foreign debt; on this point, see Devlin (1986).

18. This calculation implies that the amount of foreign credits coming from international capital markets is practically null and that the flow of foreign investments will be limited. Up to now, the flow of foreign investments into Latin America has varied between 10 percent and 15 percent of the required interest payments for its foreign debt.

19. Only an irresponsible, inappropriate, or inadequate economist would disagree with this.

20. See SELA (1986) and Grupo de los 24 (1987).

21. There is one more problem involved in the international asymmetry. The fact that there are countries with a trade deficit means that there must be other countries with a trade surplus. Why must only those countries with a deficit bear the adjustment costs in the case of a disequilibrium? A plausible answer would be that only the countries with trade deficits have liquidity problems, and these problems compel them to turn to the IMF. However, this need not be so. In the 1940s, when the establishment of the IMF and the World Bank was being discussed, Keynes advocated a symmetrical distribution of the adjustment costs.

The countries with a trade surplus must grant the countries with trade deficits access to their markets, so that the latter can generate the foreign exchange that they need in order to finance the deficit. This is exactly what the United States recently suggested to Japan. In order to lower the adjustment costs in connection with the U.S. external deficit, Japan will increase its imports from the United States and "voluntarily" decrease its exports into the North American market.

The IMF could develop various mechanisms for prompting the countries with a trade surplus to facilitate the access to their export markets from countries with a trade deficit.

22. Cited in Miller (1986), p. 84.

23. Grupo de los 24 (1987); Bacha (1985); SELA (1986).

24. The Grupo de los 24 has made other suggestions, such as the following: (a) Instead of fixing quantitative targets, the IMF should fix only the range of

the critical variables; and (b) the EFF programs should definitively replace the stand-by programs.

References

Annis, S. (1986), "The shifting grounds of poverty lending at the World Bank." In R. E. Feinberg et al., *Between two worlds: The World Bank's next decade.* Washington, D.C.: Overseas Development Council.

Bacha, E. (1983), "Prologo para a terceira carta," *Forum Gazeta Mercantil (ed.), FMI & Brasil: A armadilha da recessao,* São Paulo.

_____ (1985), "The future role of the International Monetary Fund in Latin America: Issues and proposals," Universidad Católica Rio de Janeiro (June), mimeo.

_____ (1986), "El papel futuro del FMI en América Latina: Temas y proposiciones." In Sistema Económico Latinoamericano (SELA), *El FMI, el Banco Mundial y la crisis latinoamericana,* Siglo 21, México.

Bacha, E., and R. E. Feinberg (1986), "El Banco Mundial y el ajuste estructural en América Latina." In SELA, *El FMI, el Banco Mundial y la crisis latinoamerica,* Siglo 21, México.

Balassa, B., G. Bueno, P. P. Kuczynski, and M. H. Simonsen (1986), *Hacia una renovación del crecimiento económico en América Latina.* Washington, D.C: Institute for International Economics.

Bianchi, A., R. Devlin, and J. Ramos (1987), "El proceso de ajuste en la América Latina. 1981–1986," *El Trimestre Económico,* Vol. 54, No. 216 (October).

Buira, A. (1983), "La programación financiera y la condicionalidad del FMI," *El Trimestre Económico,* Vol. 50 (1), No. 197 (January).

Cardoso, E. (1987), "Payment crisis and inflation: The IMF in Latin America," *Discussion Paper Series,* No. 70, CLADS, Boston University (May).

CEPAL (1988), *Panorama económico de América Latina.* Santiago: Comisión Económica para América Latina.

Dadzie, K.K.S. (1987), "Reviving multilateral cooperation for growth and development," *Journal of Development Planning,* No. 17.

David, W. L. (1985), *The IMF paradigm.* New York: Praeger.

De Carmoy, H. (1987), "Debt and growth in Latin America: A European banker's proposal," *Working Paper,* No. 9, Instituto de Relaciones Europeo-Latinoamericanas, Madrid.

Devlin, R. (1986), "La estructura y comportamiento de la banca internacional en los años setenta y su impacto en la crisis de América Latina," *Colección Estudios CIEPLAN,* Vol. 19 (June).

Díaz-Alejandro, C. (1983), "Some aspects of the 1982–83 Brazilian payment crisis," *Brookings Papers on Economic Activity,* No. 2.

Dornbusch, R. (1987), "Debt problems and the world macro economy," MIT (August), mimeo.

Feinberg, R. E., et al. (1986), *Between two worlds: The World Bank's next decade.* Washington, D.C.: Overseas Development Council.

Feinberg, R. E., and E. Bacha (1987), "When supply and demand don't intersect: Latin America and the Bretton Woods institutions in the 80s," *Texto para Discussao*, No. 172, Universidad Católica, Rio de Janeiro (August).

Ffrench-Davis, R. (1986), "El financiamiento externo negativo: Tendencias, consecuencias y opciones para América Latina," *Colección Estudios CIEPLAN*, Vol. 20 (December).

Ffrench-Davis, R., and R. Feinberg (eds.) (1986), *Más allá de la crisis de la deuda: Bases para un nuevo enfoque*. Santiago: Ediciones CIEPLAN.

Fishlow, A. (1987), "Capital requirements of developing countries in the next decade," *Journal of Development Planning*, No. 17.

Fraga, A. (1987), "Las reparaciones de guerra de Alemania y la deuda de Brasil: Un estudio comparativo," *Comercio Exterior*, Vol. 37, No. 4, México (April).

Ground, R. L. (1984), "Los programas ortodoxos de ajuste en América Latina: Un examen crítico de las políticas del Fondo Monetario Internacional," *Revista de la CEPAL*, No. 23 (August).

Grupo de los 24 (1987), "Deputies' report on Fund's role in promoting adjustment with growth," *IMF Survey* (August).

Guitián, M. (1981), *Fund conditionality: Evolution of principles and practices*, Pamphlet Series No. 38. Washington, D.C.: IMF.

―――― (1987), "Adjustment and economic growth: They are fundamentally complementary." In *Symposium on Growth-Oriented Adjustment Programs*. Washington, D.C.: World Bank and IMF (February).

Helleiner, G. K. (1986), "Policy-based program lending: A look at the Bank's new role." In Feinberg et al., *Between two worlds: The World Bank's next decade*. Washington, D.C.: Overseas Development Council.

International Monetary Fund (1987), *International Financial Statistics*. Washington, D.C.: IMF.

Killick, T., ed. (1984), *The Quest for economic stabilization: The IMF and the Third World*. New York: St. Martin's Press.

Krueger, A. O. (1978), *Foreign trade regimes and economic development: Liberalization attempts and consequences*. New York: NBER.

Krugman, P., and L. Taylor (1978), "Contractionary effects of devaluation," *Journal of International Economics*, Vol. 8, No. 3 (August).

Lizano, E., and S. Charpentier (1986), "La condicionalidad cruzada y la deuda externa," *Comentarios sobre Asuntos Económicos*, No. 59, Banco Central de Costa Rica, San José.

Machlup, F. (1964), *International payments, debt and gold*. New York: Scribner's.

Marshall, J. (1987), "Condicionalidad de los créditos del Fondo Monetario Internacional," *Estudios de Economía*, Vol. 14, No. 2 (December).

Massad, C. (1986), "El alivio del peso de la deuda: Experiencia histórica y necesidad presente," *Revista de la CEPAL*, No. 30 (December).

Meller, P. (1987), "Revisión de los enfoques teóricos sobre ajuste externo y su relevancia para América Latina," *Revista de la CEPAL*, No. 32 (October).

Meller, P., and A. Solimano (1987), "A simple macro model for a small open economy facing a binding external constraint (Chile)," *Journal of Development Economics* Vol. 26 (June).

Michalopoulos, C. (1987), "World Bank programs for adjustment and growth," *Symposium on Growth-Oriented Adjustment Programs*. Washington: World Bank and IMF (February).

Miller, M. (1986), *Coping is not enough: The international debt crisis and the role of the World Bank and International Monetary Fund*. Irwin, Ill.: Dow Jones.

O'Connell, A. (1986), "La deuda externa y la reforma del sistema monetario internacional," *Revista de la CEPAL* No. 30 (December).

Pastor, M. (1987), "The effects of IMF programs in the Third World: Debate and evidence from Latin America," *World Development*, Vol. 15, No. 2 (February).

Ramos, J. (1987), "Lo central de la transferencia de recursos en los procesos de ajuste, estabilización y desarrollo," CEPAL (November), mimeo.

Reisen, H. (1986), "The Latin American transfer problem in historical perspective," OECD, Paris, mimeo.

Sachs, J. (1986), "Conditionality and the debt crisis: Some thoughts for the World Bank," World Bank (June), mimeo.

_____ (1987), "Trade and exchange rate policies in growth-oriented adjustment programs," *Symposium on Growth-Oriented Adjustment Programs*. Washington: World Bank and IMF (February).

SELA (1986), *El FMI, el Banco Mundial y la crisis latinoamericana*, Siglo 21, México.

Sengupta, A. (1987), "The role of the IMF in the international monetary system and the developing countries," *Journal of Development Planning*, No. 17.

Taylor, L. (1985), "IMF conditionality: Incomplete theory, policy malpractice," MIT (April), mimeo.

World Bank (1988), "Interim Report on Adjustment Lending," World Bank, Washington, D.C., mimeo.

Acronyms

AEA	American Economic Association
ANPEC	Asociación Nacional de Pesquisas Económicas (Rio de Janeiro)
BNDE	Banco Nacional de Desarrollo Económico (Santiago)
CED	Centro de Estudios del Desarrollo (Santiago)
CEPAL	Comisión Económica para América Latina (Santiago)
CET	Centro de Estudios de Transnacionales (Buenos Aires)
CFF	Compensatory Financing Facility
CIDE	Centro de Investigaciones y Docencia Económica (México)
CIEPLAN	Corporación de Investigaciones Económicas para Latinoamérica (Santiago)
CISEA	Centro de Investigaciones Sociales sobre el Estado y la Administración (Buenos Aires)
CLACSO	Consejo Latinoamericano de Ciencias Sociales (Buenos Aires)
ECLA	Economic Commission for Latin America (Santiago)
ECLAC	Economic Commission for Latin America and the
EFF	extended fund facility
FLACSO	Facultad Latinoamericano de Ciencias Sociales (Santiago)
GDP	gross domestic product
GEL	Grupo Editor Latinoamericano (Buenos Aires)
HSFR	Social Research Council of Sweden
ILO	International Labor Office (Geneva)
IMF	International Monetary Fund
IPAL	Instituto de Planificación para América Latina (Santiago)
ISI	import-substituting industrialization
LACs	Latin American countries
LAFTA	Latin American Free Trade Association
LDC	less developed country
LIBOR	London Interest Borrowing Rate
MITI	Ministry of Trade and Industry (MITI)
NBER	National Bureau of Economic Research (Cambridge, Mass.)

OECD	Organization for Economic Cooperation and Development
ONUDI	Organización de Naciones Unidas de Desarrollo Industrial (UN)
PET	Programa de economía del Trabajo (Santiago)
PREALC	Programa Regional del Empleo para América Latina y el Caribe (Santiago)
QRs	quantitative restrictions
RIAL	Relaciones Internacionales de América Latina (Santiago)
SAF	structural adjustment facility
SAL	Structural Adjustment Lending
SDR	Special Drawing Right
SELA	Sistema Economico Latinoamericano (Caracas)
UIA	Unión Industrial Argentina
UN DIESA	United Nations Department of International Economic and Social Affairs (New York)
VAT	value added tax
VECTOR	Chilean Research Center (Santiago)
WIDER	World Institute for Development Economics Research of the United Nations (Helsinki)

About the Book and Editor

In the 1980s Latin America experienced its second worst economic crisis of the century; today the average per capita income is about 10 percent less than a decade ago. Because the crisis affected all Latin American countries regardless of their economic policies, the period has become known as "the lost decade in Latin America." In this book, eminent economists from the region reexamine strategies of development—structuralism versus monetarism, liberalism versus statism, growth versus equity—in light of new theoretical knowledge and recent economic events.

The essays offer a complex interpretation of development problems and seek to explain how different schools of thought could be compatible and how old debates must be recast in the light of structural changes in Latin American economies. In addition, contributors critically review the adjustment processes applied in various countries. Together the chapters offer a penetrating analysis of what went wrong in Latin America in the 1980s and a careful assessment of economic measures and policies that might prove viable in promoting stable and growing economies, democratic regimes, and social justice.

Patricio Meller is executive director of the Corporación de Investigaciones Económicas Para Latinoamérica (CIEPLAN) in Santiago. He received a Ph.D. in economics from the University of California at Berkeley. He has served as professor at the Economics Institute of the Catholic University of Chile and in the department of economics at the University of Chile and as visiting professor at Boston University and the Univerity of Notre Dame. Currently, he is the director of the editorial committee of the journal, *Coleccion Estudios CIEPLAN*, published by the Corporación de Investigaciones Económicas para Latinoamérica.

Series in Political Economy
and Economic Development in Latin America

Series Editor

Andrew Zimbalist

Smith College

Through country case studies and regional analyses this series will contribute to a deeper understanding of development issues in Latin America. Shifting political environments, increasing economic interdependence, and the difficulties with regard to debt, foreign investment, and trade policy demand novel conceptualizations of development strategies and potentials for the region. Individual volumes in this series will explore the deficiencies in conventional formulations of the Latin American development experience by examining new evidence and material. Topics will include, among others, women and development in Latin America; the impact of IMF interventions; the effects of redemocratization on development; Cubanology and Cuban political economy; Nicaraguan political economy; and individual case studies on development and debt policy in various countries in the region.

Index

For Product Safety Concerns and Information please contact our EU
representative GPSR@taylorandfrancis.com
Taylor & Francis Verlag GmbH, Kaufingerstraße 24, 80331 München, Germany

www.ingramcontent.com/pod-product-compliance
Lightning Source LLC
Chambersburg PA
CBHW061158220326
41599CB00025B/4530